손봉돈의
엣센스 영숙어

내신 · 수능 · 특목고 · TOEIC · TOEFL · TEPS · SAT 대비

손봉돈 저

민중서림

Prologue

머리말

이제 옛것을 그대로 사용하는 낡은 방식의 공부는 끝났다. 새 술은 새 부대에 담아야 하고 새로운 시험에는 새로운 학습법으로 대처해야 한다. 내신 및 수능·특목고·TOEIC·TOEFL·TEPS·SAT 등 각종 시험에 숙어의 비중이 매우 커지고 있다.

손봉돈의 엣센스영숙어는 현실에 맞게 쉽고 체계적으로 구성되어 있어 효과적으로 학습할 수 있다. 각 숙어의 예문은 2개 이상 쉬운 것과 어려운 것을 제시했으며, 그 내용도 우리 주변에서 발생하는 환경·과학·사회·노사 관계·속담·시사 문제 등을 다양하게 다루었다. 또한 출제 빈도가 높은 순서로 제1장, 제2장, 제3장으로 나누어져 있고 매 장마다 첫머리에 그 특색을 간단하게 설명하여 놓았다.

이 책에는 1600여 개의 표제어와 각 표제어의 동의어·반의어·유사 표현·속담 등 총 3000개 이상의 숙어를 실어 영어 실력을 크게 향상시킬 수 있으므로, 이 책 한 권이면 어떤 영어시험에서도 월등한 점수를 얻을 수 있을 것이다.

끝으로 본서가 나오기까지 애써 주신 편집부 여러분의 노고에 감사 드리고 독자 여러분들의 건강과 영어 연구에 큰 발전이 있기를 빈다.

2004. 7
저자

이 책을 사용함에 있어서

1. 이 책은 출제 빈도가 높은 순서로 제1장, 제2장, 제3장으로 구성되어 있으므로 1장부터 순서대로 익혀야 효과적이다.

2. 매일매일 자기 나름대로 일정 분량을 정하여 반복 학습을 한다면 영어 시험에서 고득점의 결과를 얻을 수 있다.

3. 이 책에 사용된 기호는 동의어(SYN.), 반의어(OPP.), 비교(*cf.*) 등으로 표시했으며, 같은 내용의 문장을 여러 개의 표현법으로 다루어 영작에 큰 도움이 된다.

4. 좀 더 연구가 필요하다면 민중서림에서 발간된 **ESSENCE ENGLISH IDIOMS DICTIONARY** (엣센스 영어 숙어 사전)을 참고하면 더욱 효과적이다.

Contents

제1장 자주 나오는 중요 숙어 /3

제2장 이것만큼은 외워야 한다 /83

제3장 시험에서 노리는 급소 /165

찾아보기 /253

제 1 장 자주 나오는 중요 숙어

제 1 장에서 공부할 것은
자주 나오는 중요 숙어!

이 장에 나오는 숙어들은
두말할 필요도 없이 외워 두어야 하는 숙어들이다.

이제 숙어 정복의 고지가 보인다.
자만감은 실패의 원인이지만
자신감은 성공의 어머니!

착실하게 노력한 자만이
성공의 비전을 만날 수 있는 법.

제1장 자주 나오는 중요 숙어

at present 지금은, 오늘날, 현재
I am busy **at present**, but soon I will be free from work.
지금은 바쁘지만 곧 일에서 해방될 것이다.
I am sorry I have no money to spare **at present**.
미안합니다만 지금은 여윳돈이 없습니다.

SYN. today; now; at this time; at the present (time)
cf. for the present 당분간, 지금 같아서는 (=for the time being; until late)

at first sight 언뜻 보아서는, 첫눈에, …을 보고
Every student liked the new teacher **at first sight**.
모든 학생들은 새로 부임한 교사를 첫눈에 좋아했다.
At first sight, these buildings have some similarities.
언뜻 보기에는, 이 건물들 간에는 어느 정도 유사점이 있다.

SYN. after a first quick look

(every) now and then / now and again
때때로, 이따금
She writes to her son **every now and then**.
그녀는 때때로 아들에게 편지를 쓴다.
After 10 years of their divorce, the two people still meet **now and again**.
이혼한 지 10년이 지났는데도 두 사람은 여전히 가끔 만난다.

SYN. occasionally; once in a while; from time to time; at intervals
cf. every once in a while 때때로, 가끔 (=at times; sometimes; at moments)

not only … but (also) ~ …뿐만 아니라 ~도
He is **not only** an artist **but also** a scientist.
그는 예술가일 뿐만 아니라 과학자이기도 하다.
(=He is a scientist as well as an artist.
=Besides being an artist, he is a scientist.)

SYN. as well as; both … and

be apt to …하기 쉽다, …할 경향이 다분히 있다
Stupid as he is, he **is apt to** be deceived and buy unnecessary things.
그는 어리석어서 잘 속고 필요하지 않은 물건들을 잘 산다.
He **is apt to** rely upon others.
그는 쉽게 타인에게 의지하고 싶어한다.

SYN. be likely to; be liable to

be accustomed to …에 익숙하다, 항상 …하다
I **am** not **accustomed to** making a speech in public.

SYN. be used to; be good at; be skillful in

나는 사람들 앞에서 연설하는 것에는 익숙하지 않다.
As far as songwriting is concerned, Frank **is accustomed to** it.
작곡에 관한 것이라면 프랭크가 잘 한다.

be responsible for …에 책임이 있다, …의 원인이 되다

I will **be responsible for** the consequences, so you must follow me.
결과에 대해 내가 책임을 질 테니 내 말을 따라야 한다.
The broken heater of the apartment **was responsible for** his cold.
그의 감기의 원인은 아파트의 고장난 난방기였다.

[SYN] be blamed, be accountable for; be caused by

one by one 하나씩, 차례차례로, 한 사람씩

Please enter the room **one by one**.
한 사람씩 입장하시오.
After the training, soldiers turned in the weapons **one by one**.
훈련을 마친 후, 군인들은 한 사람씩 무기를 반납했다.

[SYN] one at a time; in single file; one after another; in order

one after another (셋 이상이) 차례차례, 잇따라, 연속하여

One after another all his plans have failed.
그의 계획들이 잇따라 실패했다.
Many strangers visited us **one after another**.
많은 모르는 사람들이 차례로 우리를 방문했다.

[SYN] one by one; following one another; in succession

be capable of … 할 수 있다, …을 감당할 능력이 있다

Although his major is English, he **is capable of** teaching algebra.
그의 전공은 영어이지만 그는 대수를 가르칠 수 있다.
You can trust me. I **am capable of** solving the matter.
나를 믿어도 돼. 나는 그 문제를 해결할 수 있어.

[SYN] be competent for; be able to; be equal to; cope with

cannot help but+동사원형 / cannot help+동명사 …하지 않을 수 없다, …하는 것을 피할 수 없다

Her son was very sick, so she **couldn't help but** cancel the picnic.
아들이 몹시 아파서 그녀는 야유회를 취소하지 않을 수 없었다.
I **could not help** burst**ing** into laughter.

[SYN] have no choice but to; be compelled(forced, obliged) to

나는 폭소하지 않을 수 없었다.

put up with …을 참다, 견디다
I cannot **put up with** your complaining any longer.
네가 불평하는 것을 더 이상 참을 수가 없다.
I cannot **put up with** Fred's impolite conduct.
프레드의 무례한 행동을 참을 수가 없다.

[SYN] endure; bear; stand; tolerate

pay〔give〕attention to …에 주의하다, 주목하다
He never **pays attention to** anything his wife says.
그는 아내의 이야기에는 결코 주의를 기울이지 않는다.
Pay attention to what you're doing.
하는 일에 주의를 기울여라.

[SYN] attend to

do without …없이 지내다, 견디다
If there's no sugar for our coffee, we will **do without**.
커피에 넣을 설탕이 없으면 없는 대로 마시겠다.
I can **do without** this book till Monday.
월요일까지 이 책은 없어도 좋다.

[SYN] be without; go without; manage without; dispense with

do nothing but …만 하고 있다, 단지 …할 뿐이다
On Saturday he **does nothing but** play soccer.
그는 토요일에는 축구만 한다.
Teddy **does nothing but** play a joke on his brother.
테디는 남동생을 놀리기만 한다.

[SYN] only; merely; simple
cf. nothing but 다만 …뿐, …에 불과한 (=only, solely)

at best / at the best 잘해야, 고작, 기껏해야, 좋게 말해도
Life is, **at best**, a sea of troubles.
기껏해야 인생은 고해이다.
We can't finish the job before midnight **at best**.
아무리 해도 자정 전에는 그 일을 끝낼 수 없다.

[SYN] under the best condition; even saying the best about the thing

as soon as …하자마자
You may go home **as soon as** you have finished the work.
그 일을 끝내면 집에 가도 좋다.
As soon as he arrived at the station, he telephoned his mother.
역에 도착하자마자 그는 어머니께 전화했다.
(=On arriving at the station, he telephoned his

[SYN] no sooner than; just after; when; immediately after〔when〕; the moment; the instant; directly; hardly … when〔before〕; scarcely … before〔when〕

mother.)

each other (두 사람이) 서로
The two men stood facing **each other** holding a gun.
두 남자는 권총을 들고 서로 마주보고 서 있었다.
I cannot understand why they quarrel and hate **each other** so much.
나는 그들이 어째서 서로 언쟁을 하고 그렇게 미워하는지 이해할 수 없다.

[SYN] with each other; mutually; reciprocally
cf. one another (세 사람 이상이) 서로

enjoy oneself 즐기다
We **enjoyed ourselves** very much at their wedding last night.
우리는 지난 밤 그들의 결혼식에서 매우 즐겁게 지냈다.
Did you **enjoy yourself** at the party last night?
지난 밤 파티에서 재미있었나요?
(=Did you have a wonderful time at the party last night?)

[SYN] have fun; have a good time

likely to [that] …일 것 같은, …하기 쉬운
He isn't **likely to** join our dance party tonight because he is very busy helping his mother's store.
그는 어머니 가게 일을 돕느라 매우 바빠서 오늘 밤 댄스 파티에 오지 않을 것 같다.
It is not **likely that** he should have written it.
아무래도 그가 그것을 쓴 것 같지가 않다.

[SYN] apt to; inclined to

be familiar with 1. 친하다, 가깝다 2. 잘(익히) 알고 있다, 정통하다, 익숙하다
I have **been familiar with** him for years.
나는 그와 수년 간 친하게 지내고 있다.
Having spent many years in America, he **is familiar with** American things.
그는 미국에서 여러 해를 지냈기 때문에 미국 사정을 잘 안다.
He **is familiar with** French.
그는 프랑스 어에 익숙하다.

[SYN] 1. be intimate; be close; be friendly 2. be well versed in; be well acquainted with

for the most part 1. 대부분은, 대개는, 거의 2. 보통은, 여느 때는
These books, **for the most part**, were written by an American novelist.

[SYN] 1. mostly; almost; chiefly 2. usually

이 책들은 대부분 미국 소설가가 쓴 것들이다.
Jack is **for the most part** a quiet and shy boy.
잭은 보통 때는 조용하고 수줍어하는 소년이다.

from hand to mouth 그날 벌어 그날 먹는, 장래를 위한 대책 없이

They live **from hand to mouth**.
그들은 그날그날 벌어서 겨우 살고 있다.
I had spent all the money in my possession and rubbed on **from hand to mouth**.
나는 가지고 있던 돈을 몽땅 써 버렸기 때문에 하루살이 상태였다.

[SYN] with attention only to immediate needs

be absent from …에 결석하다

Being ill, she **was absent from** school today.
아파서 그녀는 오늘 학교에 결석했다.
I **was absent from** the meeting not because I was busy but because I was ill.
내가 회의에 안 나간 것은 바빴기 때문이 아니라 아팠기 때문이다.

[SYN] be not present; be not in attendance; do not appear

be rich in …이 풍부하다

This country **is rich in** natural resources.
이 나라는 천연자원이 풍부하다.
The water from this well **is rich in** minerals.
이 우물은 미네랄이 풍부하다.

[SYN] be abundant; be abound in; be plentiful

above all (things) 무엇보다도, 첫째로, 특히

Above all, you must watch your weight to maintain your health.
건강을 유지하기 위해서는 무엇보다도 체중에 신경을 써야 한다.
The refugees want, **above all**, to live with dignity as humans.
난민들은 우선 인간으로서 존엄성을 가지고 살기를 원한다.

[SYN] first of all; among all things; especially

as a matter of fact 실제로는, 사실상

As a matter of fact, I know nothing about the matter.
실은, 그 문제에 대해서 아무것도 모릅니다.
(=The fact is that I have no idea about the matter.)

[SYN] in fact; really; to tell you the truth; actually

get used to 익숙해지다

I really can't **get used to** his rude manners.
그의 무례한 태도에는 정말이지 익숙해질 수가 없다.

[SYN] become accustomed to; grow familiar (with)

It took me much time to **get used to** sharing my room with one of my friends.
친구와 방을 같이 쓰는 것에 익숙해지는 데 오랜 시간이 걸렸다.

according to …에 의하면, …에 따라서

According to today's paper, there was a fire in this town last night.
오늘 신문에 의하면 어젯밤 이 마을에서 화재가 있었다.
Cut your coat **according to** your cloth.
천에 맞추어 재단하세요. (분수에 맞게 살아야 한다.(속담))

[SYN] in conformity with; in accordance with

by turns 번갈아, 교대로

We drove the car **by turns**.
우리는 차를 번갈아 운전했다.
When Jack had a fever, he felt cold and hot **by turns** for a few days.
잭은 열이 있을 때 며칠 동안 추웠다 더웠다 했다.

[SYN] in rotation; one after another
cf. in turn 번갈아, 차례로(= alternately) (by turns와는 달리 순서가 정해져 있음)
in one's turn …의 차례가 되어

get lost 1. 길을 잃다 2. (물건이) 없어지다

It is frightening to **get lost** in an unfamiliar place.
낯선 곳에서 길을 잃는다는 것은 무서운 일이다.
Be careful that it will not **get lost**.
그것이 없어지지 않도록 조심하시오.

[SYN] 1. lose oneself; lose one's way 2. be(get) lost; be missing

all the time 처음부터 끝까지, 그동안 죽, 시종, 언제나

He remained silent **all the time** during the party.
파티 동안 그는 시종일관 침묵을 지켰다.
The bridegroom smiled **all the time** at the wedding ceremony.
신랑은 결혼식 동안 계속 미소를 지었다.

[SYN] always; at all times

run across 우연히 만나다; 발견하다

I **ran across** my old friend in Seoul last week.
나는 지난 주에 서울에서 옛 친구를 우연히 만났다.
To **run across** someone is to meet him unexpectedly.
누군가를 뜻하지 않게 만난다는 것은 우연히 만난다는 것이다.

[SYN] meet(find) by chance; come across
cf. run after …을 뒤쫓다
run into 1. 우연히 만나다 2. …에 도달하다 3. …와 충돌하다
run over 자동차에 치다

behind one's back 1. …의 등 뒤에서 2. …가 없는 자리에서

The gentlemen like me don't criticize other people **behind their back**.

[SYN] 1. at the back of 2. at the place where one is not present

나처럼 점잖은 사람들은 뒤에서 다른 사람들을 비난하지 않는다.
He speaks ill of me **behind my back**.
그는 내가 없는 곳에서 나의 험담을 한다.

so long as ···하는 한, ···이기만 하다면, ···하는 동안

So long as it is interesting, anything will do.
재미만 있다면 무엇이든 좋다.
You may stay here **so long as** you can keep quiet.
네가 조용할 수만 있다면 여기 있어도 좋다.

[SYN] while; so far as; provided that; during
cf. so long 안녕(히 가십시오〔계십시오〕)(=good-bye; cheerio; farewell)

speak well〔highly, much〕of ···을 좋게 말하다, 칭찬하다

Is this the girl you **spoke well of** the other day?
이 아가씨가 일전에 당신이 칭찬하던 그 사람입니까?
The citizens of the city **speak highly of** their mayor.
이 도시 시민들은 그들의 시장을 매우 칭찬한다.
Jane, whose help I **speak much of**, is an experienced writer.
내가 도움을 아주 많이 받은 제인은 경험 많은 작가이다.

[SYN] praise; express praise of; bestow praise on

help oneself to 1. ···을 마음대로 먹다 2. 착복하다, 횡령하다

Please **help yourself to** whatever you like.
무엇이든 좋아하는 것을 마음껏 드십시오.
(=You may take and eat whatever you like.)
Please **help yourself to** anything you like.
마음에 드는 것을 마음껏 드십시오.
He **helped himself to** the public money.
그는 공금을 횡령했다.

[SYN] 1. serve oneself 2. embezzle; misappropriate to oneself

agree on (의견·조건 등에서) 일치하다

After a long discussion, we **agreed on** the terms of the contract.
오랜 토의 끝에 우리는 계약 조건에 일치했다.
We **agreed on** a quick decision.
우리는 빨리 결정할 것에 의견이 일치했다.

[SYN] conform to; be in accord with
cf. agree to (의견·계획 등에) 동의하다
agree with (음식·기후 등이 사람에게) 맞다; 동의하다

as often as not 종종, 대체로

As often as not, the children go to bed at this time.
대개 아이들은 이 시간쯤 잠을 잔다.
As often as not, he gives me a present on a special day like birthday.

[SYN] about as many times as not; often

대체로 그는 생일과 같은 특별한 날에 나에게 선물을 준다.

have (take) a look at …을 언뜻 보다, …을 한 번 (잠깐) 보다, …을 훑어보다

SYN. look at

James **has a look at** the papers every morning.
제임스는 매일 아침 신문을 훑어본다.
Let me **take a look at** those photos.
저 사진들을 보여 주십시오.
(= Let me see those photos.)

still more 훨씬(더욱) 더, 하물며 …인, 더욱 많이 (긍정문을 받음)

SYN. much more
cf. still less 하물며(더구나) …은 아닌 (부정문을 받음) (= much less)

Everyone has a right to enjoy his / her liberty, **still more** his / her life.
모든 사람은 자유를 향유할 권리가 있다. 더구나 그 인생은 더욱 그러하다.
He can speak French, **still more** English.
그는 프랑스 어를 말할 수 있으며 하물며 영어는 말할 것도 없다.

show up 나타나다, 나오다

SYN. turn up; come out; emerge; appear

John hasn't **shown up** after two hours of the appointed time.
존은 약속 시간 두 시간 후에도 나타나지 않았다.
Jane **showed up** late, so she couldn't see all of the movie.
제인은 늦게 와서 영화를 다 보지 못했다.

in other words 바꾸어 말하면, 즉

SYN. that is to say; to put it another way

In other words, the Bible is the voice of God.
다시 말해서 성경은 하나님의 음성이다.
He became, **in other words**, a great hero.
다시 말해서, 그는 훌륭한 대장부가 되었다.

if it were not for 만약 …이 없다면 (가정법 과거로 뜻은 현재)

SYN. but for; without; were it not for

If it were not for air and water, no living things could exist.
공기와 물이 없다면 생명체는 존재할 수 없을 것이다.
If it were not for the heat of the sun, nothing could live.
태양열이 없다면 아무것도 살 수 없을 것이다.

in short 한마디로 말해서, 요컨대
In short, John loves you.
한마디로 말해서 존은 당신을 사랑하고 있습니다.
In short, he is not to be trusted.
요컨대 그를 신용할 수 없다.

SYN. in a word; to cut a long story short; after all

as much 그 정도로, 꼭 그만큼(의)
Here is 100 dollars and I have **as much** at home.
여기 100달러가 있고 집에도 그만큼 있다.
You don't have to thank me, because I would do **as much** for anyone.
나에게 감사할 필요 없습니다. 누구에게나 그렇게 하니까요.

SYN. as such degree; the same; exactly that

wait on [upon] 시중들다
She **waited on** her husband who has been ill for many years.
그녀는 여러 해째 병든 남편의 시중을 들었다.
He always **waits on** his customers respectfully.
그는 언제나 손님을 예의바르게 대한다.

SYN. attend; serve; take care of

see A off A를 전송하다, 배웅하다
I **saw** my friend **off** at the airport when he left for the United States.
친구가 미국으로 떠날 때 나는 그를 공항에서 배웅했다.
Our friends like to **see off** all their friends who are traveling overseas.
우리 친구들은 해외 여행을 하는 모든 친구들을 배웅하기를 좋아한다.

SYN. go (be) with someone to say good-bye

stand by 1. …의 편을 들다, …을 지지하다, 원조하다 2. 방관하다
I'm sure she'll **stand by** me.
나는 그녀가 내 편을 들 것임을 확신한다.
He always **stood by** his friends in difficult times.
그는 친구들이 어려울 때 항상 도왔다.
Everyone just **stood by** and did nothing.
모두가 방관하기만 하고, 아무것도 하지 않았다.

SYN. 1. take side with; side with; support 2. look on

look up to …을 존경하다, …을 우러러보다
They all **look up to** him as their leader.
그들 모두는 그를 지도자로 존경하고 있다.
He is **looked up to** by all as their leader.
그는 지도자로서 모두에게 존경받고 있다.

SYN. respect; esteem; pay respect to; have respect for
OPP. look down on …을 경멸하다 (=despise)

for an instant 잠시 동안

We had only to wait **for an instant**.
우리는 잠시 동안 기다려야 했다.
I didn't lose my presence of mind **for an instant**.
나는 조금도 마음을 흩뜨리지 않았다.

[SYN] for a moment; for a short time
cf. in an instant 순식간에, 금방 (=in a moment; a second; at once; just now)

as well ···도 또한, 마찬가지로, ··· 외에, ···도 역시

The book tells about the writer's art world and his life **as well**.
그 책은 저자의 예술 세계에 대해 이야기하며 그의 인생에 대해서도 이야기한다.
After tidying up the bedroom, please clean this room **as well**.
침실을 치우고 나서 이 방도 청소해 주세요.
(=After you have tidied the bedroom, will you also clean this room?)

[SYN] also; in addition; too; besides

look down on [upon] ···을 내려다보다, ···을 경멸하다, 업신여기다

Do not **look down upon** the poor.
가난한 사람들을 업신여기지 마라.
Well-educated people never **look down on** the poor.
교양 있는 사람들은 가난한 사람들을 결코 멸시하지 않는다.

[SYN] make light of; have a contempt for; slight

be covered with ···으로 덮여 있다

The summit of the mountain **is covered with** fresh snow.
산의 정상은 깨끗한 눈으로 덮여 있다.
More than two-thirds of the earth's surface **is covered with** water.
지구 표면의 3분의 2 이상은 물로 덮여 있다.
(=Water covers more than two-thirds of the earth's surface.)

[SYN] be crowned with; be coated with

as a whole 총괄하여, 전체로서, 전체적으로

The international sports event is in the interests of the nation **as a whole**.
국제적인 스포츠 행사는 전반적으로 국가에 이익이 된다.
I don't like his style of working. We must treat these problems **as a whole**.
나는 그의 업무 방식이 마음에 들지 않는다. 이 문제들은 총괄해서 다

[SYN] all together; not separating; generally speaking
cf. on the whole 대체로, 대략 (=generally; roughly)

루어야 한다.

at the same time 동시에

He is a famous singer and **at the same time** a talented film producer.
그는 유명한 가수이며 동시에 재능 있는 영화 제작자이다.
If my family could all have lunch **at the same time**, I will be able to have more leisure time.
나의 가족이 동시에 점심 식사를 할 수 있다면 나는 여가 시간을 더 많이 가질 수 있을 것이다.

[SYN] simultaneously; at once; at one and the same time

cannot [never] fail to 반드시 …하다

He **cannot fail to** keep his important promise.
그는 중요한 약속은 꼭 지킨다.
He **never fails to** accept my advice.
그는 내 충고를 꼭 받아들인다.

[SYN] be sure to; without fail; beyond doubt

too ... to ~ 너무 …해서 ~할 수 없다

The problem was **too** difficult for any of us **to** solve.
그 문제는 너무 어려워서 우리 가운데 누구도 풀 수가 없었다.
(=The problem was so difficult that any of us couldn't solve it.)
You are **too** young **to** understand such things.
너는 너무 어려서 그런 것들을 이해할 수 없다.
(=You are so young that you can't understand such things.)

[SYN] so ... that one cannot ~

because of … 때문에, …한 까닭으로

Because of a heavy snowstorm, the train was delayed.
심한 눈보라로 열차가 지연되었다.
(=Owing to the heavy snowstorm, the train got delayed.)
He was absent from the party **because of** illness.
그는 병중이기 때문에 그 모임에 결석했다.(단문)
(=He was absent from the party because he was ill.(복문))

[SYN] on account of; due to; in consequence of
cf. owing to … 때문에

stand for …을 뜻하다, 나타내다

WHO **stands for** the World Health Organization.
WHO는 세계보건기구를 의미한다.
Words **stand for** idea.

[SYN] mean; signify; imply; show; describe

말은 개념을 나타낸다.

turn off 1. (가스·전등을) 끄다 2. 쫓아버리다, 해고하다

Be sure that you **turn off** the gas and all the lights before you leave.
외출하기 전에 가스와 전등을 끄는 것을 잊지 마라.
She **turned** the maid **off** for a misconduct.
그녀는 하녀가 행실이 나빠 해고했다.

[SYN] 1. cause to stop; switch off; shut off 2. part with; discharge; fire; dismiss

so far as …까지는, …하는 한에서는

So far as I know, he is a very famous painter.
내가 아는 한 그는 매우 유명한 화가이다.
So far as I know, he will be away for three months.
내가 아는 한 그는 3개월 동안 출타할 것이다.

[SYN] to the place mentioned; to the extent (degree) that

make oneself understood 자신이 말하는 것을 남에게 알게 하다, 이해시키다

I could not **make myself understood** in German.
나는 독일어로 말이 통하지 않았다.
She can't **make herself understood** in English.
그녀는 자신의 의사를 영어로 전달할 수 없다.

[SYN] make somebody understand; get somebody to grasp

all of a sudden 돌연히, 불의에

All of a sudden a person in the crowd burst into a laughter.
갑자기 좌중의 한 사람이 웃음을 터뜨렸다.
All of a sudden it became dark and began to rain.
갑자기 어두워지더니 비가 내리기 시작했다.

[SYN] suddenly; all at once; abruptly; on a sudden

as if 마치 …처럼

When he saw me, he was frightened **as if** I were a ghost.
그는 나를 보고 내가 마치 유령인 것처럼 놀랐다.
At the party, Fred acted **as if** he were a lover of everybody.
파티에서 프레드는 그가 마치 모든 사람들의 애인인 것처럼 행동했다.

[SYN] as though

be composed of …으로 이루어지다, …으로 형성되다, …으로 구성되다

A community **is composed of** individuals.
사회는 개인의 집합에 의해서 구성된다.
Water **is composed of** hydrogen and oxygen.

[SYN] be made up of; consist of

물은 수소와 산소로 구성되어 있다.

be anxious about …을 걱정하다, 염려되다

She **is anxious about** her son's safety on the trip.
그녀는 여행 중에 있는 아들의 안전을 걱정한다.
His family **were** so **anxious about** him that they could not sleep.
그의 가족들은 그의 일이 너무 걱정되어 잠을 이룰 수가 없었다.

[SYN] be worried about; care about
cf. be anxious for …을 바라다 (=wish for)
be anxious to …하고 싶어하다 (=want to)

cannot but + 동사원형 …하지 않을 수 없다

I **couldn't but** laugh at his joke.
나는 그의 농담을 듣고 웃지 않을 수 없었다.
Whatever he might choose to say, his auditors **cannot but** believe him.
그가 무엇을 말하든지 간에 청중들은 그를 믿을 수밖에 없다.

[SYN] be obliged to; be compelled to
cf. cannot help -ing …하지 않을 수 없다

look after 1. 보살피다, 돌보다, 감독하다 2. …에 주의를 기울이다, …에 관심을 갖다

Barbara has **looked after** the dog for three years.
바바라는 3년 동안 그 개를 돌봐 왔다.
Look after your health.
건강 조심하세요.

[SYN] 1. take care of; care for; look after 2. attend to; take interest in

worry about 걱정〔근심〕하다, 고민하다, 안달하다

He always has something to **worry about**.
그는 걱정이 끊이지 않는다.
Don't **worry about** trifles.
하찮은 일에 고민하지 마세요.

[SYN] be anxious about; feel anxious; apprehend

to one's surprise 놀랍게도

To my surprise, the train was almost empty.
놀랍게도 열차는 거의 비어 있었다.
To my surprise, he was killed in the traffic accident.
놀랍게도 그는 자동차 사고로 사망했다.

[SYN] at one's astonishment

as many 동수의, 같은 수의

While waiting for my old friend, 10 minutes seemed **as many** hours to me.
옛 친구를 기다리는 동안 십 분이 마치 열 시간처럼 느껴졌다.
In my opinion the writer is very careless. I found 10 mistakes in **as many** pages.
내 의견으로는 그 작가는 매우 부주의한 것 같다. 10쪽에서 10개의

[SYN] of the same number; the same number of

실수를 발견했다.

it goes without saying that ... ...은 말할 필요도 없다

It goes without saying that he will win the play tomorrow.
그가 내일 경기에서 이기리라는 것은 말할 필요도 없다.
It goes without saying that health is above wealth.
건강이 부보다 낫다는 것은 말할 필요도 없다.
(=Needless to say, health is better than wealth.
=There is no need to say that health is above wealth.)

SYN. It is needless to say that ...; needless to say that ...; naturally

beside oneself (분노·공포 등으로) 자제심을 잃어, 제정신을 잃어

I was **beside myself** with terror and anxiety.
나는 공포와 불안으로 미칠 지경이었다.
Today I didn't finish my duty and the boss was **beside himself**.
오늘 내가 할 일을 끝마치지 못해서 사장은 미친 듯이 화를 냈다.

SYN. very much excited; somewhat crazy

in a word 간단히 말하면, 요컨대

In a word, they were tired of eating outside.
간단히 말하면 그들은 외식하는 것에 싫증이 났다.
In a word, you should take responsibility for the accident.
요컨대 당신은 사고에 대해 책임을 져야 한다.

SYN. in short; to cut a long story short

be likely to (that) ... ...일 것 같다, ...하기 쉽다

Susan **is** not **likely to** come, so we'd better not wait for her.
수잔은 올 것 같지 않으니 기다리지 않는 것이 좋겠다.
It **is** not **likely that** he should have written it.
아무래도 그가 그것을 쓴 것 같지가 않다.

SYN. be apt to; be inclined to

quite a few 상당히 많은, (숫적으로) 꽤 많은

Quite a few letters have arrived asking about the new product.
신상품에 대해 문의하는 편지가 상당히 많이 왔다.
These days **quite a few** people live until they are 90.

SYN. many
cf. quite a little (양적으로) 상당히 많은 (=much)

요즘은 90세까지 사는 사람들을 드물지 않게 본다.
(=Recently there are quite a few people who live to be 90.
=It is not so rare to find people who live to be 90 these days.)

for a rainy day 만일을 위하여

The man saved up money **for a rainy day**.
그 남자는 만일의 경우를 위해 돈을 저축했다.
His life had been a failure, because he had almost no money **for a rainy day**.
그의 인생은 실패였는데 왜냐하면 만일을 위해 저축한 돈이 거의 없었기 때문이다.

[SYN] against a rainy day; if anything should happen

be sure to 꼭[반드시] …하다

Be sure to lock the door before you leave.
나가기 전에 반드시 문을 잠가라.
He **is sure to** pass the examination.
그는 틀림없이 시험에 합격할 것이다.

[SYN] not forget(fail) to

in person / in the flesh 몸소, 직접

A famous sports player came to our school **in person** today.
한 유명한 스포츠 선수가 오늘 우리 학교에 직접 왔다.
The president cannot attend the ceremony **in the flesh**, but his wife can.
대통령은 행사에 직접 참석할 수 없지만 영부인은 참석할 수 있다.

[SYN] oneself; personally

It is no use[good] -ing …해 봐도 소용 없다

It is no use lament**ing** (over) your ignorance of words.
단어를 모른다고 탄식해도 소용 없다.
It is no use try**ing** to persuade him.
그를 설득해 봐도 소용 없다.
(=There is no use (in) trying to persuade him.)

[SYN] There is no use (in) -ing

before long 머지않아, 얼마 되지 않아

It is likely to rain **before long** and you'd better take your umbrella.
곧 비가 올 것 같으니 우산을 가지고 가는 것이 좋겠다.
The cherry blossoms will come out **before long**.
벚꽃은 곧 필 것이다.

[SYN] shortly after; in the near future; in the short time
cf. long before … 이전에, 오래 전에 (=a long time ago; prior to)

as a matter of course 물론, 당연한 일로서
They always check people's addresses **as a matter of course**.
그들은 당연히 사람들의 주소를 항상 확인한다.
People must not allow the gender disparity at workplaces **as a matter of course**.
작업장에서의 성차별을 당연한 일로 허용해서는 안 된다.

SYN undoubtedly; needless to say

get over 1. 회복하다, 낫다, 극복하다 2. 끝마치다, 완성하다
She **got over** her illness in a few weeks.
2, 3주가 지나 그녀는 병에서 회복되었다.
They **got** the meeting **over** in 10 minutes.
그들은 10분만에 회의를 끝냈다.

SYN 1. get better; recover; overcome 2. finish; bring to an end

at (the) most 많아야, 기껏해야, 고작해야
We can pay $100 **at (the) most** for the product and not more.
우리는 그 제품에 대해 최대한 100달러를 지불할 수 있으며 그 이상은 안 된다.
I think he is 20 **at (the) most**, but he looks much older than his age.
그는 많아야 스무 살일 텐데 나이보다 훨씬 늙어 보인다.

SYN only; not more than; at best

make use of ···을 이용하다, 사용하다
Any member can **make use of** the reading room.
회원은 누구나 독서실을 이용할 수 있다.
He **makes** good **use of** his time.
그는 시간을 잘 이용한다.

SYN utilize; harness; take advantage of

compare with 비교하다, 대조하다
No student can **compare with** Fred in running.
달리기에서는 어떤 학생도 프레드와 비교될 수 없다.
His cooking is good, but it can't **compare with** yours.
그의 요리는 훌륭하지만 너의 것과는 비교가 안 된다.

SYN make a comparison; contrast; set against (같은 종류 등을 비교할 때 많이 쓰임)
cf. compare to 비유하다 (성질이나 종류가 다른 것을 비교할 때 많이 쓰임)

in part 부분적으로, 얼마간, 일부분
You are right **in part**.
어느 정도 네가 옳다.
His success is **in part** due to her help.
그의 성공의 일부는 그녀의 도움에 의한 것이다.

SYN partly; to some extent

make sure 1. 확신하다 2. 확인하다, 확실하게 하기 위해 …이라는 수단을 강구하다

I **made sure** she would consent, but she didn't.
나는 그녀가 반드시 승낙할 것이라고 확신했는데 그녀는 승낙하지 않았다.
I had my secretary **make sure** that all our papers are in order.
나는 비서에게 서류가 모두 순서대로 되어 있는지 확인시켰다.

SYN 1. feel sure; believe firmly 2. confirm; affirm

in the first place [instance] 맨 먼저, 우선 무엇보다도

In the first place, you should be punctual.
우선 당신은 시간을 엄수해야 한다.
In the first instance, you should have enough money to buy it.
우선 당신은 그것을 살 충분한 돈이 있어야 한다.

SYN first of all; above all

due to … 때문에, …로 인해

Due to heavy smoking, he lost his health and now is lying in bed.
담배를 많이 피웠기 때문에 그는 건강을 잃어 이제 침대에 누워 있다.
Due to his lack of practice, the pianist couldn't win the contest.
연습 부족으로 그 피아니스트는 대회에서 우승하지 못했다.

SYN owing to, because of; on account of

so far 지금까지

He has eaten only bananas **so far**.
그는 지금까지 바나나만 먹었을 뿐이다.
We've had no danger **so far**.
지금까지 위험은 없었다.

SYN up to now; until now

without (a) doubt 의심할 여지없이, 틀림없이, 꼭

He is **without a doubt** the best-looking man I've ever seen!
그는 의심할 여지없이 내가 지금까지 본 가장 잘 생긴 남자다!
I believe **without doubt** that she is innocent.
나는 그녀가 결백하다고 믿어 의심치 않는다.

SYN beyond doubt; certainly; without question

from time to time 때때로

I write to her **from time to time**.
나는 때때로 그녀에게 편지를 쓴다.
From time to time he would look at my account

SYN at times; (every) now and then; now and again; on occasion; sometimes

book to see that it was all correct.
때때로 그는 나의 금전출납부를 조사하여 제대로 되어있는지 확인해 보는 것이었다.

set ... free 해방시키다

We caught a butterfly in a net, but later we **set** it **free**.
우리는 잠자리채로 나비를 한 마리 잡았지만 나중에 놓아주었다.
The committee agreed to **set** the man **free**.
위원회는 그 남자를 석방하는 데 동의했다.

[SYN] make free; liberate; let out

be free of 면제를 받다, 부과되지 않고 있다

Applicants **are** admitted **free of** entrance fee this month.
이번 달 입학생에게는 입학금을 면제한다.
For passengers older than 65, the bus **is free of** charge.
65세가 넘은 승객들에 대해 버스는 무료이다.

[SYN] be exempted from taxation

as far as 1. ⋯에 관한 한〈범위〉 2. ⋯까지〈장소〉

As far as I know, he is an honest man.
내가 아는 한, 그는 정직한 사람이다.
I'll go with you **as far as** the city.
나는 그 도시까지 당신과 동행하겠습니다.

[SYN] 1. as regards 2. until
cf. as far as ... is concerned
⋯에 관한 한

sooner or later 조만간, 머지않아

Sooner or later you will have to read this book.
조만간 너는 이 책을 읽어야 할 것이다.
We shall die **sooner or later**.
늦든 빠르든 우리는 반드시 죽는다.

[SYN] at some time or other; finally

arrive at ⋯에 도착하다, 결론에 도달하다

The train **arrived at** the station at noon.
열차는 정오에 도착했다.
When I **arrived at** the village it had already been destroyed by the typhoon.
그 마을에 도착해 보니, 이미 태풍으로 쑥밭이 돼 있었다.
(=When I got to the village it was already devastated by the typhoon.)

[SYN] get to; reach a conclusion

both [at once] ... and ~ ⋯뿐만 아니라 ~도

He is **both** a poet **and** a painter.

[SYN] not only ... but (also)~; as well as; besides

그는 시인일 뿐만 아니라 화가이기도 하다.
He speaks **both** French **and** Italian well.
그는 프랑스 어도 이탈리아 어도 능통하다.

for a while 한동안, 잠시 동안
Just wait there **for a while** and then I will help you anyway.
거기서 잠시 기다리시면 어쨌든 도와 드리겠습니다.
Please wait here **for a while**.
이 곳에서 잠시만 기다려 주십시오.

SYN. a minute; for some time; a moment

believe in 믿다, 신용하다, 진실로 받아들이다
He did not **believe in** what I was talking about.
그는 내가 하는 말을 전혀 믿지 않았다.
Do you **believe in** ghosts?
영혼의 존재를 믿는가?

SYN. trust; have trust in; give credit

to one's face …의 면전에서, 노골적으로
I refused his marriage proposal **to his face**.
나는 그의 면전에서 청혼을 거절했다.
He isn't a type of man who likes to be praised **to his face**.
그는 면전에서 칭찬받는 것을 좋아하는 그런 사람이 아니다.

SYN. in someone's presence; directly to someone

carry out (계획·약속·명령 등을) 성취하다
It is easy to make plans, but difficult to **carry** them **out**.
계획을 세우는 것은 쉽지만, 그것을 실행하는 것은 어렵다.
You are here to **carry out** orders.
너는 명령을 수행하기 위해 여기 와 있다.

SYN. perform; accomplish; execute; achieve

but for …이 없다면, …이 아니었다면 (뒤에 구가 옴)
But for your help, we couldn't have succeeded in the adventure.
당신 도움이 없었다면 우리는 모험에서 성공할 수 없었을 것이다.
But for water, nothing can live in the earth.
물이 없으면 지구 상에서 어떤 것도 살 수 없다.

SYN. unless; if not; without
cf. but that …이 없다면 (뒤에 절이 옴) (=but for the fact that)

most of all 무엇보다도
Most of all you have to learn to speak clearly in front of many people.
무엇보다도 많은 사람들 앞에서 분명하게 말하는 법을 배워야 한다.

SYN. first of all; most importantly

Most of all I want to buy a car this summer.
무엇보다도 이번 여름에는 자동차를 사고 싶다.

take part (in) (…에) 참가(관계, 공헌)하다

She **takes part in** after-school programs, like playing in the band.
그녀는 밴드부와 같은 방과 후 프로그램에 참여한다.
America is willing to **take part in** discussing worldwide reduction of armaments.
미국은 전세계적인 무기 감축 회의에 참석할 의향이다.

[SYN.] participate in; join in

may well …하는 것도 무리는 아니다(당연하다)

He **may well** be proud of his bright son.
그가 영리한 아들을 자랑하는 것도 무리가 아니다.
He **may well** be angry at your behavior.
그가 당신의 태도에 화를 내는 것은 당연하다.

[SYN.] it is natural that …; have a good reason to

be willing to 기꺼이 …하다

They **were willing to** undertake the job at that time.
그 당시 그들은 기꺼이 그 일을 떠맡았다.
He **is willing to** act the part of guide.
그는 기꺼이 안내 역할을 해 준다.

[SYN.] be ready to do something; be agreeable

all day (long) 하루 종일, 종일토록

We worked **all day** to meet the deadline.
우리는 마감일에 맞추기 위해 하루 종일 일했다.
You are complaining I didn't give you a call today, but I was busy **all day**.
당신은 내가 오늘 전화하지 않았다고 불평하지만 나는 종일토록 바빴다.

[SYN.] the whole day; for a whole day; throughout the day

be apt at …을 잘 한다, …의 명수다

He **is** uneducated, but **apt at** seeking out various means.
그는 교육은 잘 받지 못했지만 다양한 방법을 찾는 데는 명수다.
The girl **is apt at** mathematics and actually better than her teacher.
그 소녀는 수학을 잘 하는데 사실 선생님보다 더 잘 한다.

[SYN.] be good at; be proficient in

carry on 1. (임무·일을) 계속하다, 속행하다 2. 경영하다

[SYN.] 1. continue; last; maintain; keep up with 2. conduct

He has decided to **carry on** the work.
그는 그 일을 계속하기로 결심했다.
Teddy and his brother **carried on** a computer business.
테디와 그의 형은 컴퓨터 회사를 경영했다.

business; manage; run

by chance 우연히, 뜻밖에

By chance, I saw a teacher who taught me at elementary school.
초등학교 때 나를 가르쳐 주신 선생님을 우연히 만났다.
(=I happened to see one of my elementary school teachers.)
I met her **by chance** at a restuarant yesterday.
어제 어떤 음식점에서 나는 우연히 그녀를 만났다.

[SYN] accidently; by accident

surrounded by〔with〕 …에 둘러싸인, 에워싸인

The ski resort is **surrounded by** beautiful mountains.
그 스키 리조트는 경치 좋은 산으로 둘러싸여 있다.
The old man sat **surrounded by** some children.
노인은 아이들에게 둘러싸여 앉아 있었다.

[SYN] encircled by

in itself 그 자체, 본래

Human life is a mystery **in itself**.
인간의 삶은 그 자체가 신비이다.
In a capitalism, competition is not an evil **in itself**.
자본주의에서 경쟁 자체는 나쁜 것이 아니다.

[SYN] fundamentally; essentially

at once 곧, 즉시

You must start **at once**, or you will not be able to catch up your friends.
당장 출발하지 않으면 친구들을 따라잡지 못할 것이다.
We must start **at once**, or we shall miss the train.
곧 출발하지 않으면 기차를 놓칠 것이다.

[SYN] soon; right now; without delay; immediately; on the spot

no longer 이제는 …아닌

We can **no longer** imagine living without cars.
이제는 차가 없는 삶을 상상할 수 없다.
(=We cannot now imagine what life would be like without cars.
=We do not know what our daily life would be like if we had no cars.)

[SYN] not ... any longer

English is **no longer** a subject one takes just to study Western culture.
영어는 이제 단지 서양 문화를 배우기 위해 공부하는 과목이 아니다.
(=Studying English is no longer just a means of learning Western culture.
=English is not any longer a subject one takes just to study Western culture.)

in one's place ···대신에

I want you to attend the meeting **in my place**.
나 대신으로 네가 그 모임에 참석해 주었으면 한다.
You go to the concert **in my place** this evening.
나 대신 오늘 저녁 음악회에 가거라.

[SYN] in place of, instead of

of importance 중요한

This is a matter **of** real **importance** to me.
이것은 나에게 정말 중요한 문제이다.
He is a person **of importance** in the field of art.
그는 예술 분야에서 중요한 인물이다.

[SYN] important; momentous; consequential

find out 발견하다, 찾아내다, 확인하다

When did you **find** it **out**?
언제 그것을 발견했니?
We must **find out** who lost this money.
누가 이 돈을 잃어버렸는지 알아봐야겠다.

[SYN] discover or confirm a thing

as usual 여느 때와 마찬가지로, 여느 때처럼

He arrived late at the meeting **as usual**.
그는 여느 때처럼 모임에 늦게 왔다.
As usual, Tommy was late to the office and scolded by his boss.
토미는 여느 때와 마찬가지로 지각을 해서 상사에게 꾸지람을 들었다.

[SYN] in the usual way

be caught in a shower 소나기를 만나다

I **was caught in a shower** on my way home and got soaked.
집으로 돌아오는 길에 소나기를 만나 흠뻑 젖었다.
I **was caught in a** sudden **shower**.
나는 갑작스런 소나기를 만났다.

[SYN] be overtaken by a shower

from now on 지금부터는, 앞으로, 금후

[SYN] after this; in the future

What will you do **from now on**?
앞으로 어떻게 할 작정인가?
(=What is your plan for the future?)
I'll be more careful **from now on**.
지금부터 더 주의하겠습니다.

on the other hand 다른 한편으로는, 반면에, 이와 반대로

[SYN] in other respect; on the contrary

I rarely remember names; **on the other hand**, I remember numbers well.
나는 이름은 거의 기억하지 못하지만 반면에 숫자는 잘 기억한다.
He wanted to go to the park; the children, **on the other hand**, wanted to stay home.
그는 공원에 가고 싶어 했지만 반면 아이들은 집에 있기를 원했다.

at last 드디어, 결국, 마침내

[SYN] in the end; finally

He died **at last**.
그는 마침내 죽었다.
He has finished the work **at last**.
그는 드디어 그 일을 끝마쳤다.

noted for …으로 알려진, …으로 유명한

[SYN] well known for; famous for

The city is **noted for** many historic relics and tourist sites.
그 도시는 유적과 관광 명소가 많기로 유명하다.
Bill is widely **noted for** his interest in old books.
빌은 고서에 관심이 많은 것으로 널리 알려져 있다.

on behalf of 1. …을 대신하여, …을 대표하여 2. …을 위하여

[SYN] 1. as the representative of 2. for the sake of

The captain accepted the cup **on behalf of** the team.
주장은 팀을 대표하여 우승컵을 받았다.
He saves **on behalf of** his son.
그는 아들을 위해서 저축을 한다.

as … as …만큼, …와 같은 정도로

[SYN] just as much; equally
cf. not so … as ~ (부정문) ~만큼 …하지 않은

She was **as** beautiful **as** you in her highschool days.
그녀는 고등학교 시절에 너만큼 예뻤지.
The tastes of the women were **as** different **as** their faces.
여인들의 취미는 그들의 얼굴이 다른 만큼 달랐다.

by the hour 1. 시간제로 2. 몇 시간이나 계속하여

The employees of the company are paid **by the hour**.
그 회사 종업원들은 시간제로 임금을 받는다.
On Sundays, I sit reading books **by the hour**.
일요일이면 나는 앉아서 몇 시간이고 책을 읽는다.

SYN. 1. by the hour-fair system 2. for hour after hour; for considerable periods at a time

consist of …으로 되다, …으로 이루어져 있다

The Milky Way **consists of** about 100,000 million stars.
은하수는 약 천억 개의 별로 되어 있다.
The report **consists of** four parts and they are connected each other.
보고서는 네 부분으로 되어 있으며 그것들은 서로 연결되어 있다.

SYN. be made up of; comprise
cf. consist in …에 있다, …에 존재하다 (=lie in; exist in)
consist with 양립하다, 일치하다 (=coincide with; answer to)

(be) due to+동사 …할 예정이다

The ship **was due to** arrive at Busan last Monday.
그 배는 지난 월요일에 부산에 도착할 예정이었다.
The president **is due to** arrive here in an hour.
대통령은 한 시간 후 이 곳에 도착할 예정이다.

SYN. be going to, be scheduled to

at first 처음에는, 최초에

At first he was in favor of my proposal, but later he changed his mind.
그는 처음에는 내 제안에 찬성했지만 후에 마음을 바꾸었다.
English is difficult **at first**, however, you will soon find it easy to learn.
영어가 처음에는 어렵지만 곧 배우기 쉽다는 것을 알게될 것이다.

SYN. In the beginning; at the start

insist on [upon] …을 주장하다

He **insisted on** his innocence.
그는 자신의 무죄를 주장했다.
I **insisted on** the justice of my cause.
나는 내 주장이 옳다는 것을 강조했다.

SYN. persist in; demand; assert
cf. insist on [upon] one('s) -ing (사람이) …할 것을 주장하다

belong to …에 속해 있다

She **belongs to** the tennis club.
그녀는 테니스 클럽에 속해 있다.
The terrorists are believed to **belong to** the Russian mafia.
테러범들은 러시아 마피아에 속해 있는 것으로 믿어진다.

SYN. be owned by someone

side by side 나란히, 병행하여
The bride and groom were sitting **side by side**.
신랑 신부는 나란히 앉아 있었다.
The two boys walked **side by side** at the corner street.
두 소년은 모퉁이 거리에서 나란히 걸었다.

SYN in line; in order

to be frank with you 솔직하게 말하면, 사실은
To be frank with you, I do not like him.
솔직히 말하면 나는 그가 마음에 들지 않는다.
To be frank with you, he is fool.
솔직하게 말하면 그는 바보다.

SYN in plain words; to speak honestly; put it bluntly

at all 1. (부정문에서) 전혀 2. (긍정문에서) 여하튼, 어쨌든 간에 3. (의문문에서) 도대체 4. (조건문에서) 적어도
She was not **at all** happy to hear the news that she was promoted.
그녀는 승진했다는 소식을 듣고도 전혀 기뻐하지 않았다.
For the vacation, our family like to go anywhere **at all**.
휴가 때 우리 가족은 아무튼 어디든 가고 싶어 한다.
Why don't you attend the ceremony **at all**? You are the hero of today.
도대체 왜 행사에 참석하지 않는 거야? 당신이 오늘의 주인공이잖아.
If you do something **at all**, you must do it well.
적어도 무슨 일을 할 때는 잘 해야 한다.

SYN 1. in any manner; in the small amount 2. at every place; in every direction 3. on the earth 4. at least

in (the) face of …에 직면하여, …에도 불구하고, …을 정면으로 보고, …와 맞대고
They marched **in the face of** a heavy snowfall.
그들은 폭설에도 불구하고 행진했다.
They were steadfast **in the face of** disaster.
그들은 불행에 직면하여 굴하지 않았다.

SYN in spite of; notwithstanding; when confronted with

once upon a time 옛날에, 오래 전에
Once upon a time my mother was the most beautiful girl in the area.
옛날에 어머니는 이 곳에서 가장 아름다운 아가씨였다.
Once upon a time there were many wild animals in the nearby forest.
옛날에 근처 숲에는 야생 동물이 많이 있었다.

SYN sometime before now; long ago

at sea 1. 당황하여 2. 항해 중인
When it comes to higher math, Tom is completely **at sea**.
고등수학에 이르면 톰은 완전히 쩔쩔맨다.
He had never been on a ship **at sea**.
그는 배를 타고 항해해 본 적이 한 번도 없었다.

[SYN] 1. embarrassed; not knowing what to do; bewildered 2. sailing; on an ocean voyage

be born of …로 출생되다, …로부터 나오다
I know they are brothers but they **weren't born of** same mother.
그들은 형제이지만 한 어머니에게서 태어나지 않았다고 나는 알고 있다.
He **was born of** rich parents and doesn't know what the hunger is.
그는 부자 부모에게서 태어나서 배고픔이 어떤 것인지 모른다.

[SYN] come from; spring from
cf. born to …에게 탄생되다

close by 바로 곁에
You will be able to find it easily because the theater is located **close by** the station.
극장은 역 바로 옆에 있으므로 찾기가 쉬울 것이다.
Our school is **close by** the police station.
우리 학교는 경찰서 가까이 있다.

[SYN] near; nearby; not far off; near at hand

without notice 예고 없이, 무단으로
Yesterday I absented myself from school **without notice**.
어제 나는 무단결석했다.
He frequently pays a visit with his friend **without notice**.
그는 자주 친구하고 아무 예고도 없이 방문한다.

[SYN] without warning; unannounced; without leave

to be sure 과연 (…이지만), 확실히, 그렇군 (가끔 but을 동반)
To be sure, the project will require a lot of patience and hard work.
분명 그 프로젝트는 많은 인내심과 근면을 요할 것이다.
She is not bright, **to be sure**, but she is very charming.
확실히 그녀는 머리가 총명한 편은 아니지만 매우 매력적이다.

[SYN] indeed; of course; for sure

by accident 우연히
I met her at Seoul Station **by accident**.

[SYN] by chance; accidently
[OPP] on purpose 고의로 (=

나는 우연히 서울역에서 그녀를 만났다.
I came across this photo **by accident**.
나는 우연히 이 사진을 발견했다.

by name …라고 하는 이름의, 이름을 들어, 개인적으로

At a movie theater, I met a really lovely girl, Peggy **by name**.
영화관에서 나는 페기라는 이름의 정말 사랑스러운 소녀를 만났다.
I can't ask his help, because I only know him **by name**.
나는 그의 이름만 알고 있기 때문에 그의 도움을 청할 수 없다.

[SYN] called; calling name

and so on / and so forth 등등, …따위

The artist mostly draws fruit, like apples, peaches, bananas, **and so on**.
그 화가는 사과, 복숭아, 바나나 등 과일을 주로 그린다.
I love all fruits — oranges, apples **and so forth**.
나는 오렌지, 사과 등 과일은 뭐든지 좋아한다.

[SYN] etc.; and what not; and the like

a bit 조금, 소량

You look **a bit** tired.
너는 조금 피곤해 보인다.
I was **a bit** surprised.
나는 좀 놀랐다.

[SYN] a small amount; some; a little
cf. bit by bit 조금씩 (=gradually; little by little)

to begin with 우선, 첫째로

It's hopeless. **To begin with**, I have no money.
그것은 가망이 없다. 우선 나에게는 돈이 없다.
To begin with, the ratio between attackers and defenders is roughly the same.
우선 공격수와 수비수의 비율이 거의 같다.

[SYN] first of all; to start with

by halves 어중간하게, 불완전하게, 절반만

You do everything **by halves**; nothing ever gets done!
넌 무슨 일이든지 불완전하게 해. 아무것도 끝을 내지 못하잖아!
It's no good doing things **by halves**.
일을 하다 중단하면 못쓴다.

[SYN] incompletely

arrive in …에 도착하다

He **arrived in** Seoul yesterday.
그는 어제 서울에 도착했다.

[SYN] reach in; get to, gain
cf. arrive on 정각에 도착하다 (= arrive at the appointed (fixed)

You should have **arrived in** Paris two days ago.
당신은 이틀 전에 파리에 도착했어야 했다.

be famous for ···으로 유명하다, ···으로 이름이 높다
Korea **is famous for** its natural scenery.
한국은 자연 풍경으로 유명하다.
The river **is famous for** salmon even now.
그 강은 지금도 연어로 유명하다.

[SYN] well-known; renowned; famed for
cf. notorious for (나쁜 의미로) 유명한

safe and sound [sure] 무사히, 탈 없이
The package you had sent me arrived **safe and sound**.
당신이 보낸 소포는 아무 탈 없이 도착했습니다.
The scouts returned home from the camp **safe and sure**.
스카우트 단원들은 캠프에서 무사히 귀가했다.

[SYN] not harmed; not hurt

stand up for 옹호(변호)하다, ···의 편을 들다, 주장하다
We have a moral obligation to **stand up for** the poor.
우리에게는 가난한 사람들을 옹호해야 할 도덕적 의무가 있다.
Whenever John is criticized, his friend Bill **stands up for** him.
존이 비난받을 때마다 친구인 빌이 그의 편을 든다.
The workers of the factory always **stand up for** their rights.
그 공장 근로자들은 항상 자신들의 권리를 주장한다.

[SYN] defend; back up; support; vindicate
cf. stand up to ···에 (용감히) 맞서다 (=confront fearlessly)
stand in for ···의 대역을 하다

all the year round 일년 내내, 일년 중
The top of the mountain is covered with snow **all the year round**.
그 산 정상은 일년 내내 눈으로 덮여 있다.
He indulged in some sports or other **all the year round**.
그는 일년 내내 스포츠에 열중해 있다.

[SYN] throughout the year

as it were 말하자면, 이른바
You can trust what he is saying, because he is, **as it were**, a walking dictionary.
그는 말하자면 움직이는 사전이니까 그의 말을 믿어도 된다.
He stood upon a pile of eggs, **as it were**.
그는 말하자면 계란 더미 위에 서 있는 격이었다.

[SYN] so-called; as might be said to be; as if it really were; seemingly

by onself 혼자, 단독으로, 혼자 힘으로
I live (all) **by myself**.
나는 혼자 산다.
I cannot finish it **by myself**.
나는 혼자서 그것을 마칠 수 없다.

[SYN] alone
cf. for oneself 혼자 힘으로 (= by one's own effort)
of oneself 저절로, 자발적으로 (= naturally; spontaneously)

consist in …에 있다, …에 존재하다
The true wealth does not **consist in** what we have, but in what we are.
참된 부는 재산이 아니라 인격에 있다.
Wisdom does not **consist** only **in** knowing many facts.
지혜란 단지 많은 사실을 알고 있는 것만이 아니다.

[SYN] exist in; lie in; be in existence

die of (병·기아·늙음·부상 등으로) 죽다
He **died of** typhoid fever.
그는 장티푸스로 죽었다.
It is pity that she has **died of** the bite of a snake.
유감스럽게도 그 여자는 뱀에게 물려 죽었다.

[SYN] pass away; perish
cf. die from (부주의·과로·쇠약 등으로) 죽다

do away with …을 없애다, 폐지하다
Society must **do away with** racial discrimination.
사회는 인종차별을 폐지해야 한다.
We should **do away with** this regulation.
이 규칙을 없애야 한다.

[SYN] abolish; remove; get rid of

succeed in …에 성공하다, 출세하다
He **succeeded in** solving the problem.
그는 그 문제를 푸는 데 성공했다.
She **succeeded in** business and is now a millionaire.
그녀는 사업에 성공해서 지금 백만장자다.

[SYN] be successful; make good; make a good of it

one thing, another …와 ~는 별개다
To know is **one thing**, to teach **another**.
알고 있는 것과 가르치는 것은 별개다.
To make a plan is **one thing**, to carry it out (is) quite **another**.
계획하는 것과 실행하는 것은 아주 다른 문제이다.

[SYN] one is different from another

on earth 1. 도대체 2. 전혀, 조금도 (부정을 강조)
What **on earth** do you expect me to do?

[SYN] 1. in the world; under the sun; in the name of the

도대체 나더러 어떻게 하란 말이냐?
It's no use **on earth**.
그것은 전혀 쓸모가 없다.

a pair of 한 쌍의

There is **a pair of** glasses on the desk.
책상 위에 안경이 하나 놓여있다.
He packed **two pairs of** trousers and four shirts.
그는 바지 두 벌과 셔츠 네 장을 꾸렸다.

be unwilling to …하기를 좋아하지 않다

He **was unwilling** for his poems **to** be published.
그는 자기 시가 출판되는 것을 좋아하지 않았다.
I **was unwilling to** go.
나는 가고 싶지 않았다.

be bound for …행의

I should have got a train which **is bound for** Gangnung.
나는 강릉행 기차를 탔어야 했다.
Be careful not to take a bus that **is bound for** the lake.
호수로 가는 버스를 타지 않도록 주의해라.

care for 1. 돌보다 2. 좋아하다, 갈망하다

She became a nurse because she liked to **care for** people.
그녀는 사람들을 돌보는 게 좋아서 간호사가 되었다.
She doesn't **care for** spicy food.
그녀는 양념이 많이 들어간 요리는 좋아하지 않는다.

for all …임에도 불구하고

For all his wealth, he was still unhappy.
재산이 있음에도 그는 여전히 불행했다.
For all his city ways, he is a country boy at heart.
도시의 풍습대로 생활하지만, 그의 마음은 시골 소년이다.

in some respects 어떤 점에 있어(서)

In some respects John really resembles his dead father.
어떤 점에 있어서 존은 돌아가신 그의 아버지와 꼭 닮았다.
The Russians resemble the Chinese **in some**

God 2. (not) in the least; (not) at all

[SYN] a couple of
cf. a herd of cattle 소떼
a flock of geese 거위떼

[OPP] be willing to 기꺼이 …하다

[SYN] on the way to; going to

[SYN] 1. take care of; look after 2. have a liking for; be fond of (의문문, 부정문에 쓰임)

[SYN] with all; notwithstanding
cf. in spite of …에도 불구하고
(=despite; in the teeth of)

[SYN] in some ways
cf. in all respects 모든 점에서
in many respects 많은 점에서

respects.
러시아 인은 어느 점에서 중국인과 닮았다.

in order to (that) ···하기 위해서

He is working hard **in order to** pass the examination.
그는 시험에 합격하기 위해 열심히 공부하고 있다.
(= He is working hard so that he may pass the examination.)
I got up early **in order to** catch the train.
나는 기차 시간에 맞추기 위해 일찍 일어났다.

[SYN] so as to; so that ... may

succeed to ···을 계승(상속)하다, 뒤를 잇다

He has **succeeded to** family business.
그는 가업을 이어갔다.
The queen **succeeded to** the throne.
여왕은 왕위를 계승했다.

[SYN] inherit; take over; come into

were it not for 만일 ···이 없다면

Were it not for your advice, I would not know what to do.
만일 당신의 충고가 없다면 어떻게 해야 좋을지 모르겠습니다.
Were it not for his idleness, he would be a good student.
태만한 점만 없다면 그는 훌륭한 학생이 될 텐데.

[SYN] if it were not for; but for; without

year after year 해마다, 매년

He grew bigger and stronger **year after year**.
그는 해마다 더 크고 더 튼튼하게 자랐다.
I have led a very monotonous life **year after year**.
나는 해마다 매우 단조로운 생활을 해 왔다.

[SYN] every year; each year; yearly; from year to year

what we (you, they) call / what is called
소위, 이른바
This is **what we call** a brand-new idea.
이것은 소위 참신한 아이디어다.
None of his brilliant achievements were the result of **what is called** good luck.
그의 빛나는 업적 중 어느 것도 소위 행운의 결과는 아니었다.

[SYN] so-called; as it is called; as they say

by day 낮에, 주간에

As you are such an early sleeper, you must finish the study **by day**.

[SYN] during the day
[OPP] by night 밤에

너는 아주 일찍 잠을 자는 사람이므로 낮에 공부를 끝내야 한다.
Tom works at a factory **by day** and goes to school by night.
톰은 낮에는 공장에서 일하고, 밤에는 학교에 다닌다.

account for …을 설명하다, 밝히다, 해명하다

We cannot **account for** his strange behavior.
그의 이상한 행동을 설명할 수 없다.
Can you **account for** all the money you spent on your trip?
여행에 쓴 모든 돈을 설명할 수 있겠니?

[SYN] explain; prove

by the way 그런데, 겸하여서, (삽입어구로 쓰여) 말이 났으니 말이지

By the way, have you heard of him lately?
그런데 최근에 그의 소식 들은 적 있니?
Sally, **by the way**, was fired for stealing information on the new product.
말이 났으니 말이지 샐리는 신상품에 대한 정보를 빼낸 것 때문에 해고당했다.

[SYN] incidentally; however; while; and yet
cf. by the bye(by) 그런데, 말이 났으니 말이지
by way of …을 경유해서

here and there 여기저기에, 여기저기로

I looked **here and there** for my ring, but I couldn't find it.
나는 여기저기 반지를 찾아보았지만 찾지 못했다.
We went **here and there** looking for a place to camp.
우리는 야영할 장소를 찾아 여기저기 다녔다.

[SYN] in various directions

hurry up 서두르다

Hurry up, or you will miss the plane.
서두르지 않으면 비행기를 놓치겠다.
If you don't **hurry up**, you won't be able to see him.
서두르지 않으면 그를 볼 수 없을 것이다.

[SYN] make haste; be in haste
cf. in a hurry, in haste 서둘러서, 허둥지둥

what one is 사람의 현재의 모습, 인격, 인물

I owe **what I am** today to my parents.
오늘의 내가 있는 것은 부모님 덕분이다.
She is not **what she was** 20 years ago.
그녀는 20년 전의 그녀가 아니다.

[SYN] one's present self
cf. what one has 사람이 가진 것, 재산, 돈

call on 1. (사람을) 방문하다 2. 부탁하다, 요구하다, 호소하다

May I **call on** you tomorrow afternoon?
내일 오후에 찾아 뵈어도 되겠습니까?
The chairman **called on** him to make a few remarks.
의장은 그에게 몇 마디 말해 달라고 청했다.

[SYN] 1. pay a visit to; go on a visit to 2. ask; demand; appeal
cf. call at (장소를) 방문하다
call up …에 전화하다 (= telephone; ring up)

by means of …의 수단으로, …으로, …에 의하여

Thoughts are expressed **by means of** words.
생각은 말로 표현된다.
Mr. Jones succeeded **by means of** hard work.
존스 씨는 열심히 일해서 성공했다.

[SYN] by dint of; in the method of

a couple of 한 쌍의, 두 개의, 여러 개의

The vacation lasts **a couple of** weeks.
휴가는 2주일 간 계속된다.
I had only **a couple of** drinks.
나는 두서너 잔 마셨을 뿐이다.

[SYN] a pair of; a brace of; a few

in case of …의 경우에는

In case of fire, break the glass and push the red button.
화재시는 유리를 깨고 빨간 단추를 누르시오.
In case of emergency, call 119.
비상시에는 119번으로 전화하시오.

[SYN] in the event of

be superior to …보다 뛰어나다, …보다 우수하다

There are some rights which **are superior to** constitutions.
헌법에 우선하는 권리도 있다.
He **is superior to** me in mathematics.
그는 수학에서 나보다 뛰어나다.

[SYN] be better than; be above average
[OPP] be inferior to …보다 못하다 (=be lower in quality)

on account of … 때문에, …이므로

The picnic was canceled **on account of** the heavy rain.
폭우 때문에 야유회가 취소되었다.
I could not go there **on account of** the storm.
나는 폭풍 때문에 그 곳에 갈 수 없었다.
(= The storm prevented me from going there.)

[SYN] as a result of; because of

of oneself 저절로

[SYN] of its own accord;

A decayed tooth has come out **of itself**.
충치 하나가 저절로 빠져 버렸다.
The candle went out **of itself**.
촛불이 저절로 꺼졌다.

[SYN] spontaneously; naturally

engaged in …에 종사하는, …로 바쁜

Father had been **engaged in** the research job for 20 years.
아버지는 20년 동안 연구직에 종사해 오셨다.
I am **engaged in** writing a report on educational reform.
나는 교육 개혁에 대한 리포트를 쓰느라 바쁘다.

[SYN] occupied with; busy; indulged in
cf. be engaged to+명사 …와 약혼하다
engage to+동사 …하기로 약속하다 (=promise to)

(be) equal to 1. …을 감당할 수 있는, 역량이 있는 2. 같은, 동등한

Old as he is, my brother **is** still **equal to** the project.
나이는 많지만 내 형은 아직까지는 그 프로젝트를 감당할 수 있다.
You **are equal to** him in intelligence.
당신은 지적인 면에서 그와 맞먹는다.

[SYN] 1. able to+동사; competent for+명사; competent to+동사 2. same; equal

at any moment 언제 어느 때라도

Earthquakes may occur **at any moment**.
지진이 언제 어느 때 일어날지 모른다.
It may rain **at any moment** in this rainy season, so you'd better take an umbrella.
장마철에는 비가 언제라도 올 수 있으니 우산을 가져가는 것이 좋을 것이다.

[SYN] at any time; anytime; at a moment's notice

in the distance 멀리, 아주 먼 곳에

The traveler saw a light **in the distance**.
그 나그네는 멀리서 불빛을 보았다.
The valley was seen **in the distance**.
멀리 계곡이 보였다.

[SYN] far away
cf. at a distance 떨어져서

face to face 서로 마주 보고, 얼굴을 맞대고

If you have something to say, say it to me **face to face**.
하고 싶은 말이 있으면 내 얼굴을 보고 말하세요.
We came **face to face** at a street corner.
우리는 길 모퉁이에서 얼굴을 마주치게 되었다.

[SYN] facing each other

have difficulty (in) -ing …하느라 고생하다

[SYN] have a hard time -ing;

Billy speaks so fast that we **have difficulty (in)** understanding what he says.
빌리는 말을 너무 빨리 해서 그의 말을 이해하기가 어렵다.
(=The trouble is that Billy speaks too fast for us to follow.)
You'll **have difficulty[trouble] (in)** persuading him.
그를 설득하기가 힘이 들 것이다.
(=It will be difficult[hard] for you to persuade him.)

have trouble to + 동사

hundreds of 수백의
Hundreds of people will be present at the meeting tonight.
수백 명의 사람들이 오늘밤 모임에 나올 것이다.
Hundreds of people will come to see the race.
몇백 명이나 되는 사람들이 그 경주를 보러 올 것이다.

[SYN.] several hundred
cf. thousands of 수천의
tens of thousands of 수만(의)

be known to (as) …에게 알려지다
Her kindness **is known to** everybody.
그녀의 친절은 모두에게 알려져 있다.
His name **is known to** the world.
그의 이름은 세상에 알려져 있다.

[SYN.] be famous to
cf. be known by …으로 판단되다
(=can judge somebody or something)

be tired from [with] …으로 피곤하다
I **was tired from** the hard work.
힘든 일로 나는 피곤했다.
I **am tired from** walking from day to day.
연일 걸어서 피곤하다.

[SYN.] be weary with
cf. be tired of …에 싫증나다 (= be weary of)

(be) dressed in (옷을) 입고 있는
For the concert, all of our members must **be dressed in** white.
콘서트를 위해서 모든 회원들은 흰색 옷을 입어야 한다.
When the accident happened, both men **were dressed in** black.
그 사고가 났을 때 두 남자는 검은 옷을 입고 있었다.

[SYN.] clad in, wearing
cf. dress oneself 옷을 입다, 몸치장(성장)하다 (=put clothes on; get dressed)

drop in 잠시 들르다
I must be going now as I'd like to **drop in** another place on the way home.
집에 가는 길에 들를 데가 있어서 이만 가 봐야겠다.

[SYN.] stop in for a short visit

I **dopped in** on one of my old friends on my vacation trip to Florida.
플로리다로 휴가 여행을 가는 도중에 옛 친구에게 잠시 들렀다.

divide into 등분하다, 나누다
The river **divides** here **into** two branches.
강은 여기서 두 갈래로 갈라진다.
Divide 15 **into** 60.
60을 15로 나누어라.

[SYN] divide equally; deal out equally
cf. divide 두 패로 나눠 찬부를 결정하다, 표결하다 (= go into division; take a division; put to vote)

be aware of …을 알아차리다, …을 인식하다
He does not seem to **be aware of** the importance of honesty.
그는 정직의 중요성을 인식하지 못하는 것 같다.
I **was** not **aware of** how seriously ill my mother was.
나는 어머니의 병이 어느 정도 중한가를 알지 못했다.

[SYN] getting to know; recognizing

by mistake 실수로, 잘못하여
Don't scold him so much. I am sure he had done so **by mistake**.
그를 너무 나무라지 마라. 나는 그가 실수로 그렇게 한 것이라 확신한다.
Someone has taken my bag **by mistake**.
누군가 내 가방을 잘못 갖고 가 버렸다.

[SYN] as the result of a mistake; through error

the one … the other 전자는 … 후자는
I have a son and a daughter. **The one** is in New York, and **the other** in London.
나에게는 아들과 딸이 하나씩 있는데 아들은 뉴욕에 있고 딸은 런던에 있다.
Neither my elder brother nor my younger brother is in Korea; **the one** is in China and **the other** is in England.
형도 남동생도 한국에 없다. 형은 중국에 남동생은 영국에 있다.

[SYN] the former … the latter; that … this

these days 요즘
These days many students have personal computers.
요즘은 많은 학생들이 PC를 가지고 있다.
In **these days** almost every house has a car.
요즘은 거의 모든 가정이 자동차를 소유하고 있다.

[SYN] at present; nowadays; today

write down 써 두다, 기록하다

Some students **write down** every word the professors say.
어떤 학생들은 교수들이 하는 말을 한 마디도 빠지지 않고 기록한다.
I **wrote down** my friend's new address.
나는 친구의 새 주소를 적었다.

[SYN] put down in writing; put something on record

with all …에도 불구하고, …이 있으면서도

With all his merits, he was not proud.
여러 가지 장점이 있음에도 불구하고 그는 거만하지 않았다.
With all his learning, he is the simplest of men.
그만한 학식이 있으면서도 그는 정말 단순한 사람이다.

[SYN] in spite of; notwithstanding; for all

in order 1. 차례차례, 정연하게 2. (의사 진행 규칙에) 맞는

Line up and walk to the classroom **in order**.
줄을 서서 교실까지 차례차례 걸어가라.
He put his room **in order**.
그는 방을 잘 정돈했다.
It isn't **in order** to ask such inappropriate questions at the meeting.
회의 중에 그런 부적절한 질문을 하는 것은 규칙에 어긋난다.

[SYN] 1. in arrangement 2. proper; suitable
cf. out of order 1. 어지럽혀져서 2. 상태가 나쁜, 고장인

in the end 마침내, 결국

There were no people left **in the end**.
결국 아무도 없게 되었다.
All will come right **in the end**.
결국은 모든 것이 좋아질 것이다.

[SYN] finally; at last; after all; ultimately
cf. in the long run 마침내, 결국, 필경

add to …을 늘리다, 더하다, 증가시키다

The music **added to** our enjoyment.
음악이 즐거움을 증가시켜 주었다.
Books **add to** the pleasure of life.
책은 인생의 즐거움을 증가시킨다.

[SYN] increase; make greater augment

a bit of 한 조각의, 소량의

The beggar asked me **a bit of** money and I gave him it.
거지가 나에게 돈을 조금 구걸해서 나는 돈을 주었다.
There is not **a bit of** difference.
조금도 틀리지 않는다.

[SYN] a scrap of; a piece of; a dash of

back and forth 앞뒤로, 이리저리
My husband flies **back and forth** between Seoul and Moscow on business.
남편은 사업 때문에 서울과 모스크바를 왔다갔다한다.
A suspicious man is walking **back and forth** in front of our house.
수상한 남자가 우리 집 앞에서 왔다 갔다 하고 있다.

[SYN] this way and that; here and there

by degrees 서서히, 점차, 차차로
The temperature is rising **by degrees** as the summer deepens.
여름이 깊어감에 따라 기온이 서서히 오르고 있다.
You don't have to be disappointed. Your English is improving **by degrees**.
실망하지 않아도 된다. 너의 영어 실력이 점점 향상되고 있다.

[SYN] gradually; slowly; step by step

make haste 서두르다, 신속히 하다
We have to **make haste** if we are going to catch the train.
그 기차를 타려면 서둘러야 한다.
Make haste, or you will be late for your appointment.
서둘러라, 그렇지 않으면 약속에 늦겠다.

[SYN] hurry; move rapidly

die from (부주의·과로·쇠약 등으로) 죽다
The patient **died from** loss of blood.
그 환자는 출혈이 심해 죽었다.
He **died from** smoking too much.
그는 담배를 너무 많이 피워서 죽었다.

cf. die of (병·기아·늙음·부상 등으로) 죽다

make the best of (불리한 상황을) 될 수 있는대로 이용하다, …에 순응하다
Always try to **make the best of** your situation.
언제나 현재의 상황을 최대한으로 이용해라.
We Koreans must strive to **make the best of** the present situation.
우리 한국 사람들은 현 상황을 최대한 이용하기 위해 노력해야 한다.

[SYN] use something unfavorable situation fullest

what one has 사람이 가진 것, 재산, 돈
A man's worth lies not so much in **what he has** as in what he is.
인간의 가치는 재산에 있는 것이 아니라 그 됨됨이에 있다.

[SYN] possessions; fortune; money; cash

Man is rich or poor according to what he is, not according to **what he has**.
인간은 재산 여하에 의해서가 아니라 인품에 의해 부하기도 하고 빈하기도 하다.

be well off 유복하다, 형편이 좋다

He **is well off** these days.
그는 요즘 생활 형편이 좋다.
I wonder why he **is** so **well off**.
그는 왜 그렇게 잘 사는 것일까.

[SYN] be rich; be prosperous
[OPP] be badly off 가난하다, 형편이 나쁘다 (=be poor; be destitute)

say hello to …에게 안부를 전하다

Please, **say hello to** your husband.
당신 남편에게 안부 전해 주세요.
Say hello to your mother.
당신 어머니에게 안부 전해 주세요.

[SYN] give ... one's best regard; give one's compliments to

(be) satisfied with …에 만족하는

The teacher **is satisfied with** his students' progress in German.
선생님은 학생들의 독일어 향상에 만족하고 있다.
Our family **was satisfied with** the new apartment.
우리 가족은 새 아파트에 만족했다.

[SYN] satisfactory; gratifying

speak ill [evil] of …을 나쁘게 말하다, …을 헐뜯다, 욕하다

We have never heard him **speak ill of** others.
우리는 그가 다른 사람에 대해 나쁘게 말하는 것을 들어 본 적이 없다.
Abstain from **speaking ill of** others, if you are ladies and gentlemen.
당신들이 신사 숙녀라면 다른 사람 험담하는 것을 삼가시오.

[SYN] abuse; slander; scold; revile
[OPP] speak well (highly, much) of …을 좋게 말하다, 칭찬하다 (=praise; express praise of)

up to 1. (시간·공간적으로) …까지, …에 이르기까지 2. (아무의) 책임인, …가 해야 할, …을 할 수 있는

The water in the pond was only **up to** my waist.
연못 물은 겨우 내 허리까지 왔다.
I could not get **up to** him.
나는 그를 따라갈 수 없었다.
It's **up to** him to support his mother.
그가 어머니를 부양해야 한다.

[SYN] 1. as far as 2. accountable for; responsible for; able to

in particular 특히

[SYN] more than others;

All the girls performed well and Lily **in particular**.
모든 소녀들은 공연을 잘 했으며 릴리는 특히 잘 했다.
She is beautiful, her eyes **in particular**.
그녀는 아름답다. 특히 눈이 아름답다.

particularly

in place of ⋯대신에

Will you go to the meeting **in place of** me?
저 대신에 그 모임에 가 주시겠습니까?
I'll go shopping **in place of** my mother.
내가 어머니 대신에 물건을 사러 가야겠다.

[SYN] instead of; on behalf of; in one's place

be sure of ⋯을 확신하다, ⋯을 믿다

He **is sure of** passing the examination.
그는 시험에 합격할 것을 확신하고 있었다.
I **am** quite **sure of** his innocence.
나는 그의 결백을 굳게 믿고 있다.

[SYN] believe firmly
cf. be sure to 반드시 ⋯하다 (= not forget or fail to)

be possessed of ⋯을 소유하고 있다

My uncle **is possessed of** great wealth.
나의 삼촌은 막대한 재산을 갖고 있다.
He **is possessed of** intelligence.
그는 지성이 있다.

[SYN] own; have
cf. be possessed by (with) ⋯에 사로잡혀 있다 (= controlled by spirit)

get to 1. ⋯에 닿다, ⋯에 이르다 2. (어떤 결과)가 되다

This train **gets to** Busan at 10 o'clock tonight.
이 기차는 오늘 밤 10시에 부산에 도착합니다.
Where can it have **got to**?
그 일은 대체 어떻게 되었을까?

[SYN] 1. arrive at; reach 2. result in; come in effect to

go from bad to worse 더욱 악화되다, 상태가 더 나빠지다

Her school record has been **going from bad to worse**.
그녀의 학교 성적이 점점 나빠지고 있다.
With the oil shock, things **went from bad to worse**.
석유 파동으로 사태는 점점 더 심각해졌다.

[SYN] become worse

shake hands (with) (⋯와) 악수하다

After he **shook hands with** the president, he didn't wash his hands for two days.
대통령과 악수한 후 그는 이틀 동안 손을 씻지 않았다.
The popular singer **shook hands with** up to over

[SYN] shake someone by the hand; make peace with

500 fans.
그 유명 가수는 무려 500명이 넘는 팬들하고 악수를 했다.

set in 시작하다, 발전하다, 밀물이 들어오다
A strong **set in** at midnight and I couldn't sleep well.
한밤중에 강풍이 불기 시작하여 나는 잠이 잘 오지 않았다.
The rainy season had **set in** and we must prepare for it.
장마철이 시작되었으니 대비를 해야 한다.

SYN. begin; blow or flow toward the shore

be used to +(동)명사 …에 익숙하다
She **was used to** living on a small income.
그녀는 적은 수입으로 살아가는 데 익숙해져 있었다.
That beautiful woman **is used to** being treated specially any place she goes.
그 미인은 어딜 가든지 특별 대우를 받는 것에 익숙해져 있다.

SYN. be accustomed to; be familiar to

be present at …에 출석하다, …에 참석하다
How many people **were present at** the meeting?
그 모임에 사람들이 얼마나 출석했습니까?
Were you **present at** the party?
그 파티에 참석하셨나요?

SYN. attend; take one's seat
OPP. be absent from …에 결석하다

in fact 사실(은)
In fact, he did not come.
사실 그는 오지 않았다.
In fact, it's the largest I've ever seen.
사실 그것은 내가 이제까지 본 것 중에서 가장 크다.

SYN. in reality; in practice; practically; as a matter of fact

it (so) happens that 우연히(공교롭게도) …하다
It happened that she was also staying there.
공교롭게도 그녀 또한 그 곳에 머물고 있었다.
(=She happened to be also staying there.)
It happened that I could not attend the meeting.
마침 나는 모임에 나갈 수가 없었다.
(=I happened to be unable to attend the meeting.)

SYN. chance to; happen to

take care of 1. …을 돌보다, 보살피다 2. 조심하다, 주의하다 3. …을 해결(처리)하다, …을 제거하다
She **took** good **care of** the child.
그녀는 아이를 잘 돌봤다.

SYN. 1. have charge of; look after; attend to 2. take care; be careful; watch out 3. do; handle; solve; remove

(=The child was taken good care of by her.
= Good care was taken of the child by her.)
You must **take care of** your health.
건강에 주의해야 한다.
I'll **take care of** the problem myself.
내가 직접 그 문제를 처리하겠다.

cf. take care of oneself 자기 몸을 조심하다, 자기 몸을 귀중히 여기다 (= look after oneself; watch one's health); 있는 그대로 두다 (=leave; leave over)

tend to 1. …하는 경향이 있다 2. 이바지하다, 공헌하다

People **tend to** boast how big the fish was which they lost.
사람들은 놓친 고기가 엄청 컸다고 자랑하는 경향이 있다.
(=People are always boasting the fish that got away was very big.)
Education **tends to** improve human relations.
교육은 인간 관계의 개선에 이바지한다.

[SYN] 1. have an inclination to; be inclined to 2. contribute to; make for; be helpful

at length 1. 마침내, 드디어 2. 상세하게

At length my wish was realized.
마침내 내 소망이 이루어졌다.
We debated the matter **at length**.
우리는 그 사건을 상세하게 검토했다.

[SYN] 1. after all; in the end; finally 2. in detail

hurt oneself 다치다, 부상하다

Take care that children don't **hurt themselves**.
아이들이 다치지 않도록 조심하십시오.
He **hurt himself** in the traffic accident.
그는 교통 사고로 상처를 입었다.

[SYN] be injured; be(get) wounded; injure; get hurt

hand down 1. 물려주다, 남겨 주다 2. (판결을) 언도하다

This ring was **handed down** to me through four generations.
이 반지는 4대에 걸쳐 나에게 전해져 내려왔다.
The judge **handed down** the decision.
판사는 판결을 언도했다.

[SYN] 1. inherit 2. announce; declare

more often than not 대개, 자주

On Sundays she dines here **more often than not**.
그녀는 일요일이면 자주 이 곳에서 식사를 한다.
Jim is a good swimmer and he wins **more often than not**.
짐은 뛰어난 수영 선수이며 지는 경우보다는 이기는 경우가 더 많다.

[SYN] more than half the time

make efforts [an effort] 노력하다, 애쓰다

I will **make** every **effort** to make the plan successful.
나는 그 계획을 성사시키기 위해 모든 노력을 다 할 것이다.
Most of the students **make an effort** to improve their test scores.
대부분 학생들은 시험 성적을 높이기 위해 노력한다.

[SYN] exert oneself; endeavor; try

protect ... from ⋯로부터 보호하다, 지키다, 막다

He put dark glasses to **protect** his eyes **from** the strong sun-rays.
그는 강한 햇볕으로부터 눈을 보호하기 위해 짙은 안경을 썼다.
My wife **protect** her face **from** the sun with a hat.
아내는 모자를 써서 태양으로부터 얼굴을 보호했다.

[SYN] defend against

be proud of ⋯을 자랑하다, 뽐내다, 과시하다

He **is proud of** being a doctor.
그는 의사인 것을 자랑으로 여긴다.
I **am proud of** your friendship.
너의 우정이 자랑스럽다.

[SYN] be boastful; be full of pride

in a sense 어떤 의미에서

In a sense, I agree with your opinion.
어떤 의미에서 나는 당신 의견에 동의한다.
He thought she was right **in a sense**.
그는 어떤 의미에서는 그녀가 옳다고 생각했다.

[SYN] in some way but not in all; somewhat; in a way

in succession 계속해서, 다음에서 다음으로

He had fasted for three days **in succession**.
그는 3일간 계속해서 단식해왔다.
Mysterious events occurred **in succession**.
이상한 일들이 연이어서 일어났다.

[SYN] successive; one after another in a regular series

by and by 이윽고, 곧

By and by, the children went home.
곧 아이들은 집으로 돌아갔다.
Henry said he would do his homework **by and by**.
헨리는 곧 숙제를 하겠다고 했다.

[SYN] before long; soon
cf. by and large 대개 (=on the whole)

be due to+명사 ⋯에 기인하다, ⋯의 탓으로 돌려야 한다

The failure **is due to** his wrong judgment and

[SYN] be caused by; be brought about by

ignorance.
실패는 그의 잘못된 판단과 무지 탓이다.
There is no doubt that more than half of failure **are due to** hesitation.
실패의 반 이상은 확실히 주저하는 데 기인한다.

cf. due to … 때문에, …로 인해 (=owing to, because of; on account of)

as long as …하는 한(에서는), …하는 동안은

As long as you put it back afterwards, you may use my dictionary whenever you need.
쓰고 난 후 제자리에 갖다 놓기만 하면 필요할 때 언제나 내 사전을 써도 좋다.
As long as you work as my secretary, you can have an off day on Saturday.
내 비서로 일하는 동안은 토요일에 쉬어도 좋다.

SYN. while since; because; considering that; so far so
cf. so long as …하는 한, …하기만 한다면 (=provided (that))

excuse oneself 1. 변명하다, 사과하다 2. 사양하다, 의향이 없다고 말하다

Fred **excused himself** for his rudeness to the young lady.
프레드는 젊은 숙녀에게 자신의 무례함을 사과했다.
He **excused himself** from attending the party.
그는 파티 참석을 사양했다.

SYN. 1. make an excuse 2. ask to be excused

every other (second) day 하루 걸러, 격일로

It rained **every other day** last June.
작년 6월에는 하루 걸러 비가 왔다.
Mother goes shopping **every other day**.
어머니는 하루 걸러 쇼핑을 가신다.

SYN. every two days; on alternate days
cf. every fourth year 4년마다, 3년 걸러
every six hours 6시간마다, 5시간 걸러
SYN. for the sake of

in the cause of …을 위하여

He fought **in the cause of** justice.
그는 정의를 위해서 싸웠다.
She exerted herself **in the cause of** the peace of the world.
그녀는 세계의 평화를 위하여 노력했다.

in that …라는 점에서, …라는 이유로, …이므로

Men differ from animals **in that** they can think and speak.
사람은 생각하고 말할 줄 안다는 점에서 동물과 다르다.
In that he disobeyed, he was a traitor.
그는 불복했기 때문에 반역자였다.

SYN. regarding; because; since

be surprised at ⋯에 놀라다

You will **be surprised at** the number of different plastics you use every day.
매일 사용하는 플라스틱 종류가 많은 것에 놀랄 것이다.
You may **be surprised at** the results of the experiment.
당신은 실험 결과를 보고 놀랄지도 모른다.

[SYN] be startled; be taken aback; be shocked

similar to ⋯와 비슷한, 유사한, 닮은

She has a blue dress **similar to** yours, but hers has a green collar.
그녀는 네 것과 비슷한 청색 드레스를 가지고 있는데 그녀의 옷은 옷깃이 녹색이다.
Your opinion is **similar to** mine.
당신의 의견은 내 의견과 비슷하다.

[SYN] almost alike; resembling

even if(though) 비록 ⋯할지라도, 비록 ⋯라 하더라도

You must do it **even if(though)** you don't like it.
그것이 싫더라도 해야 한다.
We will go, **even if(though)** it rains(should rain).
설사 비가 오더라도 가겠다.

[SYN] no matter if; although

except for 1. ⋯을 제외하고 2. ⋯만 없다면

This is a good book **except for** a few mistakes.
이 책은 약간의 잘못을 제외하면 좋은 책이다.
Our plan should have failed **except for** his help.
그의 도움이 없었더라면 우리의 계획은 무산되었을 것이다.

[SYN] 1. except; save; but 2. but for
cf. except that ⋯임을 제외하고, ⋯라고 하는 것 말고는

so that ... may ⋯하기 위하여

He ran to the station **so that** he **might** catch the last train.
그는 마지막 기차를 타기 위해 역까지 뛰어갔다.
He is working hard **so that** he **may** finish the job in time.
그는 그 일을 시간 내에 끝내기 위해 열심히 일하고 있다.

[SYN] in order to; so as to; so that; for the purpose

search for ⋯을 찾다, 탐색하다, 수색하다

I **searched** her face **for** her true thought.
나는 그녀의 진심을 알아내려고 그녀의 얼굴을 살폈다.
Birds **search for** a good place to raise their young in summer.

[SYN] look for; make a search for; probe

새들은 여름이 되면 새끼를 키울 적당한 장소를 물색한다.

lots (plenty) of 많은
Jimmy has **lots of** friends.
지미는 친구가 많다.
He always has **plenty of** money.
그는 항상 많은 돈을 갖고 있다.

SYN. a lot of; a large number (amount) of

lead to 1. (길 등이 사람을) …에 이르게 하다, 끌고 (데리고) 가다 2. 끌어내다, 유인하다, …할 마음이 나게 하다
This road will **lead** you **to** the station.
이 길로 가면 역이 나옵니다.
Her smile **led** him **to** give her his word.
그녀의 미소에 이끌려 그는 약속을 하고 말았다.

SYN. 1. arrive at; reach 2. induce; allure

long for 그리워하다, …하기를 갈망하다
He is **longing for** her arrival.
그는 그녀가 도착하기를 애타게 기다리고 있다.
He **longs for** the day she'll come back.
그는 그녀가 되돌아올 날을 기다리고 있다.

SYN. want something very much

be supposed to …하기로 되어 있다
I **am supposed to** meet her at three this afternoon.
나는 오늘 오후 3시에 그녀를 만나기로 되어 있다.
Everybody **is supposed to** know the law, but few people really do.
누구든지 그 법을 알고 있어야 하지만 실제로 아는 사람은 별로 없다.

SYN. be expected to do; be intended to do

be tired of …에 싫증이 나다, 지치다
I **am tired of** my monotonous life.
나는 단조로운 생활에 염증을 느끼고 있다.
I **am tired of** listening to your problems.
네 문제를 들어 주는 데 지쳤다.

SYN. be sick of; be disgusted with
cf. tire out 지치게 만들다 (= wear out; exhaust)
tired with (from) 싫증난, 지친, 피곤한 (= tired; weary)

put out 끄다
Firefighters **put out** the fire with a water hose.
소방수들은 물 호스로 불을 껐다.
Mother **put out** a fire in the kitchen.
어머니는 주방의 불을 껐다.

SYN. extinguish a fire; blow out; turn out
OPP. put on (전등 따위를) 켜다

put to use …을 이용하다, 쓰다
We would like our money to be **put to** good **use**.

SYN. utilize; harness; take advantage of

우리 돈을 유용하게 써 주시기 바랍니다.
You had better **put** the lawn mower **to use**.
너는 잔디 깎는 기계를 사용하는 것이 낫다.

may as well (... as not) ···하는 것이 좋다, ···해도 나쁘지 않다, ···해도 마찬가지인 것처럼 ~해도 좋다

You **may as well** go at once.
당장 가는 것이 좋을 것이다.
You **may as well** call a cat a little tiger as call a tiger a big cat.
호랑이를 큰 고양이라고 부르는 것처럼 고양이를 작은 호랑이라고 불러도 좋다.

[SYN.] having no reason not to do something
cf. might as well ... as ~ ~하느니 ···하는 편이 낫다, ~하는 것은 ···하는 거나 매한가지이다 (may as well보다 완곡한 표현)

manage to 어떻게 해서 ···하다, 그럭저럭 ···하다

I could **manage to** earn my living.
나는 이럭저럭 생활비를 벌 수 있었다.
We **managed to** get there in time.
우리는 그럭저럭 시간에 대어 그 곳에 도착했다.

[SYN.] devise some means

be incapable of ···이 될 수 없다

The case **is incapable of** swift decision.
이 문제는 조속히 결정될 수 없다.
I **was incapable of** understanding the significance of the matter.
나는 그 일의 중요성을 이해할 수 없었다.

[SYN.] be unable to

(be) worth -ing / It is worth while to+동사원형 ···할 가치가 있다

The book **is worth reading**.
그 책은 읽을 만하다.
I don't think **it is worth while to** study Portuguese so hard.
나는 포르투갈 어를 그렇게 열심히 공부할 가치가 없다고 생각한다.

[SYN.] give a satisfactory reward, return for

in all 모두 합해서

In all we did well until now, but the next is more important.
지금까지는 모든 것이 좋았지만 앞으로가 더 중요하다.
You have 5 dollars and I have 7 dollars, making 12 dollars **in all**.
너는 5달러를 가지고 있고 나는 7달러를 가지고 있으니 모두 합하면 12달러가 된다.

[SYN.] all being counted; altogether

in spite of ···에도 불구하고, ···을 무릅쓰고

In spite of bad weather, my father went out for mountain climbing.
악천후에도 불구하고 아버지는 등산을 가셨다.
In spite of his efforts to get rid of the bad habit, he could not.
나쁜 습관을 버리려고 노력을 했는데도 불구하고 그는 실패했다.
(=He tried hard to quit the bad habit, but he failed.)

[SYN] despite; notwithstanding; in the teeth of

make it a rule to 언제나 ···하기로 하고 있다

He **makes it a rule to** do an hour's work in the field every day.
그는 매일 밭에서 한 시간씩 일하는 것을 규칙으로 하고 있다.
He **made it a rule** never **to** watch television after 9 o'clock.
그는 9시 이후에는 TV를 보지 않기로 했다.

[SYN] make it a principle to

make friends with ···와 친해지다, 친구가 되다

I want to **make friends with** that pretty girl.
나는 저 예쁜 소녀와 친구가 되고 싶다.
I shook hands and **made friends with** him.
나는 그와 악수했다. 그리고 친해졌다.

[SYN] get to know better

live on ···(만)을 먹고 살다, ···에 의지하여 살다

The tigers **live on** flesh.
호랑이는 육식을 한다.
That old scientist **lives on** his retiring allowance.
그 노 과학자는 퇴직금으로 생활한다.

[SYN] feed on; subsist on

(be) open to 받기 쉬운, 개방되어 있는, ···로 향해 있는

The jazz concert is free of charge and **is open to** everyone.
이 재즈 콘서트는 무료로 누구라도 들어갈 수 있습니다.
Children **are open to** various influences.
어린이들은 여러 영향을 받기 쉽다.

[SYN] exposed to; liable to; subject to

more or less 다소, 얼마간

Most people are **more or less** selfish.
대부분의 사람들은 다소 이기적이다.
It will cost fifty dollars **more or less** to fix this watch.

[SYN] some; somewhat; to some extent; almost

이 시계를 수리하는 데 50달러 남짓 들 것이다.

many a 많은

Many a young man went to war.
많은 젊은이가 전쟁터로 나갔다.
I've told her **many a** time to be punctual.
그녀에게 몇 번이고 시간을 지키라고 말했다.

SYN. many a man = many men

object to 반대하다, 이의를 말하다, 항의하다

His mother **objected to** John's going to Europe alone.
어머니는 존이 혼자 유럽에 가는 것에 반대했다.
They **objected to** eating dinner at the newly opened restaurant.
그들은 새로 개업한 식당에서 저녁을 먹는 것에 반대했다.

SYN. be against; be opposed to

occur to (머리에) 갑자기 떠오르다

A fresh idea **occured to** Newton.
참신한 생각이 뉴튼에게 떠올랐다.
It **occured to** me that he is the criminal in that case.
난 그가 그 사건의 범인이 아닌가 하는 생각이 문득 들었다.

SYN. hit upon; strike one's mind

get on 1. (버스·지하철 등을) 타다 2. 성공하다, 번창하다

Get on that bus and get off at the next stop.
저 버스를 타고 다음 정거장에서 내리시오.
I believe that my son will be able to **get on** in life.
나는 내 아들이 출세할 수 있으리라고 믿는다.

SYN. 1. ride; have a ride in 2. succeed; prosper

go by 1. (사람·행렬 등이) 지나가다, (시간 등이) 경과하다 2. …에 따르다, 지키다

As the time **went by**, the pain disappeared gradually.
시간이 가면서 통증이 점점 사라졌다.
All of the students should **go by** the rules.
모든 학생들은 규칙을 따라야 한다.

SYN. 1. pass; go or move past 2. follow; keep; obey

if only …하기만 한다면, …이기만 한다면

If only I could go there with you, I would be very happy.
당신과 함께 거기에 갈 수만 있다면 매우 행복할 텐데.
If I **only** had the money, I could hold a big party

SYN. provided that
cf. only if …이 있어야만 비로소, …이어야만 비로소 (= not ... until)

for your birthday.
그 돈만 있다면 당신 생일 파티를 성대하게 열 수 있을 텐데.

in turn 차례로
The students lined up and entered the theater **in turn**.
학생들은 줄을 서서 차례로 영화관으로 들어갔다.
During the trip, they drove the car **in turn**.
여행을 하는 동안 그들은 차례로 차를 운전했다.

SYN. according to a settled order; each following another

be anxious for …을 바라다
As I **was anxious for** a bicycle, I got a part-time job for six months.
자전거가 사고 싶어서 6개월간 임시직으로 일했다.
They **were anxious for** his safety.
그들은 그의 안전을 갈망하고 있었다.

SYN. be eager for; be desirous of; wish for

be anxious to …할 것을 희망하다, …하고 싶어하다
Please tell me. I **am anxious to** know what your plan is.
제발 일러 줘. 너의 계획이 무엇인지 알고 싶어.
After the party, he **was anxious to** leave as soon as possible.
파티가 끝난 후 그는 되도록 일찍 떠나고 싶어 했다.

SYN. be eager to; want to

do+사람+good …에게 도움이 되다, 이롭게 하다
A change of air will **do** you **good**.
전지요양은 당신에게 이로울 것이다.
The medicine will **do** you **good**.
그 약을 먹으면 좋아질 것이다.

SYN. do good to+사람; be helpful; useful
OPP. do+사람+harm …에게 해를 주다 (=do harm to+사람)

divide by …으로 나누다
Twenty **divided by** four equals five.
20 나누기 4는 5이다.
Divide 45 **by** three.
45를 3으로 나누어라.

SYN. divide into; part; split up

once in a while 이따금, 드물게, 때때로
My mother and father go to the park after dinner **once in a while**.
우리 부모님은 가끔 저녁 식사 후 공원으로 산책을 간다.
All of us need some refreshments from our daily life

SYN. sometimes; occasionally

once in a while.
가끔 우리 모두는 일상 생활에서 벗어나는 것이 필요하다.

of value 가치 있는, 중요한

His help will be **of** great **value** to our new project.
그의 도움은 우리의 새 프로젝트에 큰 가치가 있을 것이다.
The book is **of** most **value** to him.
그 책은 그에게 매우 중요하다.

[SYN] valuable; worthwhile; important

have no choice but to +동사원형 …하지 않을 수 없다, …할 수밖에 없다

We **had no choice but to** accept the majority decision.
우리는 다수의 결정을 받아들이지 않을 수 없었다.
They **had no choice but to** laugh at her.
그들은 그녀를 보고 웃을 수밖에 없었다.

[SYN] cannot help -ing; cannot but + 동사원형

had better …하는 것이 낫다

You **had better** not go out in such a heavy snowfall.
이렇게 폭설이 내리는 때에는 밖에 나가지 않는 것이 낫다.
He **had better** do the work before 9 o'clock.
그는 9시 전에 그 일을 하는 게 좋다.

[SYN] be better to do

ever since 그 후로 쭉, 그때 이후

She has lived alone **ever since** her husband died.
남편이 죽은 후로 쭉 그녀는 혼자 살았다.
They have been happy **ever since**.
그들은 그 후 내내 행복했다.

[SYN] after that; from that time on; since then

whether or not …이든지 아니든지, …이건 아니건 (양보를 나타내는 부사절을 인도)

Whether you like it **or not**, you still must do it now.
좋든 싫든 그 일을 지금 해야 한다.
Whether a person is smart **or not**, his success depends on his efforts.
똑똑하건 아니건 성공은 그 사람의 노력에 달려 있다.

[SYN] if or not

what for 1. 무엇 때문에, 무슨 목적으로, 왜 2. (명사로서) 엄한 벌, 질책, 비난

What do you want me **for**?
나에게 무슨 용무가 있어?

[SYN] 1. why; for what reason 2. severe punishment

What for did you do that?
무엇 때문에 그런 일을 했니?
He gave his daughter **what for**.
그는 딸을 엄하게 벌주었다.

in any case 여하튼 간에, 어떻든, 아무튼

In any case, I will call on him.
아무튼, 나는 그를 찾아가겠다.
Great men are few **in any case**.
위인이란 여하간 좀처럼 나지 않는다.

[SYN] anyway; at any rate
cf. in all cases 언제든지, 항상 (=at any time; always)
in no case 결코 …아니다

in case (that) …하는 경우에는, 만일 …이면, …의 경우에 대비하여

In case you meet Mr. Hong, give him my best regard.
홍선생을 만나면 안부를 전해 주시오.
Take an umbrella with you **in case** it rains.
혹시 비가 올지 모르니 우산을 가지고 가거라.

[SYN] if it should happen

be in need of …을 필요로 하다

He **is** much **in need of** help.
그는 도움을 매우 필요로 하고 있다.
The settlers **were in need of** many useful things.
개척민들은 여러 가지 유용한 물건을 필요로 하고 있었다.

[SYN] be in want of; needed; be necessary

be good at …을 잘 하다, …이 능하다

He **is** not **good at** putting his thoughts into words.
그는 자기 생각을 말로 표현하는 데 능숙하지 않다.
He **is good at** several foreign languages.
그는 몇몇 외국어에 능통하다.

[SYN] be at home in; proficient
[OPP] be bad(poor) at …에 서툴다

such ... that 너무 …해서 ~하다

There was **such** a crowd **that** we could hardly move.
인파가 너무 많아서 거의 움직일 수가 없었다.
Harry is **such** a nice person **that** there is no one who thinks him bad.
해리는 너무 착해서 그를 나쁘게 생각하는 사람이 아무도 없다.

[SYN] so ... that; too ... to; so great or so little that

strange to say [tell] 이상하게도, 묘하게도, 이상한 이야기지만

Strange to say, she knows (about) the plan.

[SYN] curious to say; strangely enough; though it is strange to say

묘하게도 그녀는 그 계획을 알고 있다.
Strange to say, the owl cannot see in the light as in the dark.
이상한 이야기지만 올빼미는 밝은 곳에서는 어두운 곳에서만큼 잘 보지 못한다.

in time 시간에 대어, 조만간

I arrived at the hotel **in time** to attend the party.
나는 파티에 늦지 않도록 호텔에 도착했다.
He will learn the truth **in time**.
그는 머지않아 진실을 알게 될 것이다.

SYN. soon enough; sooner or later; at some time
cf. in time for 시간에 늦지 않게, in time with …에 맞추어

in search [quest] of …을 찾아서

Many people went to the new land **in search of** the wealth.
많은 사람들이 부를 찾아서 새로운 땅으로 갔다.
I looked everywhere **in quest of** my lost ring, but I couldn't find it.
나는 사방으로 잃어버린 반지를 찾았지만 찾지 못했다.

SYN. seeking or looking for; in pursuit of

look into 알아보다, 조사하다, 연구하다

The police promised to **look into** the case again.
경찰은 사건을 재조사하겠다고 약속했다.
Barry found it difficult to **look into** the matter.
배리는 그 문제를 조사한다는 것이 어렵다는 것을 알았다.

SYN. investigate; examine; inquire into

look in the eye [face] 응시하다, 용감하게 마주치다

When Bill **looked** the thief **in the eye**, he turned and went away.
빌이 도둑의 눈을 뚫어지게 바라보자 도둑은 가 버렸다.
If I make such a mistake again, I won't be able to **look** the boss **in the face**.
그런 실수를 다시 하면 사장 얼굴을 보지 못할 것이다.

SYN. face bravely or without shame; gaze at; stare at

by no means 결코 …이 아니다

He was **by no means** happy.
그는 결코 행복하지는 않았다.
(= He was far from happy.)
What he said is **by no means** true.
그가 말한 것은 결코 진실이 아니다.

SYN. not even a little; not by any means

behind the times 시대에 뒤떨어진

Your way of thinking is **behind the times**.
당신의 사고 방식은 유행에 뒤떨어져 있어요.
Young men, above all, must take care not to be **behind the times**.
무엇보다 청년들은 시대에 뒤떨어지지 않도록 주의해야만 한다.

[SYN] old-fashioned; out of date
cf. fall behind the times 시대에 뒤떨어지다
behind time 지각하다, 늦다 (= be late)

in general 일반적으로, 일반의

In general, girls like to go shopping.
일반적으로 여자들은 쇼핑하기를 좋아한다.
In general, children are fond of candy.
어린이는 일반적으로 과자를 좋아한다.

[SYN] generally; as a general rule
cf. in particular 특히 (= particularly)

in public 공석에서, 사람들 앞에서

He expressed his opinion **in public**.
그는 공공연하게 의견을 피력했다.
They don't like speaking **in public**.
그들은 사람들 앞에서 이야기하는 것을 싫어한다.

[SYN] in the open; publicly
cf. in private 은밀하게, 비공식으로 (= secretely; in secret)

make out 1. 이해하다, 알다 2. 작성하다

I can't **make out** what he wants.
그가 무엇을 원하는지 도무지 모르겠다.
He **made out** what I said.
그는 내가 한 말을 알아들었다.
The clerk **made out** a receipt.
점원은 영수증을 썼다.

[SYN] 1. figure out, understand; distinguish 2. draw up; frame

make up one's mind 마음먹다, 결심하다

He **made up his mind** to go there.
그는 거기 갈 결심을 했다.
She **made up her mind** to be a nurse.
그녀는 간호사가 될 결심을 했다.

[SYN] make a resolution; decide; determine; make a decision; resolve

so-called 소위

Their **so-called** poverty is nothing else but a plausible lie.
그들의 소위 빈곤이란 그럴듯한 거짓말이다.
He is a **so-called** upstar.
그는 소위 벼락부자이다.

[SYN] what we (you, they) call; what is called

stare at …을 응시하다, 노려보다, 지긋이 보다

I told my son to stop **staring at** the fat woman; it

[SYN] look at someone or something steadily with wide-

wasn't polite.
나는 아들에게 뚱뚱한 여자를 그만 보라고 말했다. 그것은 예의바르지 않았다.
They all **stared at** him with equal marks of surprise.
그들은 모두 한결같이 놀란 표정을 하고 그를 말똥말똥 쳐다보았다.

opened eyes

what do you say to …이 어떨까요, …하면 어떨까요

What do you say to a walk(walking) in the park?
공원에서 산책하면 어떻겠습니까?
What do you say to a drink(drinking)?
한잔 어때요?

[SYN] why don't you; how about; let's

wish for 바라다, 원하다

I have nothing left to **wish for**.
더 이상 바랄 것이 없다.
The weather is all one could **wish for**.
날씨는 더할 나위 없이 좋다.

[SYN] desire; aspire to; yearn for; care for; hope for

no more than 단지, 겨우

I have **no more than** $3.
나는 3달러밖에 없다.
I had **no more than** a meal once a day.
나는 하루 한 끼밖에 못 먹었다.

[SYN] only; merely
cf. not more than 많아야 (=at most)

not a bit 조금도 (전혀) …않다

After walking many hours, I **don't** feel tired **a bit**.
여러 시간 걸었는데도 전혀 피곤하지 않다.
The patient's condition is **not a bit** better.
그 환자의 병세는 차도가 전혀 없다.

[SYN] not in the least; not at all

the 비교급…, the 비교급… …하면 할수록 더

The more you use your brain, **the wiser** you will become.
머리를 쓰면 쓸수록 더 현명해질 것이다.
The older one grows, **the more** knowledge and experience one acquires.
사람은 나이가 들수록 지식과 경험을 더 얻게 된다.

[SYN] all the more; more and more; still more; increasingly

this time 이번(에는)

He is sure to succeed **this time**, because he has worked so hard.

[SYN] now; the present; the current one; this one

그렇게 열심히 노력했으니 이번에는 꼭 성공할 것이다.
If you forgive me just **this time**, I will start a new life.
이번만 용서해 주면 새 인생을 시작하겠다.

on purpose 고의로, 일부러, 의도하여

Do you think he made that mistake **on purpose**?
너는 그가 고의로 그런 실수를 저질렀다고 생각하느냐?
I did not forget my books; I left them in the locker **on purpose**.
나는 책들을 잊어버린 것이 아니라 일부러 라커에 두고 온 것이다.

[SYN] purposely; intentionally; by design; deliberately

not ... until〔till〕 …하고서야 비로소

We do **not** appreciate the value of good health **until** we get ill.
병이 들고서야 비로소 건강의 고마움을 알게 된다.
(=Only when our health is broken do we appreciate its value.)

[SYN] for the first time after something has happened

for some time 잠시 동안, 얼마 동안

The political instability will remain **for some time**.
정국의 불안정은 당분간 계속될 전망이다.
I intend to stay in New York **for some time**.
나는 얼마 동안 뉴욕에 머무를 작정이다.

[SYN] for a while; a moment; for a moment; for a spell
cf. for a time 일시, 잠시, 임시로

for oneself 혼자 힘으로, 자기를 위하여

He cannot do anything **for himself**.
그는 혼자서는 아무것도 못하는 사람이다.
You are studying **for yourself**, not for anyone else.
당신은 타인을 위해서가 아니라 자신을 위해서 공부하고 있어요.

[SYN] for one's own efforts; for one's own sake
cf. by oneself 혼자서, 혼자 힘으로 (=alone; without help)

by all means 1. 반드시, 꼭 2. 아무렴, 좋다마다

You must try to keep your promise **by all means**.
반드시 약속은 지키도록 하시오.
May I use the telephone book? — **By all means**.
전화 번호부 좀 봐도 됩니까? — 좋다마다요.

[SYN] 1. by any means
cf. by no means 결코 …아니다 (=not ... at all)

call out 부르다, 소집하다

He **called out** for help.
그는 큰 소리로 구조를 요청했다.
The president **called out** the troops.
대통령은 군대를 소집했다.

[SYN] call; convene; convoke; summon

little by little 조금씩, 점차로
He developed his business **little by little**.
그는 사업을 조금씩 발전시켰다.
Little by little they grew more hopeful.
차츰 그들은 더욱 희망적으로 되었다.

SYN. by little and little; gradually

lest ... should …하지 않도록, …하면 안 되니까
You had better take your raincoat **lest** it **should** rain.
비가 올지 모르니까 우비를 가지고 가는 것이 좋겠다.
Take care **lest** you **should** be late.
늦지 않도록 조심해라.

SYN. for fear that; so that ... not

be angry with (at) +사람 …에게 화가 나다
I **was angry with** myself.
나는 내 자신에게 화가 났었다.
He **was angry with** his son.
그는 아들에게 화를 내고 있었다.

SYN. resent; get angry
cf. be angry about(at) + a thing …에 분개하다
get angry with(at, about) …에 화를 내다

be dependent on …에 의존하다, …하기 나름이다
He **is dependent on** his wife's income.
그는 자기 아내의 수입에 의존하고 있다.
She **is** always **dependent on** her boyfriend.
그녀는 언제나 남자 친구에게 의지한다.

SYN. rely on; fall back on
OPP. be independent of …로부터 독립해 있다

shut up 1. (집 등을) 잠가(닫아)두다, 폐쇄하다 2. 입을 다물게 하다, 입을 다물다
We **shut up** the garage so no one would steal the car.
우리는 아무도 자동차를 훔쳐가지 못하게 차고를 잠갔다.
I got angry at her endless nagging and I told her to **shut up**.
끝도 없는 그녀의 잔소리에 화가 나서 그녀에게 입을 다물라고 말했다.

SYN. 1. close securely; lock up 2. be quiet; stop making noise

have only to …하기만 하면 되다
You **have only to** push the button now.
지금 단추를 누르기만 하면 된다.
You **have only to** turn up by 10 o'clock at the bus station.
너는 10시까지 버스 정류장에 나타나기만 하면 된다.

SYN. all one has to do is to

rely on (upon) …에 의지하다, 신뢰하다, 기대하다

As he often breaks his words, we can't **rely on** him entirely.
그는 종종 약속을 어기므로 그를 전적으로 신뢰할 수 없다.
I **rely on** getting my money back in due time.
돈을 기일 안에 받기를 기대하고 있다.

SYN depend upon; count on

rob A of B A에게서 B를 빼앗다, 약탈하다, 강탈하다, 박탈하다

A highway man **robbed** the traveler **of** his money.
노상강도가 여행자의 돈을 빼앗았다.
Scientists have **robbed** the moon **of** its mystery.
과학자들은 달의 신비로움을 빼앗았다.

SYN deprive A of B; take by force

at the sight of …을 보고, …을 보자마자

She was very much frightened **at the sight of** the big snake.
그녀는 큰 뱀을 보고 기겁했다.
The mother wept **at the sight of** her long-lost child.
어머니는 오래 전에 잃어버린 아이를 보자마자 울었다.
(=The mother wept as soon as she saw her long-lost child.)

SYN as soon as one sees
cf. in the sight of …의 견지에서는, …이 보는 바로는, …이 보이는 곳에

for (with) the purpose of …할 목적으로, …하기 위해

Many students are going abroad **for the purpose of** studying M.B.A.
많은 학생들이 M.B.A를 공부할 목적으로 외국에 간다.
He bought the land **for the purpose of** building a house on it.
그는 집을 짓기 위해 그 땅을 샀다.

SYN with a view to; for the sake of

for the present 당분간, 지금 같아서는

The construction work is suspended **for the present**.
공사는 당분간 중단되었다.
Being busy with the new project, I can't have a vacation **for the present**.
새 프로젝트 때문에 바빠서 당분간은 휴가를 가질 수 없다.

SYN for the time being; for some time
cf. in the present 현재에
at present 현재
present oneself 나타나다 (= appear), …을 일으키다 (= happen to)

on the (one's) way …로 가는 길에, …에 가까워져서

SYN coming; going toward a place or goal; started

On the way to school Bill met a bully and was beaten by him.
학교 가는 길에 빌은 깡패를 만나서 맞았다.
Susan is well **on her way** to becoming a famous pianist.
수잔은 유명한 피아니스트가 되기 시작했다.

on the whole 전체로 보아서, 대체로
The food was, **on the whole**, satisfactory.
음식은 대체로 만족스러웠다.
On the whole, children begin speaking when they are about one year old.
대체로 아이들은 생후 1년쯤 됐을 때 말을 하기 시작한다.

[SYN] generally; mostly; in the main; by and large
cf. as a whole 전체로서 (=all together)

hear from …로부터 소식을 듣다, …로부터 편지를 받다
I have not **heard from** my brother studying in America for a long time.
미국에서 공부하고 있는 형의 소식을 오랫동안 듣지 못했다.
Have you **heard from** her since she left for Europe?
그녀가 유럽으로 떠난 이후에 소식을 들은 적이 있습니까?

[SYN] receive a message from

happen to 우연히 …하다, 마침 …하다
I **happened to** be at home when he called on me yesterday.
어제 그가 나를 찾아왔을 때 나는 마침 집에 있었다.
I **happened to** have no money with me.
나는 마침 돈이 한 푼도 없었다.
(=It happened that I had no money with me.)

[SYN] chance to; do something by chance
cf. happen to+명사 몸에 …이 미치다 (=befall)

get off 1. 내리다 2. (여행 등을) 출발하다
I **get off** the bus at the train station.
나는 기차역에서 버스를 내렸다.
They **got off** on the four o'clock train to Seoul.
그들은 4시 기차를 타고 서울로 떠났다.

[SYN] 1. alight from; step out of 2. start; leave

get along (with) 1. 사이좋게 지내다 2. 그럭저럭 해 나가다
I advise you to **get along** well **with** your co-workers.
직장 동료들과 잘 지내기 바란다.
It is not all that easy to **get along** well in the world.

[SYN] 1. get on 2. manage to do well

이 세상을 잘 헤쳐 나가기란 그리 쉬운 일은 아니다.
(= It is not so easy to get on well in society.)

take charge of 책임을 지다, 떠맡다

John will **take charge of** the all the important matters of the club.
존은 클럽의 모든 중요한 일들을 책임질 것이다.
The oldest daughter **took charge of** the kids.
큰딸이 아이들을 맡았다.

[SYN] become responsible; undertake

turn down 1. (소리를) 적게 하다 2. …을 거절하다

Turn down the radio.
라디오 소리를 줄이세요.
He was so busy that he had to **turn down** an invitation.
그는 몹시 바빴기 때문에 초대를 거절해야만 했다.

[SYN] 1. reduce the sound 2. refuse; reject
cf. turn up 1. (소리를) 높이다 2. 나타나다 (=appear; show up)

out of order 1. 순서가 잘못 되어 2. 상태가 나쁜, 고장이 나서

Little Billy wrote the alphabet **out of order**.
어린 빌리는 알파벳을 순서가 틀리게 썼다.
You can't use the copy machine, because it is **out of order**.
복사기가 고장이 나서 쓸 수가 없다.

[SYN] 1. in the wrong order 2. in poor condition; not working properly

in return 답례로서

Mother gave her some present **in return**.
어머니는 답례로 그녀에게 선물을 주었다.
I want to help you **in return** for the kindness you have shown to me.
당신이 나에게 베푼 친절의 대가로 당신을 돕고 싶습니다.

[SYN] in order to give back something; as payment; in recognition or exchange

in those days 그 당시에

In those days 10,000 won was a big amount of for him.
당시에 그에겐 1만원이 큰 돈이었다.
Abraham Lincoln was an idol of mine **in those days**.
아브라함 링컨은 그 당시 내가 숭배하는 인물이었다.

[SYN] at that time
cf. in these days 요즈음 (=at present; these days; todays)

of late 요즈음, 최근에

I started to feel very tired **of late**.

[SYN] in the recent past; not long ago; lately; recently

최근 들어 피곤함을 느끼기 시작했다.
There have been many unmarried mothers **of late**.
최근에 미혼모가 많이 생겼다.

depend on (upon) …에 의존하다, 의지하다

It **depends** entirely **upon** your ability that we are successful or not.
우리가 성공하고 못하고는 전적으로 당신 능력에 달려 있다.
It is the rule of the market economy that prices **depend on** supply and demand.
물가가 수요와 공급에 의해 결정된다는 것은 시장 경제의 원칙이다.

[SYN.] rely on; be dependent upon; fall back on; trust on

would like to / should like to ... …하고 싶다

I **would like to** read an English novel in the original.
영국 소설을 원어로 읽어 보고 싶다.
I **would like to** visit you some day.
언제고 당신을 찾아 뵙고 싶습니다.

[SYN.] feel like -ing; wish to; want to

with pleasure 기꺼이, 기쁘게

I have read your letter **with** great **pleasure**.
보내 주신 편지는 기쁘게 받아보았습니다.
"Would you take this to my house for me?" "Yes, **with pleasure**."
"이것을 집까지 운반해 주실 수 있습니까?" "예, 기꺼이 해 드리지요."

[SYN.] willingly; with delight; delightfully; joyfully; with joy; heartily

look forward to …을 기대하다, …을 즐거움으로 기다리다

She is **looking forward to** a great future for her only son.
그녀는 외아들의 유망한 전도를 기대하고 있다.
We are **looking forward to** hearing from you.
우리는 너의 소식을 고대하고 있다.

[SYN.] be eager for; expect

learn by heart …을 암기하다

Have you **learned** the poem **by heart**?
그 시를 암기했습니까?
As you have no paper, you must **learn** what I am saying **by heart**.
종이가 없으므로 내가 지금 말하는 것을 반드시 외워야 한다.

[SYN.] memorize; repeat by memory

play a part (role) 역할을 하다

[SYN.] perform one's duty;

Mark has **played a** very important **part** in the scientific research.
마크는 과학 연구에서 매우 중요한 역할을 담당해 왔다.
He **played an** important **role** in the expedition.
그는 탐험 여행에서 중요한 역할을 했다.

participate in

pick out 고르다, 선택하다, 발탁하다
She **picked out** a new dress at the store.
그녀는 가게에서 새 드레스를 골랐다.
She **picked out** a white rose.
그녀는 흰 장미를 골랐다.

[SYN] choose

for the time being 당분간
I can do with this sum of money **for the time being**.
이만한 돈이면 당분간은 걱정 없겠다.
(=This sum will be enough for the immediate express.)
For the time being we'd better not meet too often.
당분간은 자주 안 만나는 게 좋을 것이다.

[SYN] for now; temporarily; for the present; for a while

so to speak 말하자면, 즉
Two horses, **so to speak**, were dancing on their hind legs.
말 두 마리가 그야말로 뒷발로 서서 춤을 추고 있었다.
Bill is, **so to speak**, the leader of the human rights organization.
빌은 말하자면 그 인권 단체의 지도자이다.

[SYN] as it were; in other words; we might say

enter into 1. (대화·담화·교섭 등을) 시작하다, 관여하다 2. …을 이해하다, …에 동정하다
They **entered into** a discussion about the issue.
그들은 그 문제에 관한 토의를 시작했다.
We **entered** heartily **into** conviviality of the occasion.
우리는 축제 분위기를 충분히 느낄 수 있었다.

[SYN] 1. make a start; set about; take to 2. be able to understand and appreciate

cannot ... too 아무리 …해도 지나치지 않다
We **cannot** be **too** careful for our health.
건강은 아무리 주의를 해도 지나치지 않다.
We **cannot** praise him **too** much.

[SYN] it is not too much to say that ...
cf. cannot ... too, cannot ... enough

그는 아무리 칭찬해도 모자랄 정도다.
(= We cannot praise him enough.)

come along 좋아지다, 성공하다, 일이 순조롭게 진행되다

How's that Smith account **coming along**, Helen?
헬렌, 스미스사 거래 관계는 어떻게 되어 가고 있나?
Once he was critical, but after the operation he is **coming along** well.
한때 그는 위험했지만 수술 후에 많이 좋아지고 있다.

[SYN] make progress; get well; succeed; go along smoothly

in advance 미리

As it is weekend, you have to make reservation **in advance**.
주말이므로 미리 예약을 해야 한다.
If you want to start tomorrow, you had better buy the ticket **in advance**.
내일 출발하려면 표를 미리 사 두는 것이 좋다.

[SYN] beforehand; ahead of time; in anticipation
cf. in advance of …보다 앞서서

in the long run (긴 안목으로 보아) 결국은

In the long run, Ben will get to the top.
결국은 벤이 수석을 하게 될 것이다.
He will regret his foolish behavior **in the long run**.
결국은 그가 자기의 어리석은 행동을 후회할 것이다.

[SYN] eventually

take after …을 닮다

John **takes after** his father in artistic talent.
예술적인 재능에 있어서 존은 아버지를 닮았다.
In many respects, he **takes after** his mother more than his father.
여러 가지 면에서 그는 아버지보다는 어머니를 많이 닮았다.

[SYN] resemble; look after; be similar to

for the sake of / for one's sake …을 위하여

Let's be careful not to smoke too much, **for the sake of** our health.
건강을 위해 지나친 흡연을 하지 않도록 주의하자.
For your wife's sake, don't borrow so much money.
부인을 위해서라도 많은 돈을 빌리지 마세요.

[SYN] for one's good sake of; on one's account; to one's advantage

be familiar to …에 잘 알려져 있다, 익숙하다

What the speaker told us tonight were all **familiar**

[SYN] be well-known; be accustomed to

to us.
연사가 오늘밤 우리에게 이야기한 것은 잘 알려져 있는 것이었다.
Her name **is familiar to** me, though I do not know her by sight.
나는 그 여자의 얼굴은 잘 모르지만 그 여자의 이름은 잘 안다.

the day before yesterday 그저께

I saw a movie **the day before yesterday**.
그저께 영화를 구경했다.
She came to see him **the day before yesterday**.
그저께 그녀가 그를 보러 왔다.

[SYN] two days ago

on time 정각에

His lecture started **on time**.
그의 강의는 정각에 시작했다.
Our plane left **on time**.
우리 비행기는 정각에 떠났다.

[SYN] punctually

owing to … 때문에, …에 기인하여, …으로 말미암아

Owing to the traffic accident, he was late for the meeting.
교통사고 때문에 그는 회의에 늦었다.
His failure was **owing to** his negligence.
그의 실패는 그의 게으름에 기인했다.

[SYN] due to; because of; as a result of

exchange for 교환하다, 환전하다

If you want, I am willing to **exchange** this hat **for** your old one.
당신이 원한다면 이 모자를 당신의 오래된 모자와 바꿔 줄 의향이 있습니다.
Would you **exchange** these pounds **for** dollars please?
이 파운드화를 달러로 환전해 주시겠습니까?

[SYN] make an exchange; change money
cf. exchange into 환전하다
exchange with …와 (의견 등을) 교환하다
in exchange for …와 교환으로, … 대신으로

by the dozen 다스 단위로, 한꺼번에

The children ate candies **by the dozen**.
아이들은 캔디를 한꺼번에 먹었다.
People came to the picnic **by the dozen**.
많은 사람들이 소풍 왔다.

[SYN] very many at one time
cf. by the meter〔pound/hour/week〕미터〔파운드/시간/주〕단위로

by way of …을 경유하여

We went to Europe **by way of** Alaska.

[SYN] via; through

우리는 알라스카를 경유하여 유럽으로 갔다.
Most successful people are graduates of Harvard **by way of** a first-rate grammar school.
대부분의 성공한 사람들은 우수 중학교를 거친 하바드 졸업생들이다.

keep ... from -ing ⋯을 못하게 하다, ⋯로부터 보호하다, 금하다

[SYN] prevent ... from -ing

The heavy snow **kept** us **from** com**ing** in time.
우리는 폭설 때문에 제 시간에 오지 못했다.
He **kept** his son **from** fall**ing** into the lake.
그는 아들이 호수에 빠지지 않게 잘 보호했다.

no sooner ... than ⋯ 하자마자, ⋯하는 순간에, ⋯하기 무섭게

[SYN] as soon as; hardly ... when; scarcely ... before

No sooner had I left the office **than** a fire broke out.
내가 사무실에서 나오자마자 불이 났다.
No sooner had I started to read **than** he came in.
내가 책을 읽기 시작하자마자 그가 들어왔다.
(=I had no sooner started to read than he came in.)

not a little 적지 않은, 상당 양의 (양에 사용)

[SYN] much, great

He has **not a little** knowledge of the world.
그는 세상을 꽤 많이 알고 있다.
He was **not a little** ashamed of having made such a mistake.
그는 그런 실수를 한 데 대해 몹시 부끄러워했다.

come across ⋯와 마주치다, 우연히 발견하다

[SYN] run across; drop across; meet with; meet by chance
cf. happen to 우연히 만나다 (= meet by chance)

Celebrities develop a technique to deal with people they **come across**.
유명인들은 우연히 만나는 사람들을 적당히 대접하는 술수에 능하다.
I **came across** a very curious book.
기이한 책을 우연히 발견했다.

there is no room for ⋯할 여지가 없다

[SYN] leave no room for

There is no room for doubt.
의심할 여지가 없다.
There is no room for complaint.
불평할 여지가 없다.

make fun of 놀리다, 조롱하다
He often **makes fun of** his sister by imitating her.
그는 종종 누이를 흉내내어 누이를 놀린다.
It's wrong to **make fun of** an old man.
노인을 조롱하는 것은 나쁜 일이다.

[SYN] poke fun at; laugh at

make light〔little〕of …을 경시하다, 얕보다, 무시하다
He never **made light of** even small things.
그는 아무리 사소한 일도 경시하지 않았다.
He **made little of** his illness, but we knew it was serious.
그는 자신의 병을 가볍게 생각하지만 우리는 위중하다는 것을 알고 있었다.

[SYN] despise; think light of; make little account of

no more ... than …이 아닌 것은 ~이 아닌 것과 같다
A whale is **no more** a fish **than** a horse is.
고래가 물고기가 아닌 것은 말이 물고기가 아닌 것과 같다.
(=A whale is not a fish any more than a horse is.)
A bat is **no more** a bird **than** a rat (is).
박쥐가 새가 아닌 것은 쥐가 새가 아닌 것과 같다.

[SYN] not ... any more than

not ... but …이 아니고 ~이다
Not Stephen **but** Richard handed in the report.
스티븐이 아니고 리처드가 보고서를 제출했다.
That is **not** my house, **but** my uncle's.
저것은 우리 집이 아니라 삼촌의 집이다.

[SYN] instead of

keep in touch with …와 접촉〔연락〕을 유지하다
We must **keep in touch with** the scientific activity of the world.
우리는 세계의 과학 활동과 늘 접촉해야만 한다.
The man **kept in touch with** the President.
그 남자는 대통령과 접촉을 유지하고 있었다.

[SYN] keep touch with

keep on -ing 계속 …하다
He **kept on** drink**ing** all the time.
그는 줄곧 술을 마셨다.
Although I was very tired, I had to **keep on** work**ing**.
매우 피곤했지만 나는 계속 일해야 했다.

[SYN] continue to

What has become of ... ? …은 어떻게 되었는가?

I can't imagine **what has become of** those papers that I left on my desk.
책상 위에 둔 그 서류가 어떻게 되었는지 전혀 모르겠다.
Do you know **what has become of** him?
그가 어떻게 되었는지 아니?

so as to …하기 위해서

He ran to the movie theater **so as** not **to** be late for the appointment.
그는 약속 시간에 늦지 않기 위해 영화관으로 달려갔다.
He spoke loudly **so as to** be heard.
그는 들을 수 있도록 큰 소리로 말했다.

[SYN] in order to; so (that) … may

scores of 많은 수의, 많은

I've heard this story **scores of** times.
이 말을 몇 번이나 들은 적이 있다.
My father has been to Paris on business **scores of** times.
아버지는 사업차 수차례 파리에 다녀왔다.

[SYN] lots of; a great many

deal with 취급하다, 다루다, 처리하다, 거래하다

He is never a hard man to **deal with**.
그는 결코 다루기 까다로운 사람이 아니다.
I don't know how to **deal with** those juvenile criminals.
저 청소년 범죄자들을 어떻게 다루어야 할지 모르겠다.

[SYN] treat; manage; handle; engage in commercially

dwell in 거주하다, 머무르다

How you have been kind to me still **dwells in** my heart.
당신이 얼마나 나에게 친절했는가는 지금도 내 마음에 자리잡고 있다.
My husband doesn't like to **dwell in** a city.
내 남편은 도시 생활을 좋아하지 않는다.

[SYN] live in; stay at

wait for …을 기다리다, 대기하다

There are a lot of people **waiting for** you outside.
밖에 당신을 기다리는 사람들이 많이 있습니다.
I **waited for** him until five o'clock but he failed to turn up.
다섯 시까지 그를 기다렸지만 그는 나타나지 않았다.

[SYN] await; watch and wait; wait and see; abide
cf. wait on (upon) 1. 시중들다 (=attend; serve; take care of) 2. …을 방문하다 (=call on; visit)

without fail 틀림(어김)없이, 반드시, 확실히

All the participants should be here before seven, **without fail**.
모든 참가자들은 7시 전에 어김없이 와야 합니다.
Bill promised his father to return the car till the evening **without fail**.
빌은 자동차를 저녁까지 어김없이 갖다 놓겠다고 아버지에게 약속했다.

SYN. certainly; surely

needless to say 말할 것도 없이, 물론

Needless to say, honesty is the best policy.
말할 것도 없이 정직은 최선의 수단이다.
Needless to say, he kept his promise.
말할 것도 없이 그는 약속을 지켰다.

SYN. not to mention; to say nothing of; let alone

name ... after …을 본따서 이름짓다

The parents **named** their first baby **after** his grandfather.
부모는 첫 아기의 이름을 할아버지 이름을 따서 지었다.
His granddaughter was **named after** Queen Elizabeth.
그의 손녀는 엘리자베스 여왕을 본따서 엘리자베스라 이름지어졌다.

SYN. give the same name as

have nothing to do with …와 아무런 관계가 없다

Jenny **has nothing to do with** the geology department.
제니는 지질학과와 아무 관련이 없다.
His father **has nothing to do with** the firm.
그의 부친은 그 회사와 아무런 관계가 없다.

SYN. be not related with; have no connection with
cf. have little to do with 거의 관계가 없다
have something to do with …와 좀 관계가 있다

have (be) to do with 1. …와 관계가 있다 2. …을 다루다

I heard that it **is** something **to do with** the computer.
나는 그것이 컴퓨터와 관련이 있다고 들었다.
A doctor **has to do with** all sorts of people.
의사는 온갖 부류의 사람을 다룬다.

SYN. 1. be connected with something in some way 2. deal with

get on with 사이좋게 지내다

It is hard to **get on with** a suspicious man.
의심이 많은 사람과는 잘 지내기 힘들다.

SYN. get along well; be on good terms (with)

자주 나오는 중요 숙어

Do you think they can **get along with** each other?
그들이 서로 잘해 나갈 수 있을 것이라고 생각합니까?

generally speaking 일반적으로 말해서

Generally speaking, women live longer than men.
일반적으로 말해서 여성이 남성보다 오래 산다.
Generally speaking, the Germans are taller than the French.
대체로 독일 사람이 프랑스 사람보다 키가 크다.

[SYN] If you speak generally

provide ... with …에게 ~을 공급하다, 주다

He **provided** his son **with** a good education.
그는 아들에게 좋은 교육을 받게 해 주었다.
The government **provided** the flood victims **with** food and clothing.
정부는 홍수 피해자들에게 식량과 의류를 공급했다.
(= The government authorities supplied the victims of water disaster with food and clothing.)

[SYN] give; supply; provide; furnish

pass by 지나가다

On the street my ex-wife **passed by** me without saying a word.
거리에서 나의 전 부인은 아무 말도 하지 않고 내 옆을 지나갔다.
The dog sat in front of the door, barking at anyone who **passed by** our house.
개는 문 앞에 앉아서 우리 집을 지나가는 모든 사람에게 짖어댔다.

[SYN] go past without stopping

first of all 첫째(로), 우선, 무엇보다

First of all we must dismiss the cook.
무엇보다도 요리사를 해고해야 한다.
First of all, we'd better clean the table.
무엇보다도 먼저 식탁을 치우는 게 좋겠다.

[SYN] first; before everything else; above all; in the first place

fill up 채우다

They brought two baskets and **filled** them **up** by apples.
그들은 들통 두 개를 가져와서 사과로 가득 채웠다.
I want you to **fill up** my glass.
내 잔을 채워 줘.

[SYN] make a container full

used to + 동사 늘 …하곤 했다, …하는 것이 예사였다 (과거습관)

cf. would 과거의 불규칙한 습관, used to + 명사 …에 익숙한 (=

He **used to** take a walk after breakfast, shine or rain.
그는 갠 날이나 비가 오는 날이나 아침 식사 후 산책을 하곤 했다.
I **used to** like him, but now I don't.
옛날에는 그를 좋아했지만 지금은 그렇지 않다.

[SYN] accustomed to; familiar to)

under construction 건설 중, 공사 중

This road is **under construction**, so you can't travel on it.
이 도로는 공사 중이기 때문에 계속 갈 수가 없다.
The new station is now **under construction**.
새로운 역은 지금 한창 건설 중이다.

[SYN] in course of construction

get at 1. …에 달하다, 손이 미치다, 닿다 2. …을 암시하다, 넌지시 비추다, …을 의미하다

I can't **get at** the radio from here, so would you turn it on please?
여기서는 라디오에 손이 닿지 않으니 좀 켜 주겠니?
Can you understand what is the teacher trying to **get at**?
선생님이 무슨 말을 하려고 하는지 이해가 가니?

[SYN] 1. reach; attain to 2. allude; give a hint; suggest; mean

give up 포기하다, …을 그만두다

You had better **give up** drinking and smoking.
술과 담배는 끊는 편이 좋다.
He **gave up** the idea of going to America to study.
그는 미국으로 유학하려는 생각을 버렸다.

[SYN] abandon; stop doing

no matter+의문사 … may …일지라도

No matter how rich he **may** be, he cannot be called a gentleman.
아무리 부자라도 그는 신사라고 할 수 없다.
No matter how hard you **may** try, you cannot do it.
아무리 열심히 하여도 그것을 이룰 수 없다.
(=However hard you may try, you cannot do it.)

[SYN] 의문사+ever

not a few 1. 적지 않은, 상당수의 (수에 사용) 2. 꽤, 상당히

Last night **not a few** of the members were present.
간밤에는 상당수의 회원이 참석했다.
That news interested me **not a few**.

[SYN] 1. a lot of 2. quite; fairly; considerably

나는 그 소식에 꽤 흥미를 느꼈다.

day after day 매일, 날마다, 며칠이고 끝이 없이

It is cold **day after day** though it is spring now.
봄은 왔는데 매일매일 춥다.
If you do this a bit **day after day**, someday you will be able to finish it.
이것을 매일 조금씩 하면 언젠가는 끝낼 수 있을 것이다.

[SYN] every day; daily; day in and day out; without respite

put up 1. 숙박시키다, 재워 주다 2. 준비하다, 비축해 두다 3. (집 따위를) 짓다, 세우다

When I was in Paris, my old friend **put** me **up** for a few days.
내가 파리에 있을 때 옛 친구가 며칠 재워 주었다.
The hotel will **put** us **up** some foods and drinks.
호텔측이 먹을 것과 마실 것을 준비할 것이다.
They tore down the old building to **put up** a new one.
그들은 새 건물을 짓기 위해 낡은 건물을 철거했다.

[SYN] 1. give someone hospitality; provide lodging and food 2. be ready for; stock 3. build; construct; erect

boast of 자랑하다, 자랑으로 여기다

She **boasted of** her son's success.
그녀는 아들의 성공을 자랑했다.
She **boasted of** her intelligence.
그녀는 자신의 지성을 자랑했다.

[SYN] brag of; be proud of; make a boast of

take notice of …을 주목하다, 주의하다

You had better **take notice of** your mother's warning.
너는 엄마의 경고에 주의하는 것이 좋을 거야.
People **took** little **notice of** his warning.
사람들은 그의 경고를 거의 귀담아 듣지 않았다.

[SYN] give attention to; attend to; heed
cf. take no notice of …을 마음에 두지 않다, 무시하다 (= dismiss; ignore; disregard)

over and over (again) 몇 번이고 되풀이하여, 반복하여

For the test, Bill read the passage **over and over again**.
시험을 위해서 빌은 그 단락을 반복해서 읽었다.
I've warned you **over and over again** not to do it.
나는 너에게 그것을 하지 말도록 몇 번이고 주의를 주었다.

[SYN] many times; repeatedly

hang up 걸다, 수화기를 제자리에 놓다

[SYN] place on a hook, peg, or

You should **hang up** your coat first.
우선 코트를 걸어야 한다.
Jack's mother told him to **hang up** the phone.
잭의 어머니는 잭에게 전화를 끊으라고 말씀하셨다.

hanger
OPP. ring up 전화를 걸다

never ... but ···하면 반드시 ~한다
It **never** rains **but** it pours.
내렸다 하면 소나기. (속담)
They **never** meet **but** they quarrel.
그들은 만나기만 하면 반드시 싸운다.

SYN. never without

get in 1. 들어가다, (택시를) 타다 2. 도착하다, 오다
I don't like to **get in** on the driver's side.
나는 운전석 옆에 앉기 싫다.
The train **got in** on time.
기차는 정시에 도착했다.

SYN. 1. enter 2. come; arrive

near by 가까이에
Christmas is **near by**.
크리스마스가 가깝다.
She rushed to a drugstore **near by**.
그녀는 가까이에 있는 약국으로 달려갔다.

SYN. close at hand

ring up 전화하다
Did anyone **ring** me **up** while I was out?
외출 중에 전화한 사람 있었나요?
Mother **rang up** my teacher and told her that I would stay home today because of the flu.
어머니는 선생님에게 전화를 걸어 내가 오늘 독감 때문에 결석을 할 것이라고 말했다.

SYN. call up; phone

right away / right now 아주 떠나서, 즉시, 당장
I will do the job **right away** without other people's help.
다른 사람들의 도움 없이 그 일을 즉시 하겠다.
You must write down the list of things to do **right away**.
당장 해야 할 일의 목록을 작성해야 한다.

SYN. instantly; immediately; without waiting

nothing but ···밖에 없는, 다만 ···뿐
On Saturdays he does **nothing but** watch TV.
토요일에 그는 TV만 본다.

SYN. nothing except; only
cf. do nothing but 오직 ···할 뿐이다, ···하기만 하다 (= merely

자주 나오는 중요 숙어 **75**

The company manufactures **nothing but** mattresses.
그 회사는 매트리스만 제조한다.

(be) known as …으로 알려져 있다

My father **is known as** a great poet.
나의 아버지는 위대한 시인으로 알려져 있다.
He **is** better **known as** a man of letters than a physician.
그는 의사로서 보다는 문인으로 더 잘 알려져 있다.

[SYN] be generally known; be known extensively

(be) known by …을 보고 알 수 있다 (이때 by는 판단의 근거를 나타냄)

A man can **be known by** the company he keeps.
사람은 교제하는 사람들을 보면 알 수 있다.
A tree **is known by** its fruit.
나무는 그 열매를 보고 알 수 있다.

[SYN] can judge somebody or something by

for good 영원히, 이제 마지막으로

I've quit **for good**.
영원히 그만두었어.
He left home **for good** after finishing school.
그는 학교를 졸업한 뒤, 아주 집을 나가 버렸다.

[SYN] forever; permanently

later on 나중에, 후에

Finish your homework first. **Later on**, we can go out and play baseball.
숙제를 먼저 끝내. 그 후 나가서 야구를 하면 돼.
When the class started Bill couldn't solve the problem, but **later on** he could.
수업을 시작할 때에는 빌이 그 문제를 풀지 못했지만 나중에는 풀 수 있었다.

[SYN] later; not now; after; afterward(s)

become of …이 어떻게 되다

What shall **become of** my family if the war breaks out?
만약 전쟁이 터지면 내 가족은 어떻게 될까?
I wonder what will **become of** the boy.
그 소년은 어떻게 될까?

[SYN] be the end of; be the later or final condition
cf. come of … 출신이다, …에서 탄생하다, 되어 가다, 도달하다 (= descend from; come from; attain; reach)

not because … but because ~ … 때문이 아니라 ~ 때문에

I like him **not because** he is rich, **but because** he

[SYN] not that …, but that ~

is kind.
내가 그를 좋아하는 것은 그가 부자여서가 아니라 친절하기 때문이다.
I am happy **not because** I am rich **but because** I am healthy.
나는 부자여서가 아니라 건강하기 때문에 행복하다.

hit on (upon) 우연히 마주치다, 발견하다, (묘안 따위가) 문득 생각나다

I **hit on** the idea by chance on my way home.
집에 가는 길에 우연히 그 생각이 떠올랐다.
My boss **hit on** a new way of making our product.
사장은 제품을 만들 새로운 방법을 생각해 냈다.

[SYN] discover; happen to meet; run into; suddenly devise

make believe …인 체하다, …로 보이게(믿게) 하다

The boys **make believe** they are cowboys.
그 소년들은 카우보이인 척한다.
She **made believe** not to hear me.
그녀는 내 말을 못 들은 척했다.

[SYN] pretend; feign

pick up 1. (땅을) 파올리다, 줍다, 집어들다 2. (차·배 등이 승객을) 도중에서 태우다

The little girl **picked up** a ring under the tree.
어린 소녀는 나무 아래서 반지를 주웠다.
I'll **pick** you **up** at six and get you to the station.
여섯 시에 너를 태워서 역까지 데려다 주겠다.

[SYN] 1. take up; raise up; lift 2. take passengers in a vehicle

go to sea 항해를 떠나다, 선원이 되다

I don't know when to **go to sea**.
언제 항해를 떠날지 모른다.
After his marriage had failed, John decided to **go to sea**.
결혼이 실패한 후 존은 선원이 되기로 결심했다.

[SYN] earn one's living on a ship; be a sailor

with difficulty 간신히, 겨우

The survivor answered my questions **with difficulty**.
생존자는 내 질문에 간신히 대답했다.
He could pass the examination **with difficulty**.
그는 간신히 시험에 합격할 수 있었다.

[SYN] with the skin of one's teeth; barely; narrowly

lose oneself / get lost 길을 잃다

Nick **lost himself** in the bustling downtown of New

York.
닉은 복잡한 뉴욕 시내에서 길을 잃었다.
When the child **got lost**, a policeman took him to the police station.
아이가 길을 잃어버리자 경찰이 아이를 파출소로 데리고 갔다.

for sure 확실히

He didn't know **for sure** when he could finish his work.
그는 일을 언제 끝낼 수 있을지 확실히 알지 못했다.
Can you **for sure** promise me that you will invest to my business?
내 사업에 투자한다고 확실하게 약속할 수 있느냐?

[SYN] certainly; surely

keep one's promise [word] 약속을 지키다

Keeping one's promise is very important in our social life.
사회 생활에 있어서 약속을 지키는 것은 매우 중요하다.
Father **kept his promise** to buy a car for me.
아버지는 내게 차를 사 주겠다는 약속을 지키셨다.

[SYN] be true to one's promise; keep an agreement; abide by one's promise
[OPP] break one's promise [word] 약속을 어기다
cf. make a promise 약속하다

just about 1. 바로, 아주 2. 거의, 대개 3. 그럭저럭, 간신히

He is **just about** to commence the business.
그는 이제 막 그 사업을 시작하려고 한다.
He will **just about** win.
그는 가까스로 이길 것이다.

[SYN] 1. quite; right away; at once; immediately 2. almost; nearly 3. barely

result in …으로 끝나다, …에 귀결하다

Your proposal may **result in** a large profit for our company.
당신의 제안은 우리 회사를 위해 큰 이익으로 끝날지도 모른다.
Her hard work **resulted in** a big bonus for her.
그녀는 열심히 일을 하여 많은 보너스를 받았다.

[SYN] end as a consequence; have as a result; cause

on foot 1. 걸어서, 도보로 2. 착수되어, 진행 중에

It takes about two hours **on foot** to the next village.
다음 마을까지는 걸어서 두 시간 정도 걸린다.
A big birthday party for my mother is **on foot**.
어머니의 성대한 생일 파티를 계획 중이다.

[SYN] 1. by walking 2. being planned

run over 1. 자동차에 치다 2. 대충 훑어보다
A man in a red BMW just **ran over** my dog.
적색 BMW를 탄 남자가 방금 내 개를 치었다.
The professor **ran over** my report as soon as I submitted it.
교수는 내가 보고서를 제출하자마자 바로 훑어보았다.

[SYN] 1. strike and pass over with a vehicle 2. read through or study something quickly

call for 1. …을 모시러 오다 2. 요구하다, …을 필요로 하다
I'll **call for** you at 7:00 tomorrow morning.
내일 아침 7시에 모시러 오겠습니다.
It **calls for** serious consideration.
그것은 심사숙고를 필요로 한다.

[SYN] 1. drop by; visit a short time 2. need; require; ask

feel like -ing …하고 싶은 마음이 생기다
I don't **feel like** study**ing** tonight.
나는 오늘밤 공부하고 싶지 않다.
I sometimes **feel like** visit**ing** the quiet countryside.
이따금 조용한 시골에 가고 싶은 기분이 들 때가 있다.

[SYN] like to; want to do or have
cf. feel like 1. 아무래도 … 같다, 아마 …일 듯 하다 2. …을 하고 싶다
feel up to …을 견디어 내다

bear in mind 명심하다, 기억하다
Please **bear in mind** what I said.
내가 한 말을 명심하시오.
Bear it **in mind** that you must not be late for work.
지각하면 안 된다는 점을 명심해라.

[SYN] keep in mind; learn from heart

not … at all 조금도 …않다
It has **not** rained **at all** for the last few months.
지난 몇 달 동안 비가 조금도 오지 않았다.
(=We have had no rain at all for the past few months.)
I do**n't** like the way that you are behaving **at all**, so stop it.
네 행동이 전혀 마음에 들지 않으니 그만해.

[SYN] not in the least; not in the slightest degree

wrong with …에 고장이 난, …이 잘못된
Don't worry because nothing is **wrong with** me.
나는 아무 일도 없으니 걱정하지 마라.
What's **wrong with** you? I haven't seen you for a long time.
무슨 일이 있었어? 오랫동안 널 보지 못했어.

[SYN] badly off; out of order
cf. in the wrong 잘못된, 나쁜 (=bad; wrong)

of no use 쓸모 없는, 무익한
Your suggestion is **of no** practical **use**.
당신의 제안은 실제적으로 전혀 쓸모가 없다.
It's **of no use** to talk.
말해도 소용 없다.
(= It's no use talking [to talk].)

[SYN] useless; valueless

go mad 미치다, 정신이 나가다
He **went mad** because of the shock.
그는 쇼크로 정신이 나갔다.
He nearly **went mad** with vexation.
그는 분해서 거의 미칠 지경이었다.

[SYN] out of one's mind; insane

look up (사전에서) 낱말을 찾다
If you cannot make out the meaning of the word, **look** it **up** in the dictionary.
단어의 뜻이 이해가 되지 않으면 사전에서 찾아보아라.
Look up the number in the telephone book.
전화번호부에서 번호를 찾아보아라.

[SYN] try to find something in a dictionary or other reference

instead of …대신에, …하지 않고, …하기는커녕
We learned English **instead of** French.
우리는 프랑스 어 대신 영어를 배웠다.
He stayed at home all day **instead of** going out.
그는 밖에 나가지 않고 온종일 집에 있었다.
He thanked me **instead of** getting angry.
그는 화를 내기는커녕 나에게 감사를 표했다.

[SYN] in place of; in lieu of

plenty of 많은, 충분한, 다수의, 다량의
There were **plenty of** good places to camp in.
야영하기 좋은 장소가 얼마든지 있었다.
You'll arrive there in **plenty of** time.
그 곳에 도착하는 데는 시간이 충분하다.

[SYN] many; much; abundant; enough; a lot of; lots of; a good deal of; a good many

had rather 차라리 …하는 편이 좋다, 오히려 …이 좋다
She **had rather** take science than art.
그녀는 미술보다는 과학을 택하는 것이 좋다.
I **had rather** be a day-laborer than a beggar.
거지가 되느니 날품팔이꾼이 되겠다.

[SYN] had better; prefer
cf. would rather …하는 쪽이 낫다 (강한 선택) (= choose; prefer to)

thanks to …덕택에, … 때문에
Thanks to the good weather, we all enjoyed our

[SYN] because of; on account of

nice trip.
좋은 날씨 덕택에 우리는 여행을 즐겼다.
Thanks to a sudden rain, the game was put off.
갑작스런 비로 인해 시합이 연기됐다.

deal in (상품을) 취급하다

My business **deals in** all kinds of furniture.
나의 회사는 모든 종류의 가구를 취급한다.
He **deals in** art and antiques.
그는 미술품, 골동품 등을 판다.

[SYN] trade in; treat; deal with
cf. deal with 1. 처리하다, …을 취급하다 (=treat) 2. 거래하다
cope with …을 대처해 나가다 (= deal effectively)

make much of …을 중시하다, 중히 여기다

He **makes** too **much of** the event.
그는 그 사건을 너무 중시한다.
Bill **makes much of** his son who has just received a scholarship.
빌은 최근에 장학금을 받은 아들을 소중히 여긴다.

[SYN] give importance; prize
[OPP] make light(little) of …을 경시하다, 얕보다 (=despise; think little of)
make nothing of …을 아무렇지도 않게 여기다, …을 우습게 여기다

come to an end 끝나다, 중단하다

The summer vacation **came to an end** at last.
마침내 여름 휴가가 끝이 났다.
I think the war will not **come to an end** soon.
내가 생각하기에는 전쟁이 곧 끝날 것 같지 않다.

[SYN] end; stop; finish; discontinue

just as 1. 바로 …와 마찬가지로 2. 바로 …할 때

Leave the kitchen **just as** clean as you found it.
주방을 쓰기 전처럼 깨끗하게 해 놓아라.
Just as we arrived at the station, the train was leaving.
우리가 바로 역에 도착했을 때 기차는 떠나고 있었다.

[SYN] 1. exactly the same as 2. just when

up to date 최신의

All the machines are **up to date** in this factory.
이 공장의 모든 기계는 최신의 것이다.
The new car I bought yesterday is quite **up to date**.
어제 산 새 자동차는 아주 최신의 것이다.

[SYN] up-to-date; the latest

for the first time 처음으로

Seeing me **for the first time**, my uncle wept for joy.
나를 처음으로 보고 아저씨는 기뻐서 울었다.
I met him then **for the first time**.

[SYN] first; before one does anything else
cf. for the first time in… …만에 처음으로
for the last time 마지막으로

그때 처음으로 그를 만났다.

be surprised to +동사 …하고 놀라다, 아연케 하다

I **was** greatly **surprised to** see John still there.
존이 아직도 그 곳에 있는 것을 보고 무척 놀랐다.

We **are** sometimes **surprised to** find the whole tone of the color is rather dark.
전체 색조가 좀 어둡다는 것을 보고 가끔 놀라게 된다.

[SYN] be startled; be taken aback; be shocked

제 2 장   이것만큼은 외워야 한다.

제 2 장에서 공부할 것은
꼭 외워야 하는 필수 숙어들!

이것만큼은 외워 두어야 한다.
그 이유는?

숙어는 숙어로서 존재하는 것이 아니기 때문에.
풍부한 숙어 실력은
모든 영어 실력과 통하는 법!

숙어에 통달하면 영어의 절반은
마친 셈이다.

제2장 이것만큼은 외워야 한다

as likely as not 아마, 혹시 …일지 모르다
As likely as not, the game will be canceled because of heavy rain.
아마 경기는 폭우 때문에 취소될 것이다.
He knows nothing about his son's death **as likely as not**.
그는 아마도 아들의 죽음에 대해서는 모르고 있을 것이다.

[SYN] perhaps; possibly; maybe

as is often the case (with) 흔히 있는 일이지만
As is often the case with misers, the more he has, the more he covets.
구두쇠에게는 흔히 있는 일이지만 가질수록 욕심을 낸다.
As is often the case with sailors, he is too fond of alcohol.
선원들에게 흔히 있는 일이지만 그는 술을 너무 좋아한다.

[SYN] as (so) often happens

be sensitive to …에 민감하다, …을 쉽게 느끼다
His skin **is sensitive to** the sunlight.
그의 피부는 햇빛에 민감하다.
He seems to **be sensitive to** climatic changes.
그는 기후 변화에 민감한 것 같다.

[SYN] be able to sense or feel in a stronger than normal way

be crowded with …으로 붐비다
The waiting room **was crowded with** patients.
그 대합실은 환자들로 붐볐다.
The store **was crowded with** holiday shoppers.
그 점포는 휴일의 쇼핑하는 손님들로 가득 찼다.

[SYN] be jammed; be thronged
cf. be jammed with …으로 붐비다, 초만원이다 (= be overcrowded with; be filled (packed) with)

come in (into) contact with …와 접촉하다, …와 만나다
He **came into contact with** various types of men.
그는 여러 유형의 사람들을 만났다.
If you **come in contact with** him, you will find him honest.
그와 직접 부딪혀 보면 그가 정직하다는 것을 알게 될 것이다.

[SYN] touch; come in touch with; see; meet

come true 실현되다, 사실이 되다, 들어맞다

[SYN] realize; change from a

Try hard, and your dream to be a spaceman will **come true** in the end.
열심히 노력해라, 그러면 우주 비행사가 되려는 꿈이 결국 실현될 것이다.
Ann's hope of becoming an artist finally **came true**.
예술가가 되겠다는 앤의 희망이 실현되었다.

dream into a reality; really happen

do one's best 전심전력을 다하다, 최선을 다하다
All that you should do is to **do your best**.
네가 할 일은 최선을 다하는 것뿐이다.
All we can do is to **do our best** today.
우리가 할 수 있는 일은 오직 현재에 최선을 다하는 것이다.

[SYN] exert oneself to the utmost; do one's utmost; do all one can

do a favor 은혜를 베풀다, 부탁을 들어주다
Would you **do** me **a favor** and find a file for me?
나를 위해 서류를 좀 찾아 주시겠어요?
Would you **do** me **a favor** and type this letter at once?
금방 이 편지를 타이프 쳐서 받을 수 있을까요?
(=I wonder if you would be good enough to type this letter for me immediately.)

[SYN] help; comply with one's request

run into 1. …와 충돌하다, …로 뛰어 들어오다 2. 우연히 만나다
The two boys **ran into** each other when playing football.
두 소년이 축구를 하다가 서로 부딪혔다.
I **ran into** an old friend at the airport in New York.
나는 뉴욕의 공항에서 옛 친구를 우연히 만났다.

[SYN] 1. bump into; collide with; hit; run against; conflict with 2. meet by chance

run out of …을 다 써 버리다, 바닥이 나다
We have **run out of** paper for the photocopy machine.
복사기 종이가 다 떨어졌다.
I didn't finish the exam because I **ran out of** time.
시간이 다 되어 시험을 끝까지 마치지 못했다.

[SYN] use all of something; deplete; exhaust; be all gone

within (the) reach of …의 손이 닿는 곳에, …의 범위 안에
We want to live somewhere **within reach of** a bus stop.
버스 정류장에서 가까운 곳에 살고 싶다.

[SYN] within one's reach
[OPP] out of (the) reach of …의 손이 안 닿는 (=out of one's reach)
cf. above(beyond) the(one's)

I live **within** easy **reach of** my school.
나는 학교에서 아주 가까운 곳에 산다.

reach …의 힘이 미치지 않는, …의 손이 안 닿는

what is ... like …가 어떤 사람〔물건〕이냐

What is the new principal **like**?
새 교장 선생님은 어떤 분인가요?
What's it **like** going there alone?
그 곳에 혼자 가는 것은 어떤 기분인가요?

SYN what kind of person or thing

head for …로 향하다

The ships were **heading for** the land of hope.
배들은 희망의 땅을 향해 가고 있었다.
We got on the truck and **headed for** the field.
우리는 트럭을 타고 들판으로 향했다.

SYN travel towards a place

think of 1. …에 관심을 보이다, …에 마음을 쓰다, 숙고하다 2. …을 상상하다 3. 생각나다

Think of those poor children.
그 가엾은 아이들에게 관심을 보이시오.
His innocence is not to be **thought of**.
그가 결백하다는 것은 상상할 수도 없다.
I can't **think of** her name every now and then.
그녀의 이름이 이따금씩 생각나지 않는다.

SYN 1. show interest in; consider 2. imagine; fancy 3. come to mind

try on (몸에 맞는지) 입어〔신어·써〕 보다

The shopkeeper told me to **try** the blue coat **on**.
점원은 나에게 푸른색 코트를 입어 보라고 권했다.
She **tried** all the hats **on** in the store, but didn't buy anything.
그녀는 가게에 있는 모자를 전부 써 봤지만 아무것도 사지 않았다.

SYN put on a garment to test the fit

hear of 1. (다른 사람을 통해 간접적으로) 들어서 알다, 소문을 듣다 2. (흔히 부정으로 쓰여) …에 찬성하다, 들어주다

I have **heard of** his arrival.
그가 도착했다는 말을 들었다.
I have **heard of** his death.
그가 죽었다는 소리를 들었다.
I will not **hear of** your going there with her.
네가 그녀와 함께 거기 가는 것을 허락할 수 없다.

SYN 1. learn of by report 2. give one's approval to; approve of

very thing 바로 그것

SYN the exact thing that is

This is the **very thing** that I have looked for so long.
이것은 내가 그렇게 오랫동안 찾던 바로 그것이다.
You have the **very thing** that I want and it is your red dress.
너는 내가 원하는 바로 그것을 가지고 있는데 그것은 네 빨간 옷이다.

required

vote for ···에 (찬성) 투표를 하다

I shall **vote for** you to captain our team.
우리 팀 주장으로 너에게 투표할 것이다.
Most people **voted for** the measure.
대부분 사람들이 그 안에 찬성 투표를 했다.

[SYN] ballot for

participate in ···에 참가하다, 관여하다

To **participate in** the marathon, even if you can't win, is what is important.
설령 우승하지 못한다 하더라도 마라톤에 참가하는 것은 중요하다.
Many senior government officials **participated in** the scandal.
많은 고위 정부 관계자들이 추문에 연루되었다.

[SYN] take part in; have a share in
cf. participate with ... in ···와 함께 ~에 관여하다

provide for 1. 준비하다, 대비하다 2. 부양하다, 생활의 자금을 공급하다

She **provides for** her future by saving money each month.
그녀는 매달 돈을 저축함으로써 미래를 위해 준비하고 있다.
He worked so hard that he might **provide for** his large family.
그는 대가족을 부양하기 위해 열심히 일했다.

[SYN] 1. make preparations; get ready 2. support; keep up; maintain; furnish; supply

beyond question 의심할 여지 없이, 분명히

It is **beyond question** that he will get fame as a modern dancer.
그가 현대 무용가로서 명성을 얻으리라는 것은 의심할 여지가 없다.
It is **beyond question** that he will succeed in the coming entrance examination.
그가 이번 입시에 합격하리라는 것은 확실하다.

[SYN] without doubt, clearly; not in doubt; certain
cf. without question 문제 없이, 여러 말 없이, 틀림없이, 의심할 여지 없이 (=without doubt; for sure; for certain)

be occupied in [with] ···에 종사하다, ···에 여념이 없다

My mother **is occupied** herself **in** manufacturing.
어머니는 제조업에 종사하고 계신다.

[SYN] be engaged in; be absorbed in; be devoted to
cf. occupy oneself in [with] 종사시키다, 바쁘다 (=be busy;

Grandmother **is occupied with** knitting sitting by the window.
할머니는 창가에 앉아서 뜨개질에 여념이 없으시다.

engage in)

let (leave) alone ···은 말할 것도 없고, ···은 고사하고, 하물며 ···않다 (부정문에서)

I don't speak French, **let alone** Russian.
나는 러시아 어는 고사하고 프랑스 어도 모른다.
He was too tired to walk, **let alone** run.
그는 너무 피곤해서 뛰는 것은 고사하고 걸을 수도 없었다.

[SYN] not to mention; to say nothing of; not to speak of

lose one's temper 화내다

It doesn't pay you to **lose your temper**.
화를 내는 것은 너에게 이롭지 않다.
He entirely **lost his temper** with me.
그는 나에게 정말로 화가 나서 울화통을 터뜨렸다.

[SYN] get out of temper; get into a temper; get angry
cf. keep one's temper 화를 참다

yearn for ···을 동경하다, 그리워하다

James **yearns for** a better life.
제임스는 더 나은 인생을 동경한다.
She **yearns for** affection.
그녀는 애정을 그리워한다.

[SYN] long for; feel a strong desire

judging from ···으로 판단해 보면, ···을 미루어 보면, 그런 걸 보면

Judging from the rumor, he seems to run in the election.
소문에 의하면 그는 선거에 출마할 것 같다.
Judging from his accent, he must be an American.
그의 말투로 판단하면 미국인임에 틀림없다.

[SYN] if we judge from

get rid of 제거하다, 없애다, 내버리다

It is not easy to **get rid of** a bad habit.
나쁜 습관을 버리기란 쉽지 않다.
I cannot **get rid of** this headache.
이 두통을 멈추게 할 수가 없다.

[SYN] remove; escape from

get the better (best) of ···에 이기다, ···을 극복하다

I tried in vain to **get the better of** John.
나는 존을 이기려고 했지만 허사였다.
He **got the best of** John in the boxing match.

[SYN] win over; beat; defeat

그는 그 권투 시합에서 존을 이겼다.

jeer at 놀리다, 비웃다, 야유하다, 조롱하다

The audience **jeered at** the speaker who couldn't deliver the speech well.

관객들은 연설을 잘 하지 못하는 연사를 조롱했다.

The murderer was **jeered at** by the crowd as the policeman pushed him into a car.

경찰관이 살인범을 차에 밀어 넣을 때 살인범은 사람들의 야유를 받았다.

[SYN] mock; taunt; banter someone on

no less than …에 못지 않게, …만큼이나 ~하다, 자그마치 …와 같이 ~하다 (수량을 강조)

There are **no less than** 20 universities in this city.

이 도시에는 대학이 스무 개나 있다.

I know **no less than** 10 instances.

나는 그 예를 열 개나 알고 있다.

[SYN] as many as; as much as; exactly

now that …이므로, …인 까닭에, …인 이상

Now that everyone is here, we can begin the meeting.

이제 모두들 참석했으니 회의를 시작할 수 있다.

Now (**that**) you are a senior, you must study harder.

이제 4학년이 되었으니 공부를 더 열심히 해야 한다.

[SYN] since

make oneself at home 편안하게 하다

Make yourself at home until the meal is ready.

음식이 준비될 때까지 편안하게 계십시오.

Bill is an outdoor man and he could **make himself at home** in a tent at night.

빌은 야외 활동을 좋아하는 사람이어서 밤에 텐트에서 편히 있을 수 있었다.

[SYN] feel comfortable

make up for …을 배상하다, 보상하다, 벌충하다, 메우다

We cannot **make up for** the time we have lost forever.

잃어버린 시간은 영원히 보상할 수 없다.

Nothing can **make up for** the absence of someone whom we love.

이 세상의 어느 것도 사랑하는 사람을 대신할 수는 없다.

[SYN] compensate for

if anything ...의 차이가 있다면, 어느 편이냐 하면

Today, mother is worse, **if anything**.
오늘 어머니의 상태가 어떤가 하면 더 악화되었다.
She is, **if anything**, taller than her mother.
어느 편이냐 하면 그녀가 그녀의 어머니보다 키가 좀 더 크다.

[SYN] if there's any difference

in effect 1. 실제적으로, 사실상, 요컨대, 본질적으로 2. 유효한

No reply in her part was **in effect** a rejection of his proposal.
그녀가 대답을 하지 않은 것은 사실상 그의 청혼을 거절한 것이다.
The new law will be **in effect** from next month.
새 법은 다음 달부터 유효할 것이다.

[SYN] 1. effectually; in fact; really; virtually; essentially 2. valid; effective; available

run against 1. ...에 충돌하다(시키다), 부딪히다 2. ...와 우연히 만나다

The ship **ran against** a big rock.
배가 큰 바위에 부딪혔다.
He **ran against** one of his old friends in the shopping mall.
그는 쇼핑몰에서 옛 친구 한 명을 우연히 만났다.

[SYN] 1. bump into; collide with 2. meet by chance; come across

not much of a 대단한 ...은 아니다

He is **not much of a** poet.
그는 대단한 시인은 아니다.
She likes golf, but is **not much of a** player.
그녀는 골프를 좋아하지만 대단한 선수는 아니다.

[SYN] not very good at

not less ... than ...에 못지 않게 ~하다 (우월을 강조)

He is **not less** diligent **than** his brother.
그는 형 못지 않게 부지런하다.
The second daughter is **not less** beautiful **than** her mother.
둘째 딸은 어머니 못지 않게 예쁘다.

[SYN] as much or more

use up 다 써버리다

The soldiers had **used up** all their supplies.
군인들은 보급품들을 모두 다 써버렸다.
Don't **use up** all the toothpaste.
치약을 다 쓰지 마시오.

[SYN] exhaust; use something completely

set about 착수하다, ...하기 시작하다

[SYN] begin a task; undertake;

We **set about** repairing our car soon after our meal.
우리는 식사 후 곧 차를 고치기 시작했다.
Set about the homework immediately.
즉시 숙제를 시작해라.

[SYN] start; take up

set off 1. 출발하다 2. 돋보이게 하다, 드러나게 하다
She will **set off** tomorrow, if nothing happens.
아무 일도 생기지 않으면 그녀는 내일 출발할 것이다.
A light-colored dress **sets off** her, though she is not pretty.
그녀는 예쁘지는 않지만 밝은 옷이 그녀를 돋보이게 한다.

[SYN] 1. start on a journey; depart; shove off 2. make prominent by contrast

regardless of …에 관계 없이, …를 개의치 않고
I shall go **regardless of** the weather.
나는 날씨에 상관 없이 갈 것이다.
Everybody is welcome **regardless of** age.
연령에 관계 없이 누구든지 환영이다.

[SYN] irrespective of

refer to 1. 언급하다, 인용하다 2. 참조하다
The book mainly **refers to** the pollution problem.
그 책은 주로 오염 문제에 관해 언급하고 있다.
Please **refer to** the attached sheet for details.
자세한 것은 별지를 참조해 주십시오.

[SYN] 1. allude to; mention; make reference to 2. consult; see

in accordance with …에 따라서, …에 응해서
They acted **in accordance with** these rules.
그들은 이 규칙들에 따라 행동했다.
I carried it out **in accordance with** his instruction.
나는 그의 지시에 따라 실행했다.

[SYN] according to; in conformity to; agreeably to

in due course / in due time / in good time / in the course of time / in time
때가 되면
You will earn fame as an actress **in due course**.
너는 때가 되면 배우로서 명성을 얻게 될 것이다.
Your method will work out **in due time**.
네 방법은 때가 되면 효력이 있을 것이다.

[SYN] at the proper time

at a loss 어쩔 줄을 몰라서, 당황하여, 어리벙벙하여
I am **at a loss** what to do.
나는 어찌해야 좋을지 어리벙벙했다.

[SYN] embarrassed; without any idea; puzzled

If you miss the last train, you will really be **at a loss**.
마지막 열차를 놓치면 너는 정말 당황할 것이다.

ask after 안부를 묻다, 건강 상태를 묻다

I have been to Seoul to **ask after** my sick friend.
나는 서울에 친구 병문안을 갔다 왔다.
We **asked after** our sick friend.
우리들은 병에 걸린 친구의 안부를 물었다.

[SYN] inquire after
cf. ask for 간청하다, 요구하다 (=demand; beg)

kill time 한가한 시간을 보내다, 소일하다, 시간을 죽이다

While waiting for the train to come, Anne **killed time** reading newspapers.
기차를 기다리는 동안 앤은 신문을 읽으면서 시간을 보냈다.
Some people think of reading as a mere means of **killing time**.
어떤 사람들은 독서를 단지 시간을 죽이는 한 방편으로 생각한다.

[SYN] beguile; spend time by doing something

keep ... in mind …을 마음에 간직하다, 마음에 새기다, 기억하다

I always **keep** our wedding anniversary **in mind**.
나는 언제나 우리의 결혼 기념일을 기억해 두고 있다.
Repeat the words over and over till they are **kept in** your **mind**.
그 단어들이 기억될 때까지 자꾸 반복해라.

[SYN] bear in mind; remember

to tell the truth 실은, 사실대로 말하면

To tell the truth, I don't know her well.
사실대로 말하면 나는 그녀를 잘 모른다.
To tell the truth, he is very honest.
사실을 말하자면 그는 매우 정직하다.

[SYN] in fact; in reality

turn on (수도 등을) 틀다, (불을) 켜다

Could you **turn** the gas **on**?
가스를 틀어 주시겠습니까?
Don't go out with the TV **turned on**.
텔레비전을 켜 놓고 나가지 마라.

[SYN] light; kindle
[OPP] turn off (수도 등을) 막다, 불을 끄다 (=switch off)

express oneself 자기 생각을 말하다

My mother can **express herself** well in German.
어머니는 독일어로 의사 표명을 잘 할 수 있으시다.
The little boy **expresses himself** clearly every-

[SYN] demonstrate one's ability to communicate; say what one thinks or feels

where.
그 어린 소년은 어디에서나 생각하는 바를 확실하게 표현한다.

excuse+사람+from 아무의 …을 면제하다
The teacher **excused me from** the examination.
선생님은 나를 시험으로부터 면제시켜 주셨다.
I was **excused from** practice today.
오늘은 연습을 안 해도 됐다.

[SYN] exempt; release; remit
cf. excuse+사람+for …을 용서하다 (=pardon; forgive)

bring back 1. …을 상기시키다 2. 도로 데리고 오다, 돌려 주다
Her story **brought back** our happy childhood.
그녀의 이야기는 우리의 즐거운 어린 시절을 상기시켰다.
You can borrow it if you promise to **bring back** tomorrow.
당신이 그것을 내일 돌려 주겠다고 약속하면 빌려 드리겠습니다.

[SYN] 1. remind of; call something one's mind 2. take back, return

make the most of …을 최대한 이용[활용]하다, 가장 중시하다
The youth should **make the most of** their opportunity.
젊은이들은 기회를 최대한 활용해야 한다.
She's not really beautiful, but she **makes the most of** her looks.
그녀는 그다지 미인은 아니지만 자신의 용모를 최대한 이용한다.

[SYN] make the greatest use of; take fullest advantage of

do harm 해를 끼치다
Bad books **do** the children great **harm**.
나쁜 책은 아이들에게 엄청난 해를 끼친다.
The heavy rain in this season will **do** the crops a lot of **harm**.
지금 계절에 비가 많이 오는 것은 농작물에 큰 해를 끼칠 것이다.

[SYN] do damage; do injury; damage

such and such 이러저러한, 여차여차한, 이러저러한 것
They lived on **such and such** a street—I don't know the street's name.
그들은 이러저러한 거리에 살았는데 그 거리의 이름을 모르겠다.
Such and such people came to the event, but I don't remember all of them.
이런저런 사람들이 행사에 왔는데 난 그들 모두를 기억하지 못한다.

[SYN] so and so

give rise to 야기시키다, …을 일으키다

[SYN] cause; lead to; make

It may **give rise to** serious trouble.
그것은 심각한 문제를 일으킬지도 모른다.
The serious inflation **gave rise to** the riot.
심각한 인플레로 인해 폭동이 일어났다.

something happen

make room for ···을 위하여 장소를 비우다, 자리를 양보하다

He **made room for** the poor old woman in the bus.
그는 버스에서 불쌍한 할머니에게 자리를 양보했다.
Would you **make room for** my grandmother?
우리 할머니에게 자리를 양보해 주시겠습니까?

[SYN] give up one's seat to
cf. make way for 길을 비켜 주다, 장소를 양보하다

do justice to〔do ... justice〕 ···을 정당하게 다루다〔평가하다〕

His remarks do not **do justice to** the author.
그의 비평은 저자를 올바르게 평가하고 있지 않다.
It is impossible to **do justice to** the subject in a short article.
짧은 논문으로 그 문제를 충분히 다루기는 불가능하다.

[SYN] treat fairly; deal justly with

remind ... of ~ ···에게 ~를 생각나게 하다

This picture **reminds** me **of** my childhood.
이 사진을 보니 어린 시절 생각이 난다.
(=When I see this picture, I think of my childhood.)
This faded photo always **reminds** me **of** his mother-in-law.
색이 바랜 이 사진을 보면 늘 그의 장모 생각이 난다.
(=I never see this faded photo without remembering his mother-in-law.
=Whenever I see this faded photo, I am reminded of his mother-in-law.)

[SYN] put in mind of; cause someone to remember something

(be) conscious of ···을 의식하다, 알아차리다

Was he **conscious of** what he was saying at that time?
그때 그는 자신이 무슨 말을 하고 있는지 알고 있었습니까?
From the beginning she **was conscious of** being watched by many men.
처음부터 그녀는 많은 남자들의 시선을 받고 있는 것을 의식했다.
(=From the beginning she was conscious that she was being watched by many men. (복문)

[SYN] be aware of; be sensible of; feel; understand; comprehend

= She was aware that she was being watched by many men from the beginning. (복문)
= She was aware of being watched by many men from the beginning. (단문)

die out 사멸하다, 소멸하다

Dinosaurs **died out** millions of years ago on the earth.
공룡은 수백만 년 전에 지구상에서 사멸했다.
The movement **died out** of itself.
그 운동은 저절로 없어졌다.

[SYN] pass out of existence; become extinct
cf. die away (소리·바람·빛 등이) 차차 사라지다

partly ... partly 한편 … 또 한편

He traveled **partly** on business and **partly** for pleasure.
그는 출장과 관광을 겸해서 여행을 했다.
I made him agree to my proposal **partly** by force and **partly** by persuasion.
한편 힘으로 또 한편으로는 설득으로 그가 내 제의를 수락하게 했다.

[SYN] on the one hand ... on the other (hand)

be concerned with …에 관심을 갖다, …에 관계가 있다 (이때는 전치사 with, in, 또는 about을 동반)

You may not know but you **are** deeply **concerned in** this problem.
당신은 모를 수도 있지만 당신은 이 문제에 깊이 관여되어 있다.
Only last year, he **was** not **concerned with** politics.
작년만 해도 그는 정치에 관심이 없었다.

[SYN] take interest in
cf. (be) concerned for(about) …에 대해 염려하다 (= be anxious about)
concern oneself with …와 관계를 가지다, 관계하다, 관여하다 (= concern oneself in; take part in)

prepare oneself for …의 준비를 하다, 마음의 태세를 갖추다, 각오하다

It was intended that his son should **prepare himself for** the same vocation.
그는 아들에게도 같은 직업을 갖도록 준비시킬 생각이었다.
She **prepared herself for** her mother's funeral.
그녀는 어머니 장례식 준비를 했다.

[SYN] be resolved to; be ready for

at a time 동시에, 한꺼번에, 한 번에

Try to do one thing **at a time**, because it is more effective.
한 번에 한 가지 일을 하도록 하여라. 그것이 더 효율적이니까.
You can carry as many as possible **at a time**.

[SYN] at the same time; at once; at one time
cf. at one time 한때는, 어느 때는 (= once; formerly)
at that time 그 당시(에), 그때 (=

가능하면 한 번에 많이 운반해도 괜찮다.

burst into 1. (방 등에) 뛰어들다, 우르르 밀려들다 2. 갑자기 …하기 시작하다

Two armed men **burst into** the store and asked money.
두 무장 괴한이 가게로 뛰어들어와 돈을 요구했다.
The baby **burst into** tears and his mother gave him milk.
아기가 울음을 터뜨리자 어머니는 아기에게 우유를 주었다.

[SYN] 1. enter a room very suddenly 2. break into

contribute to 기여[공헌]하다, 제공하다, 주다

The player **contributed to** the victory in the game.
그 선수는 게임에서 승리에 공헌했다.
She **contributed** lots of money **to** the hospital.
그녀는 그 병원에 많은 돈을 기부했다.

[SYN] render services; be conductive to

take pleasure in …을 즐기다, 좋아하다, 기꺼이 …하다

He **takes pleasure in** driving in the country.
그는 시골로 드라이브 가는 것을 좋아한다.
She **takes** great **pleasure in** playing golf every day.
그녀는 매일 골프를 하는 것을 매우 즐긴다.

[SYN] find pleasure in; have a liking for; be fond of

yield to …에 지다, 굴하다, 응하다, 따르다

The management finally **yielded to** our demand.
회사측은 마침내 우리의 요구에 응했다.
John decided to **yield to** my advice.
존은 내 충고에 따르기로 했다.

[SYN] surrender; obey; give in

hear about …에 관해 자세히 듣다, …에 대한 비판[꾸지람, 칭찬]을 듣다

He wanted to **hear about** the news.
그는 그 소식을 상세하게 듣고 싶어했다.
He was surprised when he **heard about** my promotion.
그는 내 승진 소식을 듣고 놀랐다.

[SYN] learn about; become acquainted with

settle down 1. 정주[이주]하다, 정착하다 2. 조용해지다, 가라앉다, 진정하다

Their family **settled down** in the Midwest and

[SYN] 1. take up permanent residence 2. become calm; soothe; abate

at that moment; then; on that occasion)

began farming.
그들의 가족은 중서부에 정착하여 농사를 짓기 시작했다.
Two years after the war ended, life there finally **settled down**.
전쟁 종식 2년 후 그 곳의 삶은 마침내 조용해졌다.

would (had) sooner ... than ~ ~하기보다는 차라리 …하고 싶다

I **would sooner** die **than** do such a thing.
그런 짓을 하느니 차라리 죽겠다.
(=I would as soon die as do such a thing.
=I would rather die than do such a thing.)

SYN would rather ... than ~; would as soon ... as ~

near (close) at hand 바로 가까이에, 머지 않아서, 곁에

The summer vacation is **near at hand**.
얼마 안 있으면 여름 방학이다.
When I am ill, I want you **close at hand** to help me.
내가 아플 때 네가 가까이에 있으면서 나를 도와 주면 좋겠다.

SYN close by in distance or time

to sum up 요약하면

To sum up, the teacher is satisfied with Tom's progress in German.
요약하면 선생님은 톰의 독일어 실력 향상에 만족하고 계신다.
To sum up, within our society there still exist rampant illegality and corruption.
요컨대 우리 사회 내에는 여전히 부정부패가 만연해 있다.

SYN to make a long story short; to put it shortly; in short; in brief

weather permitting 날씨가 좋으면

Weather permitting, what do you say to going for a drive?
날씨가 좋으면 드라이브하러 가지 않겠어요?
We shall start tomorrow, **weather permitting**.
날씨가 좋으면 내일 출발할 겁니다.

SYN if (the) weather permits

as well as …와 마찬가지로, … 뿐만 아니라 ~도 (또한)

He is a scientist **as well as** an artist.
그는 예술가일 뿐만 아니라 과학자이기도 하다.
(=He is not only an artist but also a scientist.
=Besides being an artist, he is a scientist.
=He is both an artist and a scientist.)

SYN not only ... but also ~; in addition to; and also; besides

You are lucky because your bride is beautiful **as well as** rich.
당신은 운이 좋다. 왜냐하면 신부가 돈도 많고 예쁘기도 하니까.

reach (out) for (…을 잡으려고) 손을 뻗치다, 얻으려고 애쓰다

I **reached out** my hand **for** the ball.
나는 공을 잡으려고 손을 뻗었다.
The monkey **reached** (**out**) **for** the branch.
원숭이는 나뭇가지를 잡으려고 손을 뻗었다.

[SYN] try to contact someone or something physically; stretch out; extend the hand

good for nothing 전혀 쓸모가 없는, 도움이 안 되는

You can't depend on Bill, because he is **good for nothing**.
빌은 전혀 쓸모가 없기 때문에 그에게 의지할 수 없다.
Jane decided to quit her job thinking she was **good for nothing**.
제인은 자신이 아무 도움이 안 된다고 생각하여 직장을 그만두기로 결심했다.

[SYN] completely useless

speak out (up) 1. 큰 소리로 (분명히) 말하다 2. 털어놓고[솔직하게] 의견을 말하다

You should **speak** it **out** so that other people can hear you easily.
다른 사람들이 네 말을 쉽게 들을 수 있도록 큰 소리로 말해야 한다.
If you disagree, **speak out**.
불찬성이라면, 솔직하게 말하시오.

[SYN] 1. speak in a loud or clear voice 2. express one's opinion frankly

none the less 그럼에도 불구하고, 그래도, 역시

He has faults, but many people respect him **none the less**.
그에게는 단점이 있지만 그래도 많은 사람들이 그를 존경한다.
She is a clever girl, **none the less** she often makes a significant mistake.
그 여자는 똑똑한데도 불구하고 때로는 중대한 실수를 한다.

[SYN] nevertheless; for all that

on end 계속해서, 연달아

She worked for three hours **on end**.
그녀는 3시간 동안 계속해서 공부했다.
John stayed there for three weeks **on end**.
존은 3주 동안 쭉 그 곳에서 머물렀다.

[SYN] continuously; without a break; one after another

stick to 고수하다, 버티다, 순종하다
Stick to your convictions regardless of what people say.
사람들이 무슨 말을 하든 신념을 굽히지 말라.
So far he has **stuck to** the promise.
지금까지 그는 그 약속을 지키고 있다.

[SYN] preserve; be patient

have influence on …에 영향력이 있다, 영향을 미치다
The election will **have** great **influence on** politics.
그 선거는 정치에 큰 영향을 미칠 것이다.
His parents seem to **have** no **influence on** his actions.
그의 부모는 그의 행동에 전혀 영향을 미치지 않는 것 같다.

[SYN] influence; affect; have an effect on

set up 1. 준비하다, 계획하다 2. (사업 등을) 시작하다
I ordered my secretary to **set up** the room for the conference.
나는 비서에게 회의장을 준비하라고 지시했다.
My mother **set up** as a beautician.
어머니는 미용사로서 개업을 했다.

[SYN] 1. get ready; fix up; make preparations 2. start in business

by nature 날 때부터, 본래, 선천적으로
Whenever he commits a mistake, he admits it. He is frank **by nature**.
그는 실수를 저지를 때마다 그것을 인정한다. 그는 본래 솔직하다.
She is happily endowed **by nature** for a musician.
그 여자는 행복하게도 선천적으로 음악가의 자질이 있다.

[SYN] innately; originally; congenitally
cf. in nature 1. 사실상, 현실상 2. (최상급의 강조) 티 없이, 참으로 3. (의문문의 강조) 도대체 4. (부정의 강조) 어디에도 (…이 없다)

never [cannot] fail to 반드시[꼭] …하다
She **never fails to** accept my advice.
그녀는 내 충고를 꼭 받아들인다.
He **never fails to** keep his promise.
그는 약속을 어기는 일이 없다.

[SYN] be sure to do; do without fail

do well 잘 하다, 성공하다, (건강) 상태가 좋다, 번영하다
With the new medicine, the patient is **doing well**.
신약으로 환자는 좋아지고 있다.
I heard that he was **doing well** in business.
그가 사업에서 성공하고 있다고 들었다.

[SYN] prosper; succeed; get well

in view of 1. …이 보이는 곳에 2. …을 고려하여, … 때

[SYN] 1. in sight of 2. after

문에

The boy wanted to stand **in view of** the singer.
소년은 가수가 보이는 곳에 서기를 원했다.
Schools were closed temporarily **in view of** the big flood.
학교들은 대홍수 때문에 임시로 휴교했다.
The judge decided that **in view of** his youth his punishment should be light.
판사는 그의 젊음을 고려하여 형을 가볍게 판결했다.

[SYN] thinking about; because of

for one's age 나이에 비해서

Your mother looks young **for her age**.
너의 어머니는 연세에 비해 젊어 보이신다.
He looks very old **for his age**.
그는 나이에 비해 아주 늙어 보인다.

compare to 비유하다 (성질이나 종류가 다른 것을 비교할 때 많이 쓰임)

As you know, life is often **compared to** a play.
알다시피 인생은 종종 연극에 비유된다.
People often **compare** life **to** a voyage.
사람들은 흔히들 인생을 항해에 비유한다.

[SYN] liken; allegorize

do well to …하는 것이 좋다, …하는 것이 적절하다, …하는 것이 현명하다

You would **do well to** say nothing about what happened.
무슨 일이 일어났는지 말하지 않는 것이 좋을 것이다.
You will **do well to** learn from this lesson.
이 교훈을 알아 두는 게 좋을 것이다.

[SYN] had better; would rather; may as well

prior to …보다 전에[먼저]

Prior to becoming a lawyer, he worked as a legal advisor of a company.
그는 변호사가 되기 전에 어떤 회사의 법률 고문으로 일했다.
That happened **prior to** my arrival.
그것은 나의 도착 전에 일어났다.

[SYN] before; earlier than something else

change into …으로 변하다, 바뀌다

Water **changes into** steam at its highest temperature.
물은 최고 온도에서 증기로 변한다.

[SYN] become different; alter; turn; vary

You may have learned that the caterpillar **changes into** a butterfly.
유충이 변해서 나비가 된다는 것을 배웠을 것이다.

beyond description 이루 말할 수 없이; 말로 다 표현할 수 없는

The beauty of the scenery is **beyond description**.
그 풍경의 아름다움은 말로는 표현할 수 없다.
(= The scenery is too beautiful to express in words.)
Her beauty is **beyond description**.
그녀의 아름다움은 말로 표현할 수 없다.

SYN by far; indescribable; inexpressible

go beyond …의 범위를 넘다, 능가하다, …보다 낫다

The film's success **went beyond** anything we had expected.
영화의 성공은 우리의 기대 이상이었다.
She didn't just feel happy — it **went beyond** that.
그녀는 그저 행복한 것이 아니라 그 이상이었다.

SYN be much better, more serious, more advanced, etc. than something else

make for 1. …을 향해 나아가다 2. …에게 덤벼들다

He didn't turn back and **made for** the door.
그는 뒤도 돌아보지 않고 문 쪽으로 걸어갔다.
The fierce dog **made for** the visitors.
사나운 개는 손님들에게 달려들었다.

SYN 1. go in the direction of; go forward 2. rush upon; make a spring at

figure out 1. 이해하다, 알다 2. 해결하다, 생각해 내다 3. (비용 등을) 계산하다, 산정하다

I can't **figure out** what he is saying.
그의 말을 이해할 수가 없다.
Bill couldn't **figure out** several questions on the test.
빌은 시험에서 몇 문제를 풀지 못했다.
The cost of the house was **figured out** at £45.
그 집의 경비는 45파운드로 산출되었다.

SYN 1. understand; get to know; make out 2. work out 3. calculate; reckon; compute

remember -ing (과거에) …한 것을 기억하고 있다

I still **remember** go**ing** there with my ex-husband.
전 남편과 함께 거기 갔던 일을 지금도 기억한다.
Do you **remember** see**ing** him before?
그를 전에 본 것을 기억하니?

SYN recall; recollect; bear in mind

never (not) ... without ~ …하면 반드시 ~한다

I **never** listen to the song **without** thinking of my childhood.
그 노래를 들으면 반드시 어린 시절이 생각난다.
He **never** goes out for a walk **without** taking his dog.
그는 산책할 때에는 반드시 개를 데리고 나간다.
(=Whenever(Each time) he goes out for a walk, he takes his dog.)

SYN. never (not) ... but ~

at (the) least 그나마 (나쁜 상황에서 좋은 점을 강조함), 적어도, 최소한

She broke her leg, but **at the least** it was not her right one.
그녀는 다리가 부러졌는데 그나마 오른쪽 다리는 아니었다.
In the car accident, **at least** 10 people were wounded.
자동차 사고로 적어도 열 명이 부상을 입었다.

SYN. no fewer than; no less than

prefer A to B B보다 A를 좋아하다

My father always **prefers** staying at home **to** having some activities on Sundays.
아버지는 일요일이면 항상 어떤 활동을 하기보다 집에 있기를 좋아하신다.
I **prefer** horror movies **to** romantic ones.
나는 연애 영화보다 공포 영화가 좋다.

SYN. like A better than B

what by ... what by ~ 한편으로는 …하기도 하고, 또 한편으로는 ~하기도 해서 (수단을 나타냄)

What by policy, and **what by** force, he always accomplished his purpose.
정책도 쓰고 폭력도 써서 그는 항상 목적을 달성했다.
What by threats, and **what by** entreaties, he finally had his will.
그는 협박도 하고 애원도 해서 드디어 자기 뜻대로 했다.

SYN. as a result of many things
cf. what between ... and ~ …하기도 하고 ~하기도 해서

catch hold of …을 붙잡다

The climber slipped but fortunately he **caught hold of** the rope.
산악인은 미끄러졌지만 다행히도 밧줄을 붙잡았다.
Hand the branch to me so that I can **catch hold of** it.

SYN. grab; grasp quickly

내가 붙잡을 수 있게 그 나뭇가지를 내 쪽으로 건네 줘.

concentrate on (upon) …에 집중하다, 전념하다, 전력을 기울이다
You must **concentrate** your attention **on (upon)** the work.
일에 주의를 집중해야 한다.
I **concentrated** all my energies **on** English.
나는 영어에 모든 정신력을 집중했다.

SYN focus upon; centralize upon; devote oneself to

interfere with 방해하다, 훼방놓다, 상하게 하다
There is nobody who likes to be **interfered with**.
방해받고 싶어하는 사람은 아무도 없다.
His criminal record **interfered with** his effort to get a job.
그의 전과 기록이 그의 취업 노력을 방해했다.

SYN prevent; hinder
cf. interfere in …에 간섭하다, 중재하다 (=meddle in; intervene in)

strictly speaking 엄밀하게 말하면(말해서)
Strictly speaking, this answer is not perfectly right.
엄밀하게 말하면 이 대답은 완전한 정답은 아니다.
Strictly speaking, we're not allowed to give you any advice.
엄밀히 말하자면 우리는 너에게 어떤 조언도 해서는 안 된다.

SYN if we speak strictly; to be exact
cf. generally speaking 대체로 말해서
roughly speaking 대충 말해서
properly speaking 정확히 말해서

worthy of …할 가치가 있는
His speech, though brief, was **worthy of** attention.
그의 연설은 비록 짧지만 주목할 가치가 있었다.
His behavior is **worthy of** praise.
그의 행동은 칭찬받을 만하다.

SYN deserving; due; valuable; worthy; of value

provided (providing) that …을 조건으로, 만약 …이라면
I will come **provided that** it is fine tomorrow.
내일 날씨가 좋으면 가겠다.
I will consent, **provided that** all the others agree.
다른 사람들이 모두 찬성이면 나도 동의하겠다.

SYN on the condition that; if

glance at 흘끗 보다
I **glanced at** my watch and was surprised to see it was so late.
시계를 흘끗 보고는 시간이 꽤 된 것을 알고 깜짝 놀랐다.

SYN look quickly at

John **glanced at** me and walked on without saying a word.
존은 나를 보고는 한 마디 말도 없이 계속 걸어가 버렸다.

at (the) worst 아무리 나쁘더라도, 최악의 경우는

The economic situation is **at the worst**.
경제 상황은 최악이다.
At the worst, we must save the patient's life.
최악의 경우라도 환자의 목숨을 구해야 한다.

[SYN] even if it's the worst case; under the worst conditions

without (any) difficulty (아무런) 어려움 없이, 쉽사리, 수월하게

She accomplished her goal **without any difficulty**.
그녀는 목표를 무난하게 성취했다.
Bill seemed to solve the hard questions **without difficulty**.
빌은 어려운 문제들을 수월하게 푸는 것 같았다.

[SYN] with ease; easily; readily

far and wide 모든 곳에

The wind blew the ashes **far and wide**.
바람이 재를 사방으로 날려 버렸다.
His families are scattered **far and wide**.
그의 식구들은 사방으로 흩어져 살고 있다.

[SYN] everywhere; every place; in all directions

send for 1. …을 부르러 보내다 2. (물건을) 가지러 보내다

Mother being ill, the elder brother was **sent for** the doctor.
어머니가 아프기 때문에 큰 형이 의사를 부르러 갔다.
You should **send for** the baggage without delay.
당장 사람을 보내어 짐을 가져오게 해야 합니다.

[SYN] 1. ask for someone to come; summon 2. send a messenger to bring something

take into account 고려하다, 감안하다

You should **take** all risks **into account** before starting your business.
사업을 시작하기 전에 모든 위험을 고려해야 한다.
You should **take into account** the weather when camping out.
야영을 할 때는 날씨를 고려해야 한다.

[SYN] take into consideration; take account of; consider

what with … what with ~ …이라든가 ~이라든가로, …하기도 하고 ~하기도 하여 (이유나 원인 표시)

cf. what by…, what by ~; what between … and; partly

What with cooking and **what with** washing, my mother is very busy every day.
어머니는 요리도 하고 빨래도 하여 매일 매우 바쁘시다.
What with the wind and (**what with**) the rain, our trip was spoiled.
바람이라든가 비 등으로 인해 우리의 여행은 엉망이 되었다.

... partly; for one thing ... for another ···이라든가 ~이라든가 등으로, ···하기도 하고 ~하기도 하여 (수단을 표시)

on business 상용으로, 사업차 볼일이 있어

I was obliged to be absent from school **on** particular **business**.
부득이한 일로 학교를 결석해야 했다.
Mr. Jackson went over to England **on business** with his wife.
잭슨 씨는 부인과 함께 영국으로 출장을 갔다.

[SYN.] on commercial business; on an errand

give in 1. 제출하다 2. 양보하다, 굴복하다, 항복하다

The report must be **given in** by tomorrow.
보고서는 내일까지 제출해야 한다.
The strikers **gave in** and got back to work.
파업자들은 양보하고 일로 복귀했다.

[SYN.] 1. hand in; present 2. surrender; yield

run short of ···이 부족하다, ···이 떨어지나

The car **ran short of** gas before reaching the city.
그 차는 도시에 닿기 전에 기름이 떨어졌다.
We are **running short of** money.
우리는 돈이 떨어져 가고 있다.

[SYN.] have or be less than enough
cf. run out of ···을 다 써 버리다
be short of ···이 부족하다, ···에 미치지 못하다

bring about 일으키다, 초래하다

His invention **brought about** a lot of changes in our daily life.
그의 발명은 우리의 일상 생활에 많은 변화를 일으켰다.
The accident was **brought about** by his carelessness.
그 사고는 그의 부주의로 일어났다.

[SYN.] raise, cause to happen, make happen; produce; cause

set to work 일에 착수하다, 작용하기 시작하다

He **set to work** at once with his friends.
그는 친구들과 즉시 일에 착수했다.
Set to work at once, or you will not be able to finish at all.
당장 일을 시작하시오. 그렇지 않으면 끝내지 못할 것입니다.

[SYN.] get to work; set about one's business

hold good 유효하다, 지속하다

This agreement **holds good** for another year.
이 계약은 앞으로 일 년 더 유효하다.
The ticket of admission **holds good** for 10 days.
입장권은 열흘 간 유효하다.

[SYN] be effective; continue; maintain; remain in force; remain in effect; be available

remember to 잊지 않고 …하다

Remember to take these clothes to the laundry on your way to school.
학교 가는 길에 잊지 말고 이 옷들을 세탁소에 갖다 주어라.
I **remember to** see the dentist tomorrow.
내일 치과에 가는 것을 기억하고 있다.

[SYN] do something without forgetting

in the way 방해가 되어

Jim tried to help me but he was only **in the way**.
짐은 나를 도우려 했지만 방해가 될 뿐이었다.
Go away, you're always **in the way**.
저리 가, 너는 늘 방해가 된다.

[SYN] in one's way
cf. in the way of …의 방해가 되어 (=in one's way)

arise from …에서 발생하다, 일어나다, 비롯되다

Most car accidents **arise from** people's careless driving habit.
자동차 사고의 대부분은 사람들의 부주의한 운전 습관 때문에 일어난다.
Accidents **arise from** carelessness.
사고는 부주의에서 생긴다.

[SYN] be caused from; be resulted from; be brought about by

prevent ... from -ing 막아서 못하게 하다, 방해하다, 막다 (무생물이 주어 구문에서 자주 사용됨)

Circumstances have **prevented** me **from** go**ing** there.
사정이 있어서 그 곳에 가지 못했다.
Bad weather **prevented** me **from** tak**ing** outdoor exercise.
악천후 때문에 야외 운동이 불가능했다.

[SYN] stop
cf. hinder from …하는 것을 방해하다 (=prevent from)

exposed to …에 노출된, 드러난

They were **exposed to** the enemy's gunfire at night.
그들은 밤에는 적의 포화에 노출되어 있었다.
The writer is **exposed to** the ridicule of the public.
그 작가는 세인들의 조롱거리가 되었다.

[SYN] disclosed; bared

by far 훨씬, 단연, 큰 차이로, 분명하게
Jim is **by far** the best player on our team.
짐은 우리 팀에서 단연코 최우수 선수이다.
He is **by far** the greatest hero the country has ever had.
그는 분명 그 나라에 있었던 가장 위대한 영웅이다.

[SYN] very much; obviously; greatly; very

earn one's living 생계를 꾸리다
They manage to **earn their living** every day.
그들은 하루하루 생계를 간신히 꾸리고 있다.
He **earned his living** by literary work in the whole course of his life.
그는 일생 동안 문필로 생계를 꾸렸다.

[SYN] make one's living; make a living

not so much as …조차 않다
He can**not so much as** write his own name.
그는 자기 이름도 쓸 줄 모른다.
He is quite broken up, so he can**not so much as** read a newspaper.
그는 아주 쇠약해져서 신문조차 읽지 못한다.
(*cf.* He went out without so much as saying a word.
그는 한마디 말도 하지 않고 나갔다.)

[SYN] not (without) even

by any chance 만일, 행여나, 혹시 (의문문·조건문에 쓰임)
If **by any chance** I am a little late coming home, don't wait up for me.
혹시나 내가 집에 늦게 오더라도 기다리지 마라.
Do you think he will come **by any chance**?
혹시나 그가 오리라고 생각하니?

[SYN] possibly; by chance

next to 1. (부정어 앞에서) 거의 2. …와 나란히, …의 이웃(곁)에, …에 이어서
It is **next to** impossible to solve this question.
이 문제를 푸는 것은 거의 불가능하다.
She sat **next to** me in the conference room.
그녀는 회의장에서 내 옆에 앉았다.

[SYN] 1. almost; nearly; all but
2. beside; by the side of

with care 주의해서, 신중히
The ship proceeded **with care** through the channel.
배는 조심스럽게 운하를 통과했다.
You must handle the tool **with care**.

[SYN] carefully; cautiously; with caution; deliberately

그 도구는 주의해서 취급해야 한다.

idle away (때 · 시기)를 빈둥빈둥 지내다, 허비하다

He **idled away** his time at home.
그는 집에서 빈둥빈둥 시간을 보냈다.
He **idles** his time **away**.
그는 빈둥거리며 세월을 보내고 있다.

SYN. spend time unprofitably

live within one's means 수입에 맞는 생활을 하다, 수입 내에서 생활하다

You must remember that we should **live within our means**.
수입에 맞추어 살아야 한다는 것을 명심해야 한다.
She **lives within her means**.
그녀는 자기 수입 내에서 살고 있다.

SYN. spend no more than one's income
OPP. live beyond one's means 수입 이상의 생활을 하다

wear out 1. 지쳐버리다 2. 닳아 해지게 하다

Playing with those kids all day really **wore** me **out**.
하루종일 저 아이들하고 노느라 정말 지쳐버렸다.
The machine **wore out** after many years of use.
그 기계는 수년 동안 사용해 꽤 낡아 있었다.

SYN. 1. tire out; exhaust 2. use up

set out 1. 여행이나 항해를 떠나다 2. …을 설명하다

Long time ago, the pilgrims **set out** for the New World.
오래 전에 순례자들은 신세계로의 여행을 시작했다.
He **set out** his ideas in simple English.
그는 간단한 영어로 자기 생각을 설명했다.

SYN. 1. leave on a trip; make a voyage 2. explain
cf. set up 1. 준비하다, 계획하다 2. (사업 등을) 시작하다

keep off (재해 · 적 등을) 막다, 가까이 접근하지 못하게 하다, 피하다

The best way to **keep off** the bugs is to smoke in the room.
벌레들을 막는 가장 좋은 방법은 방에 연기를 피우는 것이다.
Please **keep off** the fierce dog.
그 사나운 개를 가까이 오지 못하게 해 주세요.

SYN. keep away; prevent

distinguish A from B A와 B로 구별하다, 식별하다

The twins are so much alike that I cannot **distinguish** one **from** the other.
그 쌍둥이는 너무나 닮아서 나는 둘을 구별할 수가 없다.
I cannot **distinguish** him **from** his brother.

SYN. show as different; set apart
cf. distinguish between 구별하다
distinguish oneself 눈에 띄게 하

나는 그와 그의 남동생을 구별하지 못한다.

venture to 감히 …하다, 과감하게 …하다
No one **ventured to** object to the plan.
아무도 감히 그 계획에 반대하지 못했다.
I will **venture to** ask that question.
나는 용기를 내어 그것을 물어 보겠다.

SYN dare to; presume to

previous to …의 전에, …에 앞서
Previous to leaving England he sold his house.
영국을 떠나기 전에 그는 집을 팔았다.
I'll have the house cleaned **previous to** your arrival.
당신이 도착하기 전에 집을 청소해 놓겠습니다.

SYN before; prior to

have a liking for …을 좋아하다, …에 취미를 가지다
She **has a liking for** French perfume.
그녀는 프랑스 향수를 좋아한다.
He **has a liking for** playing a trick.
그는 속임수 쓰는 것을 좋아한다.

SYN be fond of; care for; take a fancy for
OPP have a disliking for …을 싫어하다 (= be unwilling to; detest)

feed on (주로 사람 이외의 동물) …을 먹고 살다, …에게 먹이를 주다
The tiger **feeds on** flesh.
호랑이는 육식을 한다.
I **feed** my horse **on** grass.
나는 말에게 풀을 먹인다.

SYN feed off; subsist on
cf. live on (주로 사람) …을 먹고 살다

do one's utmost 최선을 다하다
We **did our utmost** to finish the work on time, but we couldn't.
우리는 시간 안에 그 일을 끝마치기 위해 최선을 다했지만 하지 못했다.
Always **do your utmost** and demand.
항상 최선을 다하고 요구해라.

SYN try one's best; do one's best

come to a standstill 멈추다, 막히다
Building construction **came to a standstill**.
건물 건설 공사가 중단되었다.
As one party violated the agreement, the peace negotiation **came to a standstill**.
한쪽이 합의안을 위반했기 때문에 평화 협상이 결렬되었다.

SYN stop; be obstructed; be clogged; be brought to a standstill

care about 염두에 두다, 관심을 갖다
I always **care about** what you have done for me.
당신이 나에게 해 준 것을 항상 염두에 두고 있다.
Don't you **care about** the environment?
당신은 환경에 관심이 없습니까?

[SYN.] give one's mind to; keep in mind; remember; be concerned about

beware of …에 주의하다, 조심하다
You must **beware of** strangers.
낯선 사람들을 경계해야 한다.
If you get on a crowded bus, always **beware of** pickpockets.
복잡한 버스에 타면 항상 소매치기를 조심해라.

[SYN.] be careful about; pay attention to; take heed to

by trade 직업은
He is a mason **by trade**.
그의 직업은 석공이다.
He is a butcher **by trade**.
그의 직업은 정육업자이다.

of one's own 자신이 …한, 스스로 …한
He showed me a letter **of his own** writing.
그는 자신이 쓴 편지를 내게 보여 주었다.
These are trees **of my own** planting.
이것들은 내가 심은 나무들이다.

[SYN.] done by oneself

go on with 계속하다
She **went on with** the work.
그녀는 일을 계속했다.
I told her to **go on with** her homework.
나는 그녀에게 숙제를 계속하라고 말했다.

[SYN.] continue; keep on

in terms of …에 관하여, …의 관점에서
My father sees the life **in terms of** money.
아버지는 인생을 돈의 관점에서 본다.
What have you done **in terms of** preparing the party?
당신은 파티 준비에서 어떤 일을 했어요?

[SYN.] in the matter of; on the subject of; about

fall back on〔upon〕 …에 의지하다
I have no savings to **fall back on**.
나는 의지할 수 있는 저금이 없다.
If he loses one thing, he can **fall back upon**

[SYN.] rely on; depend on

another.
그는 비록 하나를 잃는다 해도 다른 것에 의지할 수가 있다.

blow up 폭파하다

The guerillas **blew up** the bridge.
게릴라 대원은 그 다리를 폭파했다.
Suddenly a bag **blew up** in the waiting room.
갑자기 대합실에서 가방이 폭발했다.

SYN destroy by explosion, explode

take hold of …을 붙잡다

I **took hold of** that hot frying pan.
나는 뜨거운 프라이팬을 붙잡았다.
Someone **took hold of** him by the arm suddenly.
갑자기 누군가가 그의 팔을 잡았다.

SYN grasp; grip

like so many 마치 (동수의) …처럼

They began to work **like so many** ants.
그들은 개미처럼 열심히 일하기 시작했다.
He looked down upon us **like so many** worms.
그는 우리를 마치 벌레처럼 업신여겼다.

SYN as if they were (the same number of)

at first hand 직접적으로, 몸소

Why don't you believe me? I heard this news **at first hand**.
왜 나를 믿지 못하는 거야? 이 뉴스는 내가 직접 들었어.
It's not just a rumor that the beautiful girl will get married. I heard it **at first hand**.
그 아름다운 소녀가 결혼한다는 말은 단지 소문이 아니야. 나는 그녀에게서 직접 들었어.

SYN personally; in person; directly
cf. a second hand 간접적으로 (=indirectly)

carry through 1. 완성하다 2. 난관을 극복케 하다, 견뎌 내다

If you can't **carry through**, you'd better not set an impossible schedule.
완성하지 못하겠으면 무리한 일정을 짜지 않는 것이 낫다.
His strong will **carried** him **through** the illness.
그는 강한 의지로 병을 이길 수 있었다.

SYN 1. finish 2. support

at liberty 자유로이, 한가로이

If you are **at liberty** tomorrow, would you please help me with the report?
내일 한가하면 보고서 쓰는 것을 좀 도와 주겠니?

SYN at leisure; free to go somewhere or do something

You are **at liberty** to take any food you like.
당신이 좋아하는 어떤 음식도 마음대로 먹을 수 있다.

find fault with 흠을 잡다, 비난하다

She is always ready to **find fault with** other people.
그녀는 언제나 남의 흠을 잡으려고 벼르고 있다.
He is always ready to **find fault with** other people.
그는 항상 남의 흉을 들추어 내려고 한다.

[SYN] criticize; blame; censure

in comparison with ···와 비교해서, ···에 비하면

Autumn is far more suitable for study **in comparison with** spring.
가을은 봄과 비교해서 공부하기에 훨씬 더 적합하다.
Living here is cheap **in comparison with** in Seoul.
이 곳의 생활은 서울과 비교해서 싸다.

[SYN] compared with

with a view to -ing ···할 목적으로

He went to Paris **with a view to** study**ing** design.
그는 디자인 공부를 위해 파리에 갔다.
With a view to becom**ing** a violinist, my young sister has been practicing hard.
바이올리니스트가 되기 위해 내 누이는 열심히 연습을 하고 있다.

[SYN] for the purpose of -ing

in no time 곧, 이내

Working together, they finished the job **in no time**.
같이 했기 때문에 그들은 곧 일을 끝냈다.
After noon, the restaurant was filled with people **in no time**.
정오가 지나자 식당에는 곧 사람들로 가득 찼다.

[SYN] soon; quickly

to and fro 이리저리(로), 앞뒤로

In the park, there were children running **to and fro**.
공원에서는 아이들이 이리저리 뛰어다니고 있었다.
Mother put little Jimmy on the swing and pushed him **to and fro**.
어머니는 어린 지미를 그네에 태우고 앞뒤로 밀어 주었다.

[SYN] first in one direction and then back again

in the course of ···동안에

In the course of four months he plans to complete the work.

[SYN] during; under; in process of

4개월 동안에 그는 그 일을 완료할 계획이다.
He realized his defeat **in the course of** conversation.
그는 대화를 나누는 동안 자신의 패배를 깨달았다.

spend A on B A를 B에다 쓰다, (시간을) 보내다, 들이다

She **spends** most of her salary **on** her dresses.
그녀는 봉급 대부분을 옷 사는 데 쓴다.
He **spent** five years **on** the computer project.
그는 컴퓨터 기획에 5년을 소비했다.

[SYN] pay money for something; use time and effort on
cf. spend A (in) -ing A를 …하는 데 사용하다 (A 부분에는 시간을 사용함)

not in the least 조금도 …아닌, 조금도 …하지 않는

This book is **not in the least** interesting to me.
이 책은 내게는 조금도 재미가 없다.
She was **not in the least** surprised at the news.
그녀는 그 소식을 듣고도 조금도 놀라지 않았다.

[SYN] not at all

on an (the) average 평균하여

The novelist writes **on an average** five pages a day.
그 소설가는 하루에 평균 다섯 페이지의 글을 쓴다.
On the average our family moves to a new house every four years.
평균적으로 우리 가족은 4년마다 새 집으로 이사를 한다.

[SYN] in most cases; usually

for fear of …을 두려워하여, …을 하지 않도록, …이 없도록

For fear of accidents, please drive slowly.
사고가 나지 않도록 천천히 몰아 주세요.
The majority of students study heart and soul **for fear of** failure.
대다수의 학생들은 낙제할까 두려워서 열심히 공부한다.

[SYN] afraid of; lest ... should
cf. for fear that …을 두려워하여, …을 하지 않도록, …이 없도록 (절이 따름)

be forced to 하는 수 없이 …해야 하다, …하지 않을 수 없다

We **were forced to** accept the strict terms of agreement.
우리는 엄격한 합의 조건을 수용하지 않을 수 없었다.
They **were forced to** hide themselves during the day.
그들은 낮에는 몸을 숨기고 있지 않으면 안 되었다.

[SYN] be compelled to; be obliged to

keep up 계속하다, 유지하다, 끊임없이 …하다
I want to **keep up** my study after I graduate the college.
대학 졸업 후에도 나는 공부를 계속하고 싶다.
We **keep** our house **up** by having things fixed when they break.
우리는 물건이 부서지면 고쳐 놓아서 집을 잘 유지한다.

[SYN] continue; go on; not stop

go after …을 구하다, 꽁무니를 쫓아다니다
I heard you are **going after** Kate, but she already has a boyfriend.
케이트의 꽁무니를 쫓아다니고 있다고 들었는데 그녀에게는 이미 애인이 있어.
If you **go after** something enthusiastically, you will be able to get it.
무언가를 열정적으로 구한다면 얻을 수 있을 것이다.

[SYN] try to get; run after someone

on good terms with …와 사이가 좋은
I am not **on good terms with** Jake.
나는 제이크와 사이가 좋지 않다.
Since I had a big quarrel with Paul, we have been **on good terms with** each other.
폴과 크게 싸운 후 우리는 사이가 좋아졌다.

[SYN] friendly with; in good relationship with
[OPP] on bad terms with …와 사이가 나쁜
cf. on intimate terms with …와 절친한

grow into (성장·발전 등을 해서) …이 되다
She's **grown into** a beautiful young lady.
그녀는 성장해서 아름다운 숙녀가 되었다.
Their work **grew into** a great idea of freedom for everybody.
그들의 일은 만인을 위한 자유라는 대 사상으로까지 발전해 갔다.

[SYN] become; get; grow; be

not so much A as B A라기보다는 오히려 B다
He is **not so much** a scholar **as** a statesman.
그는 학자라기보다는 오히려 정치가이다.
A man's worth lies **not so much** in what he has **as** in what he is.
인간의 가치는 그 사람의 재산보다는 사람됨에 있다.

[SYN] B rather than A

in regard to …에 관해서(는)
What have you to say **in regard to** this matter?
이에 대해서 무엇인가 의견이 있으십니까?
In regard to this, I wish to say a few words.

[SYN] concerning; in regard of; as regards

이 문제에 관해서 몇 마디 하고 싶다.

blame ... for …의 책임〔원인〕으로 돌리다

They **blamed** me **for** accident.
그들은 사고에 대한 책임을 내게 돌렸다.
He will **blame** you **for** neglecting your duty.
그는 직무태만이라고 너를 책할 것이다.

[SYN] place(lay) the responsibility on

hand over 양도하다

Do you expect any trouble when power is **handed over** to the new government?
새 정부에 정권이 이양되면 문제가 있을 것으로 봅니까?
The president **handed over** the company to his eldest son.
사장은 장남에게 회사를 넘겨주었다.

[SYN] give control of

get back 1. 돌아오다〔가다〕 2. 회복하다, 되찾다

When Bill **gets back**, please tell him to stop by my office.
빌이 돌아오면 내 사무실에 잠깐 들르라고 말해 주세요.
If you lend the book to Tom, you will never be able to **get** it **back**.
그 책을 톰에게 빌려 주면 다시는 그 책을 되찾을 수 없을 것이다.

[SYN] 1. return to one's starting point 2. recover something which belongs to one

with regard to …에 관해서(는)

I have nothing particular to mention **with regard to** the affair.
그 사건에 대해서는 특별히 할 말이 없다.
With regard to this, I wish to say a few words.
이 문제에 관해서 몇 마디 하고 싶다.

[SYN] concerning; in regard of; as regards

look out 주의하다

Look out! There's a hole in the road.
조심해! 길에 구멍이 있어.
Look out! There's a car coming.
조심해! 차가 오고 있어.

[SYN] watch out
cf. look out for …에 주의하다 (=be careful on)

it is not until ... that ∼ …하고서야 비로소 ∼하다

It was not until a few days later **that** I got the news.
나는 며칠 지나서야 비로소 그 소식을 들었다.
It is not until we injure our health **that** we realize

[SYN] not ... till ∼

its blessing.
사람들은 건강을 잃고서야 그 고마움을 알게 된다.
(=We do not realize the blessing of good health until we lose it.)

within hearing 들리는 곳에서, 매우 가까운 곳에

I called out for help, but nobody was **within hearing**.
나는 도와 달라고 외쳤지만 아무도 그 소리를 듣지 못했다.
She lives **within hearing** of the sea.
그녀는 바다 소리가 들리는 곳에 살고 있다.

[SYN] within call; near; close by
[OPP] out of earshot

for the benefit of / for one's benefit …을 위하여

He used all his money **for the benefit of** the poor.
그는 그의 돈을 모두 가난한 사람들을 위하여 썼다.
He wasn't really angry; that was just an act **for his girl friend's benefit**.
그는 정말 화가 난 것이 아니었다. 그건 단지 그의 여자 친구를 위한 시늉이었을 뿐이었다.

[SYN] for one's interest; for the sake of

count on 의지하다, 기대하다, 의존하다

We're **counting on** completing the opinion research by the end of the year.
우리는 올해 말까지 여론 조사를 완료할 것으로 기대하고 있다.
Jim always **counts on** his brother Tom for everything.
짐은 늘 매사를 자기 형인 톰에게 의존한다.

[SYN] rely on(upon); fall back on; lean on

take somebody by surprise 1. 기습하다 2. …을 깜짝 놀라게 하다

The sudden cold weather **took us** all **by surprise**.
갑작스러운 추운 날씨가 기습했다.
The offer of a high-paying position with another company **took me by surprise**.
봉급이 더 많은 자리를 주겠다는 다른 회사의 제의가 나를 놀라게 했다.

[SYN] 1. come upon suddenly or without warning 2. cause to feel wonder or astonishment

at the mercy of …에 좌우되어, …의 처분대로, …의 마음대로

The small boat drifted **at the mercy of** high waves.
작은 배는 높은 파도에 밀려 떠다녔다.

[SYN] in the power of; without defense against

The baseball game is **at the mercy of** the weather.
야구 경기를 하고 안 하고는 날씨에 달려 있다.

break out 1. (전쟁·화재·유행병 등이) 일어나다 2. 갑자기 …하기 시작하다

[SYN] 1. begin showing a rash or other skin disorder 2. occur suddenly; happen; take place

A fire **broke out** last night, and about fifty houses were reduced to ashes.
어제 저녁에 불이 나서 집 50채 정도가 재로 변했다.

A case of smallpox has **broken out** in the country.
천연두 환자가 시골에 발생했다.

Upon seeing a big dog, the little boy **broke out** crying.
큰 개를 보자마자 어린 소년은 울음을 터뜨렸다.

a short cut 지름길

[SYN] a shorter way(road)

If you want to go there fast, you'd better take **a short cut** instead of this way.
그 곳에 빨리 가고 싶으면 이 길보다는 지름길을 택하는 것이 좋다.

Without knowing **a short cut**, many people take this road.
많은 사람들은 지름길을 몰라서 이 도로를 이용한다.

in the world 1. 도대체 (의문사를 강조) 2. 세상에서

[SYN] on earth; the devil

What **in the world** does he mean?
도대체 그는 어떻게 할 예정인가요?

He is the greatest man **in the world**.
그는 세상에서 가장 위대한 사람이다.

pass away 1. 지나가다 2. 죽다, 멸망하다

[SYN] 1. pass; slip by; go by 2. cease to exist; die; vanish

Thirty years have **passed away** since he had gone to America.
그가 미국으로 가버린 지 30년이 지났다.

Grandfather **passed away** during the night without notice.
할아버지는 아무도 모르는 채 밤 동안에 돌아가셨다.

wonder if …인지 모르겠다, …이 아닐까 하고 생각하다

[SYN] wonder whether

I **wonder if** you'd look after my dog while I go shopping.
제가 쇼핑하러 나간 동안 제 개를 봐 주실 수 있는지요.

I **wonder if** something has happened to him.
그에게 무슨 일이 생기지 않았는지 모르겠다.

devote oneself to ⋯에 전념하다, 몰두하다
He **devotes himself to** the task.
그는 그 일에 전념하고 있다.
(=He is devoted to the task.)
She **devoted herself to** the improvement of women's rights body and soul.
그녀는 여성 권익 향상에 몸과 마음을 다 바쳤다.

[SYN] apply oneself to; be absorbed in; concentrate on
cf. devote A to B A를 B에 바치다, 심신을 맡기다

to advantage 1. 유리하게, 형편 좋게 2. 뛰어나게, 훌륭히, 돋보이게
The situation turned out **to** his **advantage**.
상황은 그에게 유리해졌다.
Her hairstyle showed her figure **to advantage**.
그녀의 헤어스타일은 그녀의 모습을 돋보이게 했다.

[SYN] 1. advantageously; favorably 2. finely; nicely; excellently; splendidly

there is no -ing ⋯할 수 없다
There is no know**ing** what may happen in the future.
미래에 어떤 일이 일어날지는 알 수 없다.
(=It is impossible to know what may happen in the future. =No one can know what may happen in the future. =We cannot know what may happen in the future.)

[SYN] it is impossible to do something

be disappointed at ⋯에 실망하다
The teacher **was disappointed at** the result of the study.
그 교사는 연구 결과에 실망했다.
Everybody **was disappointed at** your irresponsible behavior today.
오늘 네가 보여 준 무책임한 행동에 다들 실망했다.

[SYN] despair; lose one's heart or hope
cf. be disappointed to+동사 ⋯에 낙담하다, ⋯에 실망하다 (=lose one's heart)

by birth 태생은, 타고난
He is a pianist **by birth**.
그는 타고난 피아니스트이다.
He is a nobleman **by birth**.
그는 귀족 태생이다.

[SYN] born; natural; innate

suited for〔to〕 ⋯에 맞아 떨어지는, 어울리는, 적합한
The young man is quite **suited for** the position.
그 청년은 그 자리에 아주 잘 어울린다.
He is **suited for**〔**to** be〕 a teacher.

[SYN] fit; suitable to; matching well; becoming

그는 교사가 적격이다.

call off 취소하다, 중지하다
I **called off** the previous appointment.
나는 이전의 약속을 취소했다.
The strike was **called off**.
파업은 중지되었다.

[SYN] cancel; drop; abandon; stop

in the event of …의 경우에는
In the event of my father's death, I shall have to give up my study.
만약 아버지가 돌아가신다면 공부를 포기해야 할 것이다.
In the event of raining, you may stay here until it stops.
만약 비가 오면 그칠 때까지 여기 있어도 좋다.

[SYN] on the occasion of; in case of

devote to …에 바치다
Her father **devoted** his life **to** the religious advancement.
그녀의 아버지는 종교 발전에 일생을 바쳤다.
She told me (that) her father **devoted** his life **to** science.
그녀는 자신의 아버지가 과학에 일생을 바쳤다고 말했다.

[SYN] sacrifice

bring on (병 등을) 일으키다, 야기시키다, 만들어 내다
Our manager has **brought on** an illness by overdrinking.
우리 지배인은 과음으로 병이 났다.
The governor's speech has **brought** suspicion **on** him.
그 지사의 연설은 그의 신변에 의혹을 야기시켰다.

[SYN] cause; lead; make

under way 진행 중에
Preparations are **under way** for their wedding.
그들의 결혼식 준비가 진행 중에 있다.
We have several plans **under way**.
우리는 몇 가지 계획을 진행 중이다.

[SYN] in progress; making progress; advancing

of necessity 필연적으로, 당연히
He must **of necessity** succeed.
그는 필연적으로 성공하지 않을 수 없다.
She will **of necessity** fail in the plan of going to

[SYN] necessarily; inevitably; because there is no other way

Europe this summer.
그녀는 이번 여름에 유럽으로 가려는 계획에 당연히 실패할 것이다.

ever so 1. 매우, 대단히 2. (양보절에서) 비록 …하더라도

I want to thank you **ever so** much for the kindness you have shown me.
저에게 보여 주신 친절에 진실로 감사하고 싶습니다.
Home is home, be it **ever so** humble.
아무리 초라해도 내 집만 한 곳은 없다.

SYN 1. very; greatly 2. though, even though

up and down 여기저기, 위아래로, 우왕좌왕

We walked **up and down** the streets to look for a house to rent.
우리는 셋집을 찾아 여기저기 돌아다녔다.
She ran **up and down** among the soldiers in order to look for her son.
그녀는 아들을 찾기 위해 군인들 사이를 이리저리 뛰어다녔다.

SYN to and fro; in every direction; backwards and forwards

such ... as …와 같은, …처럼

We can't trust **such** a dishonest man **as** he.
우리는 그와 같은 부정직한 사람을 믿을 수 없다.
I've never seen **such** an attractive girl **as** Alice.
지금까지 앨리스처럼 매력적인 소녀를 본 적이 없다.

SYN of a kind like; of a kind or amount shown or named; such

off guard 방심하여

The criminals were caught **off guard** by the police.
범인들은 방심하다 경찰에 잡혔다.
Bill put Susan **off** her **guard** and she revealed an important secret to him.
빌이 수잔을 방심케 하여 그녀는 중대한 비밀을 그에게 털어놓았다.

SYN in a careless attitude; not alert to coming danger; not watching

come after …의 뒤를 쫓다, 뒤에 오다

The pickpocket found that a policeman was **coming after** him.
소매치기는 순경이 그의 뒤를 쫓고 있는 것을 발견했다.
She knew that Fred would **come after** her wherever she went.
그녀는 어디를 가든 프레드가 따라 올 것임을 알았다.

SYN follow; chase or search for someone

turn out (to be) …로 판명되다, 결국 …이 되다

Harry and Susan **turned out** to be spies from outer space.

SYN result in; prove to be; be discovered to be
cf. turn over 뒤집히다 (=turn

해리와 수잔은 외계에서 온 스파이로 밝혀졌다.
The plan **turned out** to have had no effect.
그 계획은 아무런 효과도 없었다.

bring up 1. 키우다, 교육하다 2. (문제 등을) 끄집어 내다, 소개하다, 언급하다

Since her mother's death, the little girl has been **brought up** by her aunt.
어머니가 돌아가신 후 어린 소녀는 숙모의 손에서 자랐다.
At the lunch time, Ben **brought up** the idea of a picnic.
점심 시간에 벤은 야유회 이야기를 꺼냈다.

[SYN] 1. raise, educate, train; instruct 2. begin a discussion of; introduce, mention

on board 배(비행기)에 타고, 차 안에

Standing on the port, I saw people **on board** waving their hands.
부두에 서서 나는 배에 탄 사람들이 손을 흔들고 있는 것을 보았다.
There are about 200 passengers **on board** this jet.
이 비행기에는 200여 명의 승객이 타고 있다.

[SYN] aboard; on a ship

clear of …이 없는, …이 면제된

It took me two hours to get **clear of** the village.
그 마을을 벗어나는 데 두 시간 걸렸다.
I want to **clear of** exams for a while.
당분간 시험이 없었으면 좋겠다.

[SYN] free or freed from something

hold back 억제하다

I'm afraid we'll have to **hold back** supplies until we sign a new contract.
새로운 계약을 체결하기까지 물품 인도를 보류해야 할 것 같습니다.
The police had difficulty **holding back** the crowd.
경찰은 군중을 제지하기 어려웠다.

[SYN] restrain; refuse to release

there is no use (whatever) -ing …해도 소용이 없다

There is no use try**ing** to persuade her, for she is obstinate by nature.
그 여자는 본래 고집이 세기 때문에 설득하려고 해 봤자 소용이 없다.
(= It is no use trying to persuade her, ~.
= It is of no use to persuade her, ~.
= It is useless to persuade her, ~.)
There is no use whatever try**ing** to help people

[SYN] it is useless to; it is no use -ing; it is of no use

upside down)

who do not help themselves.
스스로를 돕지 않는 사람들은 도우려고 해도 소용이 없다.

cheer up 격려하다, 기운 나게 하다
We went to a hospital to **cheer up** a friend.
우리는 친구를 격려하러 병원에 갔다.
The support of the fans **cheered up** the losing team.
팬들의 응원은 지고 있는 팀을 기운 나게 했다.

[SYN] make cheerful or happy; encourage

weigh on (upon) 압박하다, 괴롭히다
The rucksack **weighed** heavily **on** the boy's shoulders.
배낭이 소년의 어깨를 무겁게 압박했다.
The sadness from her dog's death **weighed upon** the little girl.
개의 죽음으로 인한 슬픔이 어린 소녀의 마음을 괴롭혔다.

[SYN] press; oppress; suppress

run away 1. 가출하다 2. 도망치다, 달아나다
He **ran away** from home to be an actor when he was a little boy.
그는 어렸을 때 배우가 되려고 가출했다.
As soon as he saw the policeman, the pickpocket **ran away**.
소매치기는 경관을 보자마자 달아나 버렸다.

[SYN] 1. leave home 2. escape; get away quickly

separate from 떼어 버리다, 분리시키다
We should **separate** education **from** religion.
교육과 종교는 분리되어야 한다.
No one could **separate** me **from** him.
아무도 나와 그를 갈라놓을 수 없었다.

[SYN] move something apart or away from something else

as though 마치 …처럼, 마치 …이기나 한 듯이
He speaks **as though** he knew everything. Actually he knows nearly nothing.
그는 모든 것을 다 알고 있는 것처럼 말하지만 사실은 거의 아무것도 알지 못한다.
He acts **as though** he were my husband and I don't like it.
그는 마치 내 남편인 것처럼 행세하는데 나는 그것이 싫다.

[SYN] as if; apparently

rid A of B A에서 B를 제거하다

[SYN] disencumber; get rid of;

We must **rid** the house **of** rats.
집에서 쥐를 없애야 한다.
We must **rid** the world **of** the menace of atomic warfare.
이 세상에서 핵전쟁의 위험을 제거해야 한다.

[SYN] clear

at any time 언제든지, 언제라도
Come to see me **at any time** tomorrow evening.
내일 저녁 아무 때라도 오십시오.
You can visit patients at the hospital **at any time**.
그 병원 환자들은 언제라도 면회할 수 있다.

[SYN] always; all the time; at all times

fix on (upon) 1. 정하다 2. (눈·주의 등을) …에 고정시키다, 쏟다
The place was **fixed upon** the exhibition grounds.
그 곳은 박람회의 부지로 결정되었다.
His eyes are **fixed on** the ground as he strides along.
그는 큰 걸음으로 거닐면서 눈은 땅을 보고 있었다.

[SYN] 1. decide on; settle on
2. fix one's attention on what one's doing

be at home in …에 정통하다, …에 익숙하다
Although Ted is a scientist, he **is** also **at home in** music.
테드는 과학자이지만 음악에도 조예가 깊다.
Don't worry, as I **am at home in** this city.
나는 이 도시에 익숙하니까 걱정하지 마라.

[SYN] be at one's own wit; be familiar with

be acquainted with …을 알고 있다, …에 정통하다
When it comes to mathematics, go to Jim. He **is acquainted with** it.
수학 문제라면 짐에게 가 봐. 그는 수학에 정통해.
It is said that Mary **is acquainted with** Oriental medicines.
메리는 한약을 잘 안다고 사람들은 말한다.

[SYN] be familiar with; know well; be well informed about
cf. become acquainted with …을 알게 되다, 친하게 되다 (= become familiar with)

talking of …으로 말하면, 말이 났으니 말인데
Talking of Mt. Seorak, have you been there in winter?
설악산 말이 났으니 말인데 겨울에 가 봤나요?
Talking of travel, I am on tour about six month of a year.
여행 이야기가 났으니 말인데 나는 일년 중 6개월은 여행을 해.

[SYN] speaking of

bring down 1. (물가를) 하락시키다 2. 쏘아 떨어뜨리다

The good harvest **brought down** the price of rice.
풍작으로 쌀값이 내렸다.
A bomber was **brought down** by a ground-to-air missile.
지대공 미사일에 의해 폭격기 한 대가 격추되었다.

[SYN] 1. decline, fall, come down 2. shoot down

with the result that 그 결과

They talked on for hours **with the result that** the strike was called off.
그들은 몇 시간 동안 계속 대화를 하여 그 결과 파업이 취소되었다.

[SYN] as the result; consequently; in the sequel

respond to 1. …에 반응하다, 좋은 반응을 보이다 2. 대답하다, 응답하다, 응하다

The plane **responds** well **to** the controls.
그 비행기는 조종 장치가 잘 듣는다.
The wireless calls were soon **responded to**.
무선으로 호출하자 바로 응답이 왔다.

[SYN] 1. react; change as result of something 2. reply

sufficient for …에 충분한, 족한

Our money was **sufficient for** a two-week vacation.
우리 돈은 2주 동안 휴가를 보내기에 충분했다.
The pension is **sufficient for** living expenses.
연금은 생활비로 쓰기에 충분하다.

[SYN] enough; ample; sufficient; adequate

derive from 1. …에게서 빼내다, 획득하다, 손에 넣다 2. (종종 수동태) …의 기원을 찾다

I also **derive** great pleasure **from** looking through the mail that I get.
내게 오는 우편물을 훑어보는 것에서 또한 큰 즐거움을 얻는다.
These words were **derived from** Latin language.
이 단어들은 라틴어에서 나왔다.

[SYN] 1. obtain; get; have; secure 2. be originated in; be resulted from

take pains 수고를 하다

She always **takes pains** with her appearance.
그녀는 항상 외모에 신경을 쓴다.
They **took** great **pains** with the preparations for the party.
그들은 파티 준비에 몹시 애썼다.
(=They took great pains preparing for the party.)

[SYN] take the trouble; make efforts

see through …을 간파하다, 꿰뚫어 보다, 이해하다

[SYN] perceive the true mean-

I can **see through** him like a pane of glass.
나는 그를 유리창을 보듯 꿰뚫어 볼 수 있다.
Mother **saw through** little Billy's excuses not to go to bed on Saturday.
어머니는 어린 빌리가 토요일에 잠을 자지 않으려고 핑계를 대는 것을 알아챘다.

ing, character, or nature of

command a fine view 전망이 좋다

We can **command a fine view** from the top of the hill.
언덕 위에서의 전망이 아주 좋다.
This room **commands a fine view**, so the rent is more expensive than that of other rooms.
이 방은 전망이 좋아서 다른 방들보다 임대료가 비싸다.

[SYN] have a fine view
cf. command a view of …을 훤히 내려다 보다

for sale 팔려고 내놓은

We don't want our car anymore; it is **for sale**.
이제 자동차가 필요하지 않아 팔려고 내놓은 것이다.
This suit is not **for sale**.
이 양복은 비매품이다.

[SYN] available for purchase
cf. on sale (싸게 팔려고) 내놓아, 특가로 (= available for a lower price than usual)

look to 1. 감시하다, 주의하다 2. …에 의존하다, 기대를 걸다

Look to it that such mistakes will never happen again.
다시는 그런 실수가 생기지 않도록 주의해라.
We are fond of **looking to** the future.
우리는 미래에 기대를 걸기를 좋아한다.

[SYN] 1. attend to; consider 2. depend on(upon); place one's hope on
cf. look to … for ~ …에게 ~을 의존하다 (= depend on; rely on; be dependent on)

be astonished at …에 깜짝 놀라다

Students **were astonished at** getting unexpectedly high grade.
학생들은 예상 외로 높은 점수를 받고서 놀랐다.
I **was astonished at** the news.
나는 그 소식에 깜짝 놀랐다.

[SYN] be surprised at

in proportion to …에 비례하여

The air becomes cooler **in proportion to** its distance from the ground.
지면으로부터의 거리에 비례해서 공기는 차가워진다.
Are you paid **in proportion to** your working hours?
노동 시간에 비례해서 보수를 받습니까?

cf. in proportion as …하는 것에 비례하여

it follows that ···라고 말하는 대로다, 당연한 결과로 ···되다

If that is true, **it follows that** he didn't attend the meeting.
그것이 사실이라면 자연히 그가 회의에 참석하지 않았다는 말이 된다.
If that is true, **it follows that** Susan wasn't there with her husband.
그 말이 사실이라면 수잔은 남편과 함께 그 곳에 있지 않은 셈이다.

[SYN] occur as a consequence
cf. it does not follow that ··· 반드시 ···하는 것은 아니다 (=not necessarily; not always)

hang on 1. 매달리다, 버티다, 끝까지 노력하다 2. 전화를 끊지 않고 기다리다

He managed to **hang on** until the aid workers came.
그는 구조대가 올 때까지 간신히 매달려 있었다.
Hang on a moment, I am almost ready.
잠깐만 기다려. 거의 다 됐어.

[SYN] 1. cling to; hold fast to the end 2. wait

as ... as possible 될 수 있는 대로, 가능한 한, 가급적

I can't wait for so long, so please come **as** soon **as possible**.
나는 그렇게 오래 기다릴 수가 없으니 가능한 한 빨리 오기 바란다.
Remembering the last failure, he took **as** much care **as possible**.
지난번의 실패를 떠올리며 그는 가능한 한 조심했다.

[SYN] as ... as one can, as much(far) as possible

with interest 1. 흥미를 가지고 2. 이자를 붙여서

Everybody will read the novel **with interest**.
누구든 그 소설을 흥미를 가지고 읽을 것이다.
He promised to pay back the money **with** high **interest**.
그는 높은 이자를 붙여서 그 돈을 갚겠다고 약속했다.

[SYN] 1. taking interest; feeling an interest in 2. adding interest

as many as ···와 같은 수의, ···만큼, 그렇게도 많이

You are allowed to take apples **as many as** you want.
너는 사과를 원하는 만큼 가져가도 좋다.
Why do you want more? I don't have **as many** books **as** you have.
너는 왜 더 원하는 거야? 나는 책을 너만큼 가지고 있지 않아.

[SYN] the same number as

lose oneself in ···에 열중하다, 빠지다

He **lost himself in** silent meditation.

[SYN] be lost in

그는 조용하게 명상에 잠겨 있었다.
He often **loses himself in** his job.
그는 곧잘 일에 몰두하곤 한다.

irrespective of ···에 관계 없이

It must be done **irrespective of** cost.
비용과는 관계 없이 그것을 해야만 한다.
I shall go **irrespective of** the weather.
나는 날씨에 상관 없이 갈 것이다.

[SYN] regardless of; without regard to

ashamed of ···을 부끄럽게 여기는, 창피하게 여기는

She was **ashamed of** her old clothes.
그녀는 자신의 낡은 옷들이 부끄러웠다.
Don't be **ashamed of** your poor education.
교육을 제대로 받지 못했다고 창피하게 여기지 마라.

[SYN] feeling shame about

upside down 뒤집혀서, 거꾸로, 엉망이 된

The picture was hung **upside down**.
그림이 거꾸로 걸려 있었다.
We found the room turned **upside down** by the thieves.
도둑이 들어 방이 엉망이었다.

[SYN] topsy-turvy; in disorder or confusion

turn over 1. 뒤집다, 쓰러뜨리다 2. 넘겨주다, 인계하다, 이양하다

I saw the truck leave the road and **turn over**.
나는 트럭이 길에서 벗어나 전복되는 것을 보았다.
The inventory was **turned over** to the broker.
재고 목록은 중개인에게 인계됐다.

[SYN] 1. turn upside down; invert 2. hand over; transfer

as good as ···와 거의 같은, 사실상 ···와 같은, ···나 다름없는

When the car was repaired after the accident, it looked **as good as** new.
사고 후 자동차를 수리하고 나니 거의 새 차처럼 보였다.
My homework is **as good as** finished.
숙제는 다 한 것이나 다름없다.

[SYN] nearly the same as; almost

yell out 큰 소리로 외치다

Susan **yelled out**, but Tom across the street couldn't hear.
수잔은 큰 소리로 외쳤지만 길 건너 있는 톰은 듣지 못했다.

[SYN] shout out; say something in a loud voice

On the street I heard someone **yell out** my name.
거리에서 누군가가 내 이름을 크게 부르는 소리를 들었다.

clear away 1. (구름·안개가) 걷히다 2. 치우다

The clouds **cleared away** and we could see the blue sky again.
구름이 걷히고 우리는 푸른 하늘을 다시 볼 수 있었다.
Before you go to bed, you should **clear** all the toys **away**.
잠자리에 들기 전에 장난감을 모두 치워야 한다.

[SYN] 1. brighten up 2. put away; remove

make both ends meet 수지를 맞추다

I made great efforts to **make both ends meet**.
나는 수지를 맞추기 위해 대단한 노력을 했다.
I found it hard to **make both ends meet**.
나는 수지 균형을 맞춘다는 것이 힘들다는 것을 알았다.

[SYN] balance the budget; make ends meet

at any price 어떤 대가를[희생을] 치르더라도, 기어코, (부정문에서) 무슨 일이 있어도 …않다

The two parties must agree to resume the peace talks **at any price**.
양측은 어떤 대가를 치르더라도 평화 회담 재개에 동의해야 한다.
You should not have allowed such a tragic accident to take place **at any price**.
당신은 무슨 일이 있어도 그처럼 비극적인 사고가 발생하지 않도록 했어야 했다.

[SYN] at all costs; by any means; at whatever cost in money, honor, happiness, etc.

come into use 사용하게 되다, 활용케 하다

This word **came into** common **use** only recently.
이 단어는 최근에야 일반적으로 사용하게 되었다.
Those scientific terms **came into** general **use** three years ago.
그 과학 용어들은 3년 전에 일반화되어 사용하게 되었다.

[SYN] put to use; allow the use of

hold one's breath 숨을 죽이다

Holding my breath, I gazed at the scene behind the door.
나는 숨을 죽이고 문 뒤에서 그 광경을 지켜보았다.
He **held his breath** under water for 30 seconds.
그는 물 속에서 30초 동안 숨을 쉬지 않았다.

[SYN] not breathe; inhale and not breathe
cf. out of breath 숨이 차서

get down 1. (사다리·지붕·말 등에서) 내리다 2. 삼키

[SYN] 1. get off; alight from 2.

다
Get down from your horse.
말에서 내리세요.
The pill was small enough for the child to **get down**.
그 알약은 아이가 삼킬 정도로 작았다.

[SYN] swallow; choke down; take down

think over …을 잘 생각하다, 숙고하다
We'll **think over** your offer and give you our answer tomorrow morning.
당신의 제안을 검토해 보고 내일 아침에 답을 드리겠습니다.
She **thought over** his marriage proposal for several weeks before accepting.
그녀는 몇 주 동안 그의 청혼에 대해 심사숙고한 후 받아들였다.

[SYN] muse on; think deliberately; ponder

set aside 따로 챙겨 두다
You'd better **set** this **aside** for future use.
이것을 따로 챙겨 두었다가 나중에 쓰는 것이 좋겠다.
Anne **set aside** some of the toys which she wanted to keep.
앤은 장난감 중에서 갖고 싶은 것 몇 개를 따로 챙겨 두었다.

[SYN] set apart and keep for a purpose; reserve; put aside; save

feel for 더듬다, 찾다
After making a mistake, Bill **felt for** an excuse.
빌은 실수한 후 핑계거리를 찾았다.
I **felt** my pocket **for** a lighter.
라이터를 찾으려고 호주머니에 손을 넣어 뒤적거렸다.

[SYN] feel around for

cling to 달라붙다, 고착하다
People say barnacles **cling to** the hulls of ships.
사람들은 삿갓조개가 선체에 달라붙는다고 말한다.
Wet clothes **clung to** the body.
젖은 옷이 몸에 달라붙었다.

[SYN] stick to; adhere to; hold on to; fasten oneself on; attach oneself to

talk over 1. …에 관해 상담[이야기]하다, 논하다 2. (…을 인정하도록) 설득하다
Now I don't have time, so let's **talk over** the matter later.
지금은 시간이 없으니 그 문제는 나중에 이야기합시다.
He tried to **talk** me **over** to the current situation.
그는 현 상황을 인정하도록 나를 설득하려고 애썼다.

[SYN] 1. discuss a matter, especially to reach an understanding 2. persuade; prevail on

go through 1. 자세히 조사하다, 검토하다 2. 경험하다, 겪다

They **went through** the drawer.
그들은 서랍을 뒤졌다.
Many people **went through** dangers during the war.
많은 사람들이 전쟁 동안 위험을 겪었다.

SYN 1. examine carefully 2. experience; suffer

store up 저축[저장]하다, 비축하다

We are **storing up** oil for the cold winter.
우리는 추운 겨울을 위해 기름을 비축하고 있다.
What food do they **store up**?
그들은 어떤 식량을 비축합니까?

SYN accumulate; save for emergency; store; reserve

put down 1. (힘·권력으로) 억누르다, 진정시키다 2. 적다, 기입[기장]하다

The troops soon **put down** the rebellion.
군대는 즉시 반란을 진압했다.
She **put** her thoughts **down** on paper not to forget them.
그녀는 잊어버리지 않기 위해 생각을 종이에 적었다.

SYN 1. press down; force down; make calm 2. write down; make a note of

drink to 건배하다, 축배를 들다

All the guests **drank to** the bride and groom.
모든 하객들은 신랑 신부를 위해 건배했다.
Ladies and gentlemen, let's **drink to** the prosperity of our company.
신사 숙녀 여러분 우리 회사의 번영을 위해 건배합시다.

SYN drink a toast; toast

be obliged to 1. 하는 수 없이 …하다 2. 남에게 감사하다

We **were obliged to** put off our departure because our child became ill.
우리 아이가 병이 나서 출발을 연기하지 않으면 안 되었다.
I **am** much **obliged to** you for your help.
도와 주셔서 정말 감사합니다.

SYN 1. be forced to; be compelled to 2. be grateful; be very thankful

of moment 중요한

I hold that the matter is **of** great **moment**.
나는 그 일이 대단히 중요하다고 생각한다.
It is a matter **of moment** to remove the superstition in our society.

SYN of importance; important

우리 사회에서 미신을 제거하는 것은 중요한 문제이다.

stretch out 1. (손발을) 뻗다 2. 길게 눕다

For a few moments he was unable to **stretch out** his hand.
잠시 동안 그는 손을 뻗칠 수 없었다.
John **stretched out** on the sofa and fell asleep soon.
존은 소파에 길게 누워서는 곧 잠이 들었다.

[SYN] 1. hold out; extend the hand 2. relax by lying at full length

put away 1. 치우다, 정리하다 2. 남겨두다, 저축하다, 따로 남겨두다

You may **put** these things **away**.
이 물건들을 치워도 좋아요.
Every week I'd like to **put away** $55 toward buying a new car.
나는 새 차를 구입하기 위해 매주 55달러씩 저축하려고 한다.

[SYN] 1. take away; clear away; clear off; remove 2. set aside; save; lay by; store up

without exception 예외 없이(없는), 남김없이

There is no rule **without exception**.
예외 없는 규칙은 없다.
Everybody **without exception** was sent away from the place.
한 사람도 남김없이 그 곳에서 쫓겨났다.

[SYN] entirely; wholly

form the habit of -ing …하는 습관을 붙이다, 버릇을 들이다

It is important to **form the habit of** read**ing** good books in our youth.
젊을 때 양서를 읽는 습관을 들이는 것은 중요하다.
It is important to **form the habit of** think**ing**.
사고하는 습관을 들이는 것이 중요하다.

[SYN] make a habit of -ing

attempt to …하려고 시도하다, 노력하다

Why don't you **attempt to** be a song-writer instead of a singer?
가수보다는 작곡가가 되도록 노력해 보는 게 어때?
The moment the student **attempted to** answer the question, his teacher interrupted him.
그 학생이 질문에 답을 하려는 순간 선생님이 그를 가로막았다.

[SYN] try to; make an attempt to

on the part of …의 편에서는

[SYN] on one's part

There was no objection **on the part of** the laborers.
노동자측에서는 전혀 반대가 없었다.
Some accidents happen through carelessness **on the part of** pedestrians.
일부 사고들은 보행자측 부주의로 발생한다.

escape from ···에서 도망치다, 벗어나다

We must **escape from** the old bad traditions.
우리는 낡은 나쁜 전통에서 벗어나야 한다.
A prisoner on a death row killed a guard and **escaped from** the prison.
사형수 한 명이 교도관을 죽이고 탈옥했다.

[SYN] break free from; be released involuntarily from

next door 1. 옆집 2. 매우 가까이

I am glad that a very nice family moved into the **next door**.
매우 좋은 가족이 옆집으로 이사 와서 기쁘다.
My grandmother is **next door** to death.
할머니는 임종이 가깝다.

[SYN] 1. in or to the next house or apartment 2. very close

look through 1. (유리창·렌즈 등을) 통해 보다 2. 보고도 못 본 척하다

Looking through the keyhole, I saw a man asleep on the floor.
열쇠 구멍으로 들여다보았더니 한 남자가 마룻바닥에서 자고 있는 것이 보였다.
When we meet outside by chance, Tom always **looks through** me.
밖에서 우연히 마주치면 톰은 항상 나를 못 본 척한다.

[SYN] 1. turn one's gaze through 2. pretend not to see

run down 1. (기계·시계 등이) 멈추다, (건전지 등이) 떨어지다 2. 부딪혀(받아) 쓰러뜨리다

I kept the machine working for a long time, so the battery has **run down**.
기계를 오랫동안 가동했더니 건전지가 다 떨어졌다.
A man was **run down** by a car as he crossed the street.
거리를 건너다가 한 남자가 차에 치였다.

[SYN] 1. run short of 2. hit; throw someone to the ground

within one's reach [grasp] 거의 손에 넣을 듯한

[SYN] almost in the possession of someone

Victory is **within our reach**, so try a little bit harder.
승리는 바로 우리 눈앞에 있으니 조금만 더 노력하자.
The deal was **within their grasp**, but at the last moment, the negotiation failed.
계약이 거의 체결될 듯 했지만 막판에 협상은 결렬되고 말았다.

disagree with 1. 의견이 일치하지 않다 2. (풍토·음식 등이 체질에) 맞지 않다, 해가 되다

On almost all topics, the two brothers **disagree with** each other.
거의 모든 문제에 있어서 그 두 형제는 서로 의견이 일치하지 않는다.
The climate here **disagrees with** me.
여기 기후는 나에게 맞지 않다.

[SYN] 1. not match; not agree 2. prove unsuitable for; have bad effects on

be weary of 싫증이 나다, 지긋지긋하다

I'm never **weary of** (doing) the job.
그 일은 정말 싫증이 안 난다.
I'm **weary of** his preaching.
그의 설교에는 진력이 난다.

[SYN] be tedious; be tiresome

hand in 제출하다

Please **hand in** your report by Thursday.
목요일까지 보고서를 제출해 주세요.
I forgot to **hand in** my expense account for last month.
지난달 분 경비 보고를 깜박 잊고 제출하지 않았다.

[SYN] submit; turn in

stand in for …의 대역을 하다

I am **standing in for** the mayor because he is ill.
시장이 병이 나서 제가 시장 대행을 하고 있습니다.
Susan **stood in for** Nancy who suffered from broken leg.
수잔이 다리가 부러진 낸시 대역을 했다.

[SYN] play the part for; replace

lose heart 낙담하다

He tried again and again in vain, so he **lost heart**.
그는 여러 번 시도했으나 실패하여 의기소침해졌다.
His job became so boring that he **lost heart** and stopped trying.
그의 일이 너무 지루해져서 그는 낙담하여 노력하기를 중단했다.

[SYN] become disappointed; be in despair
[OPP] take heart 기운을 내다

point out 1. 가리키다, 지적하다 2. 주목하게 하다, 설명하다

Nancy **pointed out** her friend to me among the huge crowd.
낸시는 엄청난 군중 속에서 그녀의 친구를 나에게 가리켜 주었다.
The police **pointed out** that we shouldn't cross the street.
경찰은 우리에게 길을 건너면 안 된다고 주의를 주었다.

SYN. 1. show by pointing with the finger; point to 2. bring to notice; call to attention; explain

be better off 살기가 더 나아지다, 보다 행복하다, 더 좋은 상태이다

To get there before dark, he'd **be better off** leaving right now.
어두워지기 전에 거기에 도착하려면 지금 당장 떠나는 것이 더 나을 것이다.
He would **be better off** if he had worked harder.
더 열심히 일했더라면 그는 더 잘 살 텐데.

SYN. be richer; be happier; be in better situation

what if 1. …라면 어떨까, …하면 어떻게 될까 2. …한들 상관없지 않은가

What if she comes back now?
그녀가 지금 돌아온다면 어떻게 될까?
What if we should fail?
우리가 실패해도 상관없잖아?

SYN. 1. what will happen if 2. what matters if

on the spot 1. 그 자리에서, 즉석에서 2. 현장에서

I was so foolish to give him such a big amount of money **on the spot**.
그런 거금을 즉석에서 그에게 주다니 정말 내가 어리석었다.
The policeman caught the criminal **on the spot**.
경찰관은 범인을 현장에서 붙잡았다.

SYN. 1. immediately; at once; right away 2. then and there

know A from B A와 B를 구별하다

It is hard to **know** a good book **from** a bad one.
양서와 악서를 구별하기란 어렵다.
They are twins and it's difficult to **know** one **from** the other.
그들은 쌍둥이여서 분간하기가 어렵다.

SYN. tell A from B; distinguish A from B

close at hand 1. 가까이에 2. 임박하여

We always need a reliable English dictionary **close at hand**.

SYN. 1. nearby; at a short distance; at close hand 2. become acute; grow tense

우리는 늘 믿을 만한 영어 사전을 곁에 두어야 한다.
The final examination is **close at hand**, so we must study hard.
기말 시험이 가까워서 우리는 열심히 공부해야 된다.

cf. near at hand 임박하다 (= draw near; be imminent)

know of ···(이 있는 것)을 알고[듣고] 있다, ···의 일을 들어서 알고 있다
I **know of** the man, but I have never met him.
그에 대해서는 들어서 알고 있지만 만난 적은 없다.
I **know of** the politician, but I don't know him.
그 정치인에 대한 이야기는 들었지만 직접 알지는 못한다.

[SYN] be familiar with but not know everything

Indeed ..., but 과연 ···이기는 하지만 그러나
Indeed he may be a little dull, **but** he is very honest.
과연 그는 좀 머리가 둔하기는 하지만, 그러나 아주 정직하다.

[SYN] It is true ..., but

come to life 활기를 띠다
When Mary showed up, people at the party began to **come to life**.
메리가 나타나자 파티에 참석한 사람들은 활기를 띠기 시작했다.

[SYN] become lively; animated

as a result (of) ···의 결과로서
He was injured seriously **as a result of** a boiler explosion.
그는 보일러 폭발로 중상을 입었다.
I was late **as a result of** the train delay.
나는 기차가 연착했기 때문에 늦었다.

[SYN] consequently; in consequence

be accountable for 책임지다
We should **be accountable for** our actions.
우리는 각자 자기의 행동에 책임을 져야 한다.
Who **is accountable for** this state of affairs?
이 사태에 대한 책임은 누구에게 있는가?

[SYN] be responsible for; be liable for

be guilty of 죄를 범하다
He **is guilty of** the crimes.
그가 죄를 범했다.
Are **you guilty** or innocent **of** his death?
그의 죽음에 대해 너는 죄가 있는가 결백한가?

[SYN] commit a crime

bring out 1. ···을 꺼내다 2. ···을 명백히 하다, 폭로하

[SYN] 1. take out; draw out;

다, (색·성질을) 뚜렷이 나타내다 3. (신제품·책을) 시장에 내놓다, 출판하다

I saw the criminal **bringing out** a gun from his pocket.
나는 범인이 호주머니에서 권총을 꺼내는 것을 보았다.
Marriage seems to have **brought out** the better side of him.
결혼에 의해서 그의 좋은 면이 드러난 것 같다.
Her husband intends to **bring out** a new monthly magazine.
그녀의 남편은 새 월간지를 출판하려고 한다.

[SYN] pick out 2. show clearly; make clear; disclose 3. introduce; publish; put on sale

throw away 1. (물건을) 내버리다, (카드놀이에서) (패를) 버리다 2. (…에 돈·일생 등을) 헛되이 쓰다, 낭비하다, 허비하다

It's no good. **Throw** it **away**.
그것은 못 쓰겠다. 갖다 버려라.
The advice was **thrown away** on him.
그에게 해 준 충고는 허사였다.

[SYN] 1. discard; get rid of 2. be wasteful of; waste

all the same / just the same 그렇지만, 그래도 역시

He has some faults, but I like him **all the same**.
그에게는 결점이 있다. 그럼에도 나는 그가 좋다.
He is not rich and has no job now, but I love him **all the same**.
그는 부자도 아니고 현재 직업도 없지만 그래도 나는 그를 사랑한다.

[SYN] nevertheless; anyhow; still

shake up 1. 세게 흔들다, …의 신경을 뒤흔들어 놓다 2. 섬뜩하게 하다, 놀라게 하다

The violent murder **shook up** the small, peaceful town.
참혹한 살인사건이 평온한 소도시를 뒤흔들어 놓았다.
The employees were **shaken up** by the news that a new chairman will come.
종업원들은 신임 사장이 온다는 소식에 놀랐다.

[SYN] 1. wave; disturb; stir up 2. shock; startle

break up 1. (물건이) 박살나다, (배가) 산산조각이 나다, 부수다 2. (회의·군중이) 해산하다, 흩어지다

When spring came, river ice began to **break up**.
봄이 오자 강의 얼음이 깨어지기 시작했다.
The workmen **broke up** the pavement to dig up

[SYN] 1. break into pieces 2. disperse

the pipes under it.
인부들은 보도 밑에 묻힌 관을 드러내기 위해 보도를 부수었다.
When the people began to fight each other, the meeting **broke up**.
사람들이 서로 싸우기 시작하자 회의는 해산되었다.

turn up 1. 모습을 나타내다 2. (사물이) 우연히 나타나다
He **turned up** an hour later.
그는 한 시간이나 지난 뒤에 나타났다.
I fear something extraordinary might **turn up**.
어떤 심상치 않은 일이 일어날까봐 걱정이다.

[SYN] 1. show up; appear 2. occur; happen, especially unexpectedly

something of 얼마간, 조금, 어느 정도, 약간, 다소
There is **something of** uncertainty in it.
그것에는 뭔가 불확실한 데가 있다.
John's mother is **something of** a musician.
존의 어머니는 조금은 알려진 음악가이다.

[SYN] somewhat; more or less

at the risk of …을 걸고, …의 위험을 무릅쓰고
Policemen went to catch the murderer **at the risk of** their lives.
경찰들은 목숨의 위험을 무릅쓰고 살인범을 검거하러 갔다.
He saved me **at the risk of** his own life.
그는 자신의 목숨을 걸고 나를 구해 주었다.

[SYN] in danger of; in the face of danger

be sensible of …을 알아채고 있다
I **am** very **sensible of** your kindness.
나는 당신의 친절을 잘 알고 있습니다.
Ellen **is** not **sensible of** her own defects.
엘렌은 자신의 결점을 알아채지 못한다.

[SYN] be aware of
cf. be sensitive to …에 민감하다 (=susceptible)

in brief 간단하게, 요약하여, 요컨대
In brief, the negotiations were unsuccessful.
요컨대 교섭은 실패했다.
In brief, I want some money.
요컨대 난 돈이 좀 필요하다.

[SYN] briefly; in summary

share out 분배하다, 할당하다
Mother told me to take some cookies and **share** them **out** to the kids.
어머니는 내게 과자를 가지고 가서 아이들에게 나누어 주라고 말씀하셨다.

[SYN] divide up; assign; allot; parcel out

We bought two pizzas and **shared out** among four people.
우리는 피자 두 판을 사서 네 사람이 나누어 먹었다.

as it is 있는 그대로, 그런데 실은, 사실은

[SYN] actually; without changes or improvements

As it is, we are just fooling around wasting time all day.
사실 우리는 하루 종일 빈둥빈둥 시간을 낭비하고 있다.
He tried to keep calm but **as it was** he was in confusion.
그는 냉정하게 있으려고 했지만 실제로는 혼란스러웠다.

build up 1. (부·명성을) 쌓아 올리다 2. (건강을) 증진시키다

[SYN] 1. accumulate wealth or fame 2. improve one's health

He has **built up** an excellent business.
그는 놀라운 사업 실적을 쌓아 올렸다.
The baseball player jogs every morning to **build** his strength **up**.
그 야구 선수는 힘을 강하게 하기 위해 매일 아침 조깅을 한다.

the former ..., the latter ~ / that ... , this ~ 전자는 …, 후자는 ~

[SYN] the one ... the other ~
cf. one thing, another …와 ~는 별개의 것이다
one ... the other ~ 하나는 ... 다른 하나는 ~
some ... others ~ 몇몇 중에 일부를 some이라 하면 나머지는 others

They keep horses and cattle; **the former** for riding, **the latter** for milking.
그들은 말과 소를 키운다. 말은 타기 위함이고 소는 우유를 얻기 위함이다.
Work and play are both necessary to health; **this** gives us recreation, and **that** gives us energy.
일과 놀이는 모두 건강에 필요하다. 놀이는 우리에게 휴식을 주고 일은 우리에게 에너지를 준다.

to the purpose 요령있게, 적절히

[SYN] relevantly; pertinently
cf. to no (little) purpose 전혀 (거의) 헛되이, 아주 (거의) 예상 밖으로 (= with no (little) result (effect))

He talked much **to the purpose**.
그는 말을 매우 요령있게 했다.
His interference was very much **to the purpose**.
그의 개입은 매우 시의적절했다.

to say nothing of …은 말할 것도 없고, …은 제쳐놓고(고사하고), …은 물론

[SYN] not to mention; not to speak of; let alone

He can ski very well, **to say nothing of** tennis.
그는 테니스는 말할 것도 없고 스키도 잘 탄다.
He has no scholarship, **to say nothing of**

experience.
그는 경험은 말할 것도 없고 학식도 없다.

odds and ends (이것저것) 잡동사니, 시시한 것
We moved all our things from one apartment to another, except for a few **odds and ends**.
우리는 몇몇 잡동사니를 제외한 모든 물건을 한 아파트에서 다른 아파트로 옮겼다.
She went to the big supermarket and bought new **odds and ends** for her kitchen.
그녀는 큰 슈퍼마켓에 가서 잡다한 주방 기기를 새로 샀다.

[SYN] a mix of items; bits and pieces

bear out 지지하다, 확인하다, 증명하다
The president will **bear** me **out** in what I propose.
회장은 내가 제의하는 것을 지지해 줄 것이다.
I hope my suspicions that my father is the criminal are not **born out**.
내 아버지가 범인이라는 내 추측이 사실로 증명되지 않기를 바란다.

[SYN] show to be right; support; ascertain; prove

sum up 요약하다
I would like to **sum up** the main reasons for this reform.
이번에 개혁을 하게 된 주요 원인들을 요약해서 설명하고 싶습니다.
The lecturer **summed up** today's speech in three rules.
강사는 오늘 한 연설 내용을 세 가지 규칙으로 요약해서 말했다.

[SYN] summarize; epitomize; digest; condense

at any rate 어쨌든지간에, 여하튼, 하여간
At any rate, I must finish this job.
하여튼 나는 이 일을 끝내야만 한다.
I know it's not much of a car, but **at any rate** it is not expensive.
썩 좋은 차가 아니라는 것은 나도 알지만 아무튼 비싸지는 않다.

[SYN] however; anyhow; in any case

at a distance 조금 떨어져서, 떨어진 곳에
Oil paintings show to advantage **at a distance**.
유화는 좀 떨어져서 보면 한결 낫게 보인다.
We could see a small island **at a distance**.
우리들은 좀 떨어진 곳에 섬이 있는 것을 볼 수 있었다.

[SYN] at some distance
cf. in the distance 멀리서 (=far away)

if any 만일 (조금이라도) 있다면, 비록 있다 하더라도
There is little, **if any**, hope to recover his health.

[SYN] if there is any at all

그의 건강이 회복될 가망이 있다 하더라도 거의 없는 것이나 마찬가지다.
There is little, **if any**, hope.
설사 있다 하더라도 희망은 거의 없다.

to the point 간단명료한, (말 등이) 군더더기가 없는, 적절한

His explanation is very much **to the point**.
그의 설명은 참으로 간단명료하다.
What he says is always terse and **to the point**.
그의 말은 항상 짧고 간단명료하다.

[SYN] to the purpose; relevant

be equipped with …을 갖추고 있다

The ship **is equipped with** many modern facilities.
그 배는 많은 현대적 시설들을 갖추고 있다.
The factory **is equipped with** the most modern machinery.
그 공장은 최신 기계설비가 갖추어져 있다.

[SYN] be completed; be furnished

in company 사람 틈에서, 사람 앞에서

We must behave well **in company**.
다른 사람들과 함께 있을 때는 행동을 잘 해야 한다.
You must be a good boy **in company**.
(남자 아이에게) 사람들 앞에서는 얌전해야 한다.

[SYN] amidst other people

hold on 1. (전화를) 끊지 않고 놔두다 2. 버티어 나가다

Hold on, please.
끊지 말고 기다리세요.
I **held on** and finally succeeded.
나는 계속 버텨내어 결국 성공했다.

[SYN] 1. hold the time; keep the telephone on 2. endure; stand

all the way 내내, 멀리(서)

I was **all the way** with them during the hard times.
나는 어려운 시절 동안 내내 그들과 함께 있었다.
They traveled **all the way** from Los Angeles to New York.
그들은 로스앤젤레스부터 뉴욕까지 멀리 여행했다.

[SYN] from start to finish; during; from the distance
cf. the whole way 내내, 멀리(서)

share A with B A를 B와 나누다

I will **share** my dinner **with** you if you are really hungry.
당신이 정말 배가 고프다면 내 저녁밥을 나누어 주겠다.

[SYN] share or divide something equally

He **shared** his food **with** the poor man.
그는 가난한 사람에게 자기 음식을 나누어 주었다.

too ... not to ~ 몹시 …이기 때문에 ~이다〔하지 않으면 안 된다〕 (이중부정으로 긍정의 뜻)

He is **too** wise **not to** know it.
그는 아주 현명해서 그것을 깨닫고 있다.
(= He is so wise that he cannot but know it.)
He is **too** wise **not to** see it.
그는 아주 현명해서 그것을 알 수 있을 것이다.
(= He is so wise that he can surely see it.)

[SYN.] so ... that cannot but ~

as a rule 대체로, 일반적으로

As a rule, we don't have much snow in winter in Jejudo.
일반적으로 제주도에는 겨울에 눈이 많이 오지 않는다.
I work overtime at least twice a week **as a rule**.
나는 대체로 일주일에 적어도 두 번은 시간외 근무를 한다.

[SYN.] in general; at large; generally; in the main

slow down (자동차 등의) 속력을 떨어뜨리다, 속도를 늦추다

Due to the last night's snow, the road is slippery, so, please **slow down**.
어젯밤에 내린 눈 때문에 도로가 미끄러우니 속도를 늦추십시오.
If you don't **slow down**, you won't be able to digest your food well.
천천히 먹지 않으면 음식을 제대로 소화시킬 수 없을 것이다.

[SYN.] reduce the speed; make slow

be welcome to do something …을 마음대로 해도 좋다

You **are welcome to** use telephone.
전화를 마음대로 써도 됩니다.
I told Jim that he**'s welcome to** join our fishing club whenever he wants to.
나는 짐에게 원한다면 언제든지 우리 낚시 클럽에 들어와도 된다고 말했다.

[SYN.] be free to do something; be allowed to do something

take to 1. …을 좋아하게 되다 2. …에 몰두하다

The students have **taken to** their new teacher.
학생들은 새 선생님을 좋아하게 되었다.
These days, John is **taking to** fishing.
요즘 존은 낚시에 몰두해 있다.

[SYN.] 1. be attracted to; care for; become fond of 2. be absorbed in

as yet 현재까지는, 지금까지는, 아직

The plan is working well **as yet**.
그 계획은 지금까지는 잘 돼 가고 있다.
It has not been successful **as yet**.
지금까지는 성공하지 못했다.

[SYN] until now; so far; up to the present time

starve to death 아사하다, 굶어 죽다

I am afraid that the homeless girl will **starve to death**.
그 집없는 소녀가 굶어 죽을까봐 걱정이 된다.
At last the old man **starved to death**.
마침내 그 노인은 굶어 죽었다.

[SYN] die of hunger; be starved to death

by dint of …에 의해서, …의 힘으로

His success as a writer was purely **by dint of** his natural talent.
작가로서의 그의 성공은 순전히 그의 천부적인 재능 덕분이었다.
By dint of real courage, the war orphan overcame many difficulties of the life.
진정한 용기의 힘으로 그 전쟁 고아는 인생의 많은 어려움들을 극복했다.

[SYN] by the strength of; by the power of; thanks to

in proportion as …에 비례하여, …을 따라서, …에 준하여

Generally speaking, a man will succeed **in proportion as** he perseveres.
일반적으로 말해서 사람은 인내에 비례해서 성공한다.
A man is happy **in proportion as** he is content.
사람은 만족도에 비례해서 행복하다.

[SYN] in proportion to

take pride in …을 자랑하다

He **takes** great **pride in** his ability to fix things.
그는 물건을 고칠 수 있는 자신의 능력을 무척 자랑스러워한다.
She **takes pride in** her skill in cooking.
그녀는 자신의 요리 솜씨를 자랑한다.
(=She prides herself on her skill in cooking.
 =She is proud of her skill in cooking.)

[SYN] make a boast of; be proud of; pride oneself on

at hand 가까이, 가까운 장래에

With the final exam **at hand**, how can you go to the movies tonight?
마지막 시험이 코앞에 닥쳤는데 너는 어떻게 오늘 밤에 영화를 보러

[SYN] in the near future; easy to reach; nearby

갈 수가 있니?
Don't forget to keep a dictionary **at hand** so as to use it when necessary.
필요할 때 사용할 수 있도록 사전을 가까이 두는 것을 잊지 마라.

think nothing of …을 아무렇지 않게 여기다, 얕보다
She seems to **think nothing of** lying.
그녀는 거짓말 하는 것을 아무렇지 않게 여기는 것 같다.
Think nothing of doing shopping for you.
당신 대신 쇼핑해 준 것을 마음에 두지 마세요.

SYN care nothing for; defy; consider something normal, routine; make light of

by the day 일당으로, 하루 단위로
We are paid **by the day** at the construction site.
우리는 공사장에서 일당을 받는다.
He couldn't get a regular job, so he was hired **by the day**.
정규직을 구할 수가 없어서 그는 일용직으로 고용되었다.

SYN on a daily basis; by daily wages

suppy A with B A에게 B를 공급하다
The school **supplies** the students **with** books.
학교는 학생들에게 책을 지급한다.
Sheep **supply** us **with** wool.
양은 우리에게 양털을 공급한다.

SYN provide someone with something; furnish with

at all events 어쨌든, 여하튼지 간에
Tom wasn't bright, but **at all events** he worked hard.
톰은 총명하지는 않았지만 어쨌든 열심히 공부했다.
At all events we must carry out the plan.
어쨌든 우리는 그 계획을 실행해야 한다.

SYN however; in any case

be exposed to …에 노출되다, 드러나다
They **were exposed to** the enemy's gunfire at night.
그들은 밤에는 적의 포화에 노출되어 있었다.
The writer **is exposed to** the ridicule of the public.
그 작가는 세인들의 조롱거리가 되었다.

SYN be disclosed; be bared

in sight 보이는 곳에, 보이는 거리에, 눈 앞에
The war started last year, and there is no end **in sight**.
전쟁은 작년에 시작했는데 끝이 보이지 않는다.

SYN able to be seen; able to see
OPP out of sight 보이지 않는 (= not visible)

The children are nowhere **in sight**.
아이들은 어디에도 보이지 않는다.

take leave of …에게 작별인사를 하다
I **took leave of** them at the door and took a car.
나는 현관에서 그들에게 작별인사를 하고 차를 탔다.
It's time for us to **take leave of** you.
우리가 여러분과 작별해야 할 때가 되었다.

[SYN] say good-bye to

show off 자랑해 보이다, 과시하다
He attended the meeting to **show off** her fine clothes.
그는 자신의 멋진 옷을 자랑하기 위해 회의에 참석했다.
She **showed off** her ruby ring when she met two friends for dinner.
그녀는 저녁식사를 하기 위해 만난 두 친구에게 자신의 루비 반지를 자랑했다.

[SYN] make a display of; parade

at the cost of …을 희생하고
The rescuer saved a little boy from the fire **at the cost of** his own life.
구조대원은 자신의 생명을 희생해서 화재로부터 어린 소년을 구했다.
The scientist developed a new medicine **at the cost of** his health.
그 과학자는 자신의 건강을 희생시켜 신약을 개발했다.

[SYN] at the price of; at the expense of

a rainy day 궁한 시기, 만일의 경우
You must save money for **a rainy day**.
너는 만일의 경우를 대비하여 저축을 해야 한다.
If you put aside little by little, you will not have to worry about **rainy days**.
조금씩 저축해 놓으면 궁핍하게 되더라도 걱정할 필요가 없을 것이다.

[SYN] a time of need, especially a time when one really needs money

that is (to say) 다시 말하면, 즉
My father was born in 1945, **that is to say**, when World War II ended.
아버지는 2차 세계대전이 종식되던 해인 1945년에 태어나셨다.
The budget, **that is to say**, the 2005 budget, is still under consideration.
예산, 즉 2005년 예산은 아직 검토 중이다.

[SYN] in other words; namely

in the main 대개는, 대체로

[SYN] in most cases; generally;

In the main, kids like small dogs.
대개 아이들은 조그만 개를 좋아한다.
In the main, the participants did well in the singing contest.
대체로 참가자들은 노래 경연대회에서 잘 했다.

usually

be bound to 틀림없이 …하다, …하지 않을 수 없다, 꼭 …하다

He **is bound to** come here.
그는 꼭 여기에 와야 한다.
Everybody **is bound to** obey the laws.
모든 사람은 법률에 따라야만 한다.

SYN be certain to; be impelled to; be compelled to; be constrained to

as such 그와 같은 것으로서, 그러한 자격에 있어서

He is a child, and must be treated **as such**.
그는 어린아이니까 어린아이로 취급돼야 한다.
You are a lady and you can expect to be treated **as such**.
당신은 숙녀이므로 숙녀 대우 받기를 기대해도 좋다.

SYN in that particular capacity, manner, form or function

sit up 1. (밤 늦게까지) 자지 않고 있다 2. 일어나 앉다, 단정히 앉다

My mother will **sit up** until I get home from the dance party.
어머니는 내가 댄스파티를 마치고 집에 올 때까지 주무시지 않고 나를 기다리실 것이다.
The doctor **sat up** all night with the sick man.
의사는 병든 사람과 함께 밤을 새웠다.

SYN 1. not sleep till late at night 2. rise to a sitting position; sit erect

answer for …을 책임지다, …을 보증하다

Do you expect me to **answer for** the accident?
내가 그 사고의 책임을 져야 한다고 생각하십니까?
Please give him a job, as I will **answer for** his sincerity and ability.
그에게 일자리를 주세요. 그의 성실성과 능력은 제가 보증하겠습니다.

SYN be responsible for; guarantee

inside out 1. 뒤집어서, 안팎으로 2. 철저하게, 완전히

For some reason John had put his sweater on **inside out**.
웬일인지 존은 스웨터를 뒤집어 입었다.
I searched the village **inside out** for the dog.
나는 개를 찾으러 마을을 구석구석 다 돌아다녔다.

SYN 1. so that the inside is turned outside 2. in every part; throughout; completely
cf. upside down 거꾸로

take away 1. …을 제거하다, 없애다 2. 효과를 줄이다

Two of his children were **taken away** by the recent flood.
최근의 홍수로 그는 아이들 중 둘을 잃었다.
The bad news **took away** my appetite.
그 나쁜 소식을 들으니 식욕이 사라졌다.

SYN 1. remove; get rid of; withdraw 2. reduce the effect of something

wake up 1. (정신적으로) 깨닫게 하다, 눈뜨게 하다, 분발시키다 2. 잠에서 깨게 하다, 일어나게 하다

We've got to **wake** him **up** from his laziness.
그를 나태로부터 벗어나 분발토록 해야 한다.
I asked mother to **wake** me **up** at five.
나는 어머니에게 다섯 시에 깨워달라고 했다.

SYN 1. make someone realize; open someone's eyes to 2. make someone awake; rouse from sleep

at once A and B A이기도 하고 B이기도 하다

She was **at once** beautiful **and** intelligent.
그녀는 아름다우면서 동시에 지적이다.
They are **at once** wise **and** kind-hearted.
그들은 현명할 뿐 아니라 다정하다.
(=They are both wise and kind-hearted.
=They are alike wise and kind-hearted.
=They are kind-hearted as well as wise.)

SYN both A and B; alike A and B

by virtue of …의 힘으로, …의 덕택에, …에 의하여

By virtue of the position he holds, he can move about freely.
지위 덕분에 그는 자유롭게 돌아다닐 수 있다.
By virtue of frugality he has made a fortune.
검소함으로 그는 큰 재산을 만들었다.

SYN by dint of; thanks to

to the letter 정확하게, 엄밀히, 자세히, 문자 그대로

When writing a test, you are required to follow some rules **to the letter**.
시험을 치를 때는 몇 가지 규칙을 그대로 따라야 한다.
If you give Tom an order, he will carry it out **to the letter**.
톰에게 어떤 지시를 하면 그는 그대로 할 것이다.

SYN just as written or directed; precisely; literally

at one's best 활짝 피어, 가장 좋은 상태에서

When we visited the national park, cherry blossoms were **at their best**.
우리가 국립공원에 갔을 때는 벚꽃이 만발해 있었다.

SYN at one's peak; at one's highest point

German literature was **at its best** in the beginning of the 19th century.
독일 문학은 19세기 초가 전성기였다.

watch over 지키다, 경호하다

[SYN] guard; take care of

Don't worry. God will **watch over** us.
걱정하지 말아라. 하나님이 우리를 지켜 주실 것이다.
Would you **watch over** my kids tonight?
오늘 밤 우리 아이들 좀 보살펴 주시겠어요?

at home 1. 편히 2. 집에서, 본국에

[SYN] 2. in the place where one lives or comes from

Why are you standing there? Make yourself **at home**, please.
왜 그 곳에 서 있는 거야? 편하게 있어.
The artist is very popular **at home** and abroad.
그 예술가는 국내외에서 인기가 매우 높다.

peculiar to …에 특유한, 고유의, 독특한

[SYN] characteristic; unique; special; original

Language is **peculiar to** mankind.
언어는 인간 특유의 것이다.
The construction style is **peculiar to** the 18th century.
그 건축 형식은 18세기 특유의 것이다.

in honor of …에게 경의를 표하여, …을 기념하여

[SYN] as an honor to
cf. in memory of …을 기념하여

They gave a dinner **in honor of** the great scholar.
그들은 그 위대한 학자에 경의를 표하고자 만찬회를 가졌다.
A party was given **in honor of** Mr. Tracy.
트레이시 씨를 축하하기 위해 파티가 열렸다.

together with …와 함께, 더불어, …도

[SYN] in addition to; in the company of; along with

Nancy went to the party **together with** her mother.
낸시는 어머니와 함께 파티에 갔다.
The police found a gun, **together with** the dead body, hidden in the forest.
경찰은 시신과 더불어 숲속에 숨겨진 권총을 발견했다.

be free from …이 없다, …을 면제받다

[SYN] be saved from; escaped from
cf. be free of …이 없다, …이 면제돼 있다 (= be exempted

John **is**, by nature, **free from** pecuniary anxiety.
존은 천성적으로 돈에 대한 걱정이 없다.
He **is free from** the duty of military service.

그는 군 복무 의무를 면제받았다. | from)

at random 닥치는 대로, 되는 대로, 함부로, 임의로
I picked 20 people **at random** for the survey.
나는 조사를 위해서 임의로 스무 명을 골랐다.
He called the students **at random**.
그는 학생들을 닥치는 대로 지적했다.

[SYN] with no order or plan or purpose

to some extent / to a certain extent 어느 정도(까지는)
The violence of the storm lulled **to some extent**.
사나운 폭풍우는 어느 정도 가라앉았다.
To some extent I agree with you.
어느 정도는 너에게 동의한다.

[SYN] in some measure; to some degree

at the foot of …의 기슭에, …의 아래쪽에
The orphanage is located **at the foot of** a scenic hill.
고아원은 경치 좋은 언덕 기슭에 있다.
The chairman's villa was **at the foot of** a mountain.
회장의 빌라는 산기슭에 있었다.

[SYN] at the downside of

part from+사람 사람과 헤어지다
I **parted from** my friends at the station.
나는 역에서 친구들과 헤어졌다.
I **parted from** her at Busan last year.
그녀와는 작년에 부산에서 헤어졌다.

[SYN] separate; part company with
cf. part A from B B에서 A를 분리하다
part with+사물 사물을 내놓다

suitable for …에 적합한, 어울리는, 알맞은
The book, written in an easy style, is **suitable for** children.
그 책은 쉬운 문체로 씌어 있기 때문에 어린이들에게 적합하다.
You should wear clothes **suitable for** the occasion.
당신은 경우에 적합한 옷을 입어야 한다.

[SYN] appropriate; fitting; apt

warn+사람+of〔against〕 사람에게 …에 대하여 경고하다〔주의시키다〕
He **warned** me **of** their evil plot.
그는 그들에게 무서운 흉계가 있다고 나에게 경고했다.
Birds attract each other's attention by **warning of** danger.
새들은 서로서로 위험을 경고하여 주의를 끈다.

[SYN] give warning on; admonish

at peace 평화롭게, 마음 편히, 사이좋게

We are now **at peace** with all the nations of the world.
우리들은 지금 세계의 여러 국민들과 평화롭게 살고 있다.
Now her mind is **at peace** because her son passed the college exam.
아들이 대학 시험에 합격하여 이제 그녀의 마음이 편하다.

[SYN] peacefully; in a state of friendship

be true to …에 충실하다

He **is** always **true to** his word.
그는 언제나 자신의 말에 충실하다.
The translation **is** quite **true to** the original.
그 번역은 원문에 꽤 충실하다.

[SYN] be faithful to
cf. be true of …의 경우에 들어맞다, …에 해당하다 (= be applicable to)

some or other(s) 1. 무언가 2. 누군가 3. 어딘가

Some man **or other** spoke to me on the street.
거리에서 누군가가 내게 말을 걸었다.
Some bunch of idiots **or others** have done it.
누군가 바보들이 그 짓을 했다.

[SYN] 1. what; what kind of 2. somebody 3. somewhere; somehow

twice as ... as 배의

The house rent is **twice as** high **as** three years ago.
집세는 3년 전보다 배가 올랐다.

at work 일을 하고, 작업 중인, 작동 중인

He got hurt **at work** at the construction site.
그는 공사장에서 작업 중에 부상을 입었다.
He was **at work** till late at night.
그는 밤 늦게까지 일을 하고 있었다.

[SYN] busy at a job; doing work

abide by (규칙·결정 등에) 따라 행동하다, 지키다, 고수하다

The citizens must **abide by** the national law.
시민들은 국법을 따라야 한다.
You had better **abide by** your resolution whatever may happen.
무슨 일이 생기더라도 네 결심을 고수하는 것이 좋다.

[SYN] follow; agree to accept a rule or decision
cf. abide with …와 동거하다, …에 머물다 (= live(stay) with)

at times / at intervals 때때로, 가끔

At times he behaves like an alien, and then he seems a stranger to me.

[SYN] now and then; not often
cf. between times 때때로, 틈틈이 (= sometimes; now and

가끔 그는 이방인처럼 행동해서 낯선 사람처럼 느껴질 때가 있다.
I feel my husband as my dead father **at times**.
때때로 남편이 돌아가신 아버지처럼 느껴질 때가 있다.

then)

according as …에 의하면, …에 따라서

We see things differently, **according as** we are rich or poor.
우리는 우리가 부자인가 가난한가에 따라서 사물을 달리 본다.
You may either go or stay, **according as** you decide.
결심여하에 따라 가도 되고 안 가도 된다.

SYN. in proportion as; to the degree that

turn to advantage 이용하다, 이롭게〔유리하게〕하다

We must **turn** this situation **to our advantage**.
우리는 현 상황을 우리에게 이롭게 만들어야 한다.
The umbrella store owner could **turn** the rainy season **to his advantage**.
우산 가게 주인은 우기를 이용하여 돈을 벌 수 있었다.

SYN. make use of; put to good use of; turn to account

breathe one's last 마지막 숨을 거두다, 죽다

My grandfather **breathed his last** at four o'clock in the morning.
할아버지께서는 오전 4시에 돌아가셨다.
After lying in bed for a long time, grandmother **breathed her last** yesterday.
오랫동안 누워 계신 후 할머니께서는 어제 돌아가셨다.

SYN. die; pass by

in favor of …에 찬성하여, …의 이익이 되도록

They are **in favor of** your plan with a unanimous approval.
그들은 만장일치로 당신의 계획에 찬성하고 있다.
All the students are **in favor of** postponing the exams.
모든 학생들은 시험을 연기하는 것에 찬성이다.

SYN. on the side of; in support of

wind up 1. 태엽을 감다 2. (보통 수동태) 흥분시키다, 긴장시키다

I **wind up** the grandfather's clock once a week.
나는 일주일에 한 번씩 할아버지 시계 태엽을 감는다.
He was all **wound up** before the game.
그는 경기 전에 완전히 얼어 있었다.

SYN. 1. turn and tighten; crank 2. make someone very tense, nervous, excited

be contented with ···에 만족하고 있다

He **is contented with** his present situation.
그는 현재의 상황에 만족하고 있다.
He can never **be contented with** it.
그는 결코 그것에 만족하지 못한다.

[SYN] be satisfied with

at large 1. 자세히, 상세히 2. 일반적으로 3. 자유롭게, 붙잡히지 않고

Please describe **at large**.
좀 자세하게 진술하시오.
The people **at large** are against war.
일반 대중은 전쟁에 반대하고 있다.
The murderer is still **at large**.
그 살인범은 아직 잡히지 않았다.

[SYN] 1. at full length; in detail; at length; minutely 2. in general; as a whole; on the whole 3. escaping; fleeing; not kept within walls; free

take the place of ···을 대신하다, 대리하다

He will **take the place of** the mathematics teacher.
그는 수학선생님을 대신할 것이다.
The sewing machine **took the place of** women's hand.
미싱은 부인들의 손을 대신했다.

[SYN] take one's place; replace

be subjected to ···을 받다; ···을 당하다, ···에 시달리다

Anyone who has violated this rule shall **be subjected to** severe punishment.
누구든 이 규칙을 위반하는 사람은 엄벌에 처해질 것이다.
They **were subjected to** unfair treatment.
그들은 부당한 대우를 받았다.

[SYN] be confronted by; be caught in

allow for ···을 참작하다, 고려하다

You must **allow for** his youth.
당신은 그의 젊음을 고려해야 한다.
Although he is a robber, we must **allow for** his poverty.
비록 그가 도둑이긴 하지만 우리는 그의 가난을 참작해야 한다.

[SYN] take into account; take into consideration
cf. allow to 허락하다, 인정하다 (= admit; permit; tolerate)

be proficient in ···에 숙달하다, ···에 능숙하다

He **is proficient in** using the guns.
그는 총을 능숙하게 다룬다.
As he lived in the States for 10 years, he **is**

[SYN] be skilled in; be good at

proficient in English.
그는 10년 동안 미국에서 살아서 영어에 능숙하다.

tie up 1. 단단히 묶다, 고정하다 2. (교통을 파업 등으로) 통하지 못하게 하다 3. (보통 수동태) 꼼짝 못하게 되다

I **tied up** old newspapers and put them outside for recycling.
지나간 신문들을 묶어서 재활용을 위해 밖에 내놓았다.
All the traffic was **tied up** by the snow storm.
눈보라로 모든 교통이 두절됐다.
We were **tied up** in conference yesterday.
어제는 회의 때문에 꼼짝할 수가 없었다.

[SYN] 1. bind; fasten together 2. block 3. be held with no way out

apply for …에 신청하다, 지원하다, 부탁하다

I made up my mind to **apply for** scholarship.
나는 장학금을 신청하기로 결심했다.
Why didn't you **apply for** the job? This is a rare opportunity for you.
왜 그 일자리에 지원하지 않았니? 이것은 네게 드문 기회인데.

[SYN] ask for; go in for; seek for; make application (for)

grow up 자라다

He **grew up** in a small village near the lake.
그는 호수 근처 조그만 마을에서 자랐다.
John **grew up** to be a scientist.
존은 자라서 과학자가 되었다.

[SYN] increase in size or height; become taller or older

attend to …에 신경 쓰다, …에 주의하다, …에 유의하다

You have to **attend to** your lessons.
너는 네 학업에 신경 써야 한다.
Please see to it that all things are **attended to**.
모든 일에 주의가 가도록 마음을 써 주세요.

[SYN] pay attention to; give heed to
cf. attend on(upon) 시중들다, 간호하다, 수행하다, 섬기다

aim at …을 노리다, 겨냥하다, …을 목표로 하다

As a photographer, he **aims at** winning the Pulitzer Prize.
사진작가로서 그는 퓰리처상 수상을 목표로 하고 있다.
You must **aim at** the proper target from the start.
너는 처음부터 올바른 표적을 겨냥해야만 한다.

[SYN] set a goal of; set one's sights on

ten to one 십중팔구, 틀림없이

Ten to one you will win the election.

[SYN] in nine cases out of ten; nine-tenths; almost; nearly

선거에서 네가 이길 것이 거의 확실하다.
Ten to one he will arrive late.
십중팔구 그는 늦을 것이다.

take advantage of 1. …을 이용하다, …의 틈을 타다 2. 속이다, …을 유혹하다

They escaped by **taking advantage of** disturbance.
그들은 소란한 틈을 타 도망쳤다.
The salesperson **took advantage of** me by charging too much.
판매원은 나에게 바가지를 씌웠다.

SYN. 1. use an opportunity; make use of for one's own benefit 2. cheat; exploit; tempt; entice

(it is) no wonder (that) ... …하는 것은 당연하다

It is no wonder he has failed in the business.
그가 사업에 실패한 것은 조금도 이상하지 않다.
No wonder he didn't come.
그가 오지 않은 것도 무리는 아니다.

SYN. take for granted; take as a matter of course

start up 1. 작동하다 2. (일·사업을) 시작하다 3. 마음에 떠오르다

He **started up** the motor of the car.
그는 자동차 모터를 가동시켰다.
He **started up** his company last year.
그는 작년에 회사를 시작했다.
A new idea has **started up** and I wrote it down not to forget.
새로운 생각이 떠올라서 나는 잊지 않기 위해 써 두었다.

SYN. 1. turn on an engine; function; operate 2. begin something; start an enterprise 3. occur to; hit upon

pass for (as) …으로 통하다, …으로 간주되다

Among his friends, Bill **passes for** a gentleman.
친구들 사이에서 빌은 신사로 통한다.
Judging from your accent, you could **pass for** an Englishman.
액센트로 판단하면 너는 영국 사람으로 생각될 정도다.

SYN. look like; seem to be; be known as

be alive to …에 민감하다, …을 눈치채다, 꿰고 있다, 통달하다

He **is alive to** interests.
그는 사리(私利)에 밝다.
She **is alive to** pain.
그녀는 고통에 민감하다.

SYN. be completely aware of; be tactful

bear fruit 열매를 맺다, (노력 등이) 결실을 보다
This plum **bears fruit** every other year.
이 자두나무는 한 해 걸러서 열매를 맺는다.
The general public expected the president's economic reform to **bear fruit**.
국민들은 대통령의 경제 개혁이 좋은 성과를 가져올 것으로 기대했다.

SYN produce something; produce a result

take one's place 자리잡다, 착석하다
Everybody, **take your place** at the table.
모두 식탁에 앉아 주십시오.
If all of you **take your place**, the meeting will begin.
모두 착석하면 회의를 시작할 것이다.

SYN take one's seat; sit down

take turns 교대로 하다, 번갈아 …하다, 차례대로 하다
He and his wife **take turns** washing the dishes.
그와 그의 아내는 교대로 설거지를 한다.
Susan and her sister **took turns** at looking after her sick mother.
수잔 자매는 병든 어머니를 번갈아 돌보았다.

SYN act in sequence

to one's disappointment 유감스럽게도, 낙심천만하게도
To our disappointment, the picnic was canceled.
유감스럽게도 소풍이 취소됐다.
To my disappointment, the book was out of print.
실망스럽게도 그 책은 절판이었다.

SYN to one's regret

abound in (with) …이 풍부하다
The sea **abounds in** diverse fish.
그 바다에는 다양한 물고기가 풍부하다.
Some parts of the nation **abound in** minerals.
그 나라의 일부 지역들은 광물이 풍부하다.

SYN be rich in; be affluent in

and that 더욱이, 그것도, 게다가
My brother can play violin, **and that** like an expert.
내 남동생은 바이올린을 켤 줄 안다. 그것도 마치 전문가처럼.
He gave me a phone call, **and that** in the middle of the night.
그는 나에게 전화를 걸었다. 그것도 한밤중에.

SYN furthermore; in addition

it will not be long before 머지않아, 곧
It will not be long before he comes.
그는 곧 올 것이다.
(=He will come soon.)
It will not be long before the rainy season sets in.
곧 장마철에 접어들 것이다.
(=The rainy season will come before long.)

[SYN] soon; before long; by and by

in private 비밀히, 비공식적으로, 사생활에 있어
I told him **in private** yesterday morning.
나는 어제 아침 그에게 비밀히 말했다.
The boss said he had something to talk to me **in private**.
사장은 내게 비공식적으로 할 말이 있다고 말했다.

[SYN] secretly; in secret; in confidence

as for …에 대하여 말하면, …에 관해서는
As for me, I would like to visit Paris this winter with her.
나로서는 이번 겨울 그녀와 함께 파리에 가 보고 싶다.
As for the agenda of the meeting, we can decide tomorrow.
회의 안건에 대해서는 내일 결정해도 된다.

[SYN] concerning; to say about; in regard to; speaking of; concerning
cf. as to …에 관해서, …에 대해서 (= about, regarding)

so ... as to ~ 1. ~할 만큼 …한(하게) 2. ~하게도 …하다
He is not **so** foolish **as to** believe it.
그는 그것을 믿을 만큼 그렇게 어리석지 않다.
(=He is not such a fool as to believe it.)
He was **so** fortunate **as to** pass the examination.
그는 운 좋게 시험에 합격했다.

[SYN] 1. so ... that; enough to 2. enough ... to

at the beginning of …의 초에, 최초에, 맨처음에
He left for America **at the beginning of** this year.
그는 금년 초에 미국으로 떠났다.
The film festival will take place **at the beginning of** next month.
영화제는 내달 초에 열릴 것이다.

[SYN] in the early part of; early

put ... together 1. 조립하다, 짜맞추다 2. (생각 등을) 한 데 모으다, 종합하다, 정리하다
We followed the direction but could not **put** the

[SYN] 1. fix up; frame; assemble 2. concentrate one's strength on

machine **together**.
우리는 설명대로 했지만 기계를 조립할 수 없었다.
They **put** their heads **together** to settle the complicated situation.
그들은 복잡한 상황을 해결하기 위해 이마를 맞대었다.

take off 1. (옷·모자·신 등을) 벗다 2. 이륙하다

She has **taken off** her overcoat because she felt too warm.
너무 따뜻하다고 느꼈기 때문에 그녀는 외투를 벗었다.
The airplane **took off** at 11:20 a.m.
비행기는 오전 11시 20분에 이륙했다.

SYN 1. get out of one's clothes; strip oneself; remove one's hat 2. leave the ground; rise in the air
OPP put on 옷을 입다

avail oneself of …을 이용하다

You had better **avail yourself of** this opportunity.
이 기회를 이용하는 편이 좋다.
I **availed myself of** a holiday to visit him.
나는 휴일을 이용하여 그를 방문했다.

SYN take advantage of; make use of; utilize; exploit

in addition (to) (…에) 더하여, …외에, 게다가

The taxi driver drove recklessly; **in addition** the cab was very dirty.
그 택시 운전사는 무모하게 운전했다. 게다가 그 차는 매우 더러웠다.
Father bought me a dress and a pair of shoes **in addition**.
아버지께서 내게 양복을 사 주시고 게다가 구두도 사 주셨다.

SYN besides; as well as; moreover
cf. in addition to …뿐만 아니라

along with …와 함께, 더불어

Put the box there **along with** others.
다른 것들과 함께 그 상자를 거기 두어라.
The group of people came **along with** us.
그 그룹도 우리와 함께 왔다.

SYN together; in company with; with

tire out 녹초가 되게 하다, 지치게 하다

The continued night duty **tired** me **out**.
계속된 야근으로 나는 녹초가 됐다.
My wife's never-ending chattering **tired** the guests **out**.
아내의 끊임없는 수다는 손님들을 지치게 만들었다.

SYN make someone very tired

speak of …에 관하여 말(평)하다, …이라는 말을(용어를) 쓰다

SYN talk about; comment on

Is this the book you **spoke of** the other day?
이 책이 요전날 네가 말하던 그 책이니?
Language is often **spoken of** as a living organism.
언어는 종종 살아 있는 유기체라고 일컬어진다.

take on 1. 떠맡다 2. 고용하다, 채용하다 3. (성질을) 띠다

He asked me to **take on** a project developing a new overseas market.
그는 나에게 새로운 해외 시장 개발 프로젝트를 맡으라고 말했다.
I hear you've **taken on** 20 new workers.
현장 작업원을 20명 새로 고용했다고 들었습니다.
Many people joined the fist fight and it began to **take on** the look of a riot.
많은 사람들이 주먹 다툼에 가담하여 폭동의 양상을 띠기 시작했다.

[SYN] 1. undertake; assume; bear the responsibility 2. hire; employ; take someone into service 3. assume; put on

as much as ⋯만큼, 마찬가지로, 비록

She loves you **as much as** she does her son.
그녀는 자기 아들을 사랑하는 만큼 너를 사랑한다.
As much as I hate to do it, I must go to the library and study overnight.
하긴 싫지만 나는 도서관에 가서 밤을 새워 공부해야 한다

[SYN] although; even though; alike; as ... as
cf. half as much as 그 절반 정도

ask for 간청하다, 요구하다, 자청하다

My father **asked for** my opinion regarding my sister's marriage.
아버지는 누이의 결혼 문제에 대한 내 의견을 물어 보셨다.
When you were very busy, Frank was **asking for** you on the phone.
네가 아주 바쁠 때 프랭크가 전화로 너를 바꿔 달라고 했어.

[SYN] demand; beg
cf. ask to 부탁하다 (= beg, make (a person) a request), 초대를 받다 (수동태)

in the air 1. (소문 등이) 퍼져 2. 미결의

There's another rumor **in the air** that the firm is going into bankruptcy.
그 회사가 도산하게 될 것이라는 소문도 퍼져있다.
Our plans are still **in the air**.
우리 계획은 아직 미정이다.

[SYN] 1. prevailed; spread 2. unsettled; undecided
cf. on the air 생방송 중에, 방송되어

as it happened 마침, 공교롭게도

As it happened, we took the same bus yesterday morning.
우연히 우리들은 어제 아침 같은 버스를 탔다.

[SYN] be coincidence; by chance; as chance will have it

As it happened, no one was in the house when the fire started.
불이 났을 때 공교롭게도 집에는 아무도 없었다.

to make matters worse 설상가상으로, 엎친 데 덮친 격으로

[SYN] what is worse

To make matters worse, it began to rain.
설상가상으로 비가 오기 시작했다.
To make matters worse, I was robbed of my purse.
설상가상으로 나는 지갑을 도난당했다.

at the end of 마지막에, 다해서

[SYN] finally; at the last point

When she was **at the end of** her patience, the bus came.
그녀의 인내심이 막바지에 이르렀을 때 버스가 왔다.
My father's birthday comes **at the end of** the year.
아버지 생신은 연말이다.

take up 시작하다, 착수하다

[SYN] begin; commence; launch

My wife is thinking of **taking up** aerobics.
아내는 에어로빅을 시작할 생각을 하고 있다.
I am going to **take** the business **up** with him.
나는 그와 사업을 시작하려고 한다.

set sail 항해를 시작하다, 출항하다

[SYN] begin a sea voyage; start sailing

The ship carrying over 200 passengers **set sail** for Europe.
200명이 넘는 승객을 태운 배는 유럽으로 항해를 시작했다.
A few ships **set sail** before dawn.
배 몇 척이 새벽이 되기도 전에 출항했다.

inquire into …을 조사하다

[SYN] look into; investigate
cf. inquire after …의 안부를 묻다

The police **inquired into** his past.
경찰은 그의 경력을 조사했다.

to the minute 1분도 틀리지 않고, 정각에

[SYN] at the appointed hour (time); just (right) on time

The train left at five o'clock **to the minute**.
기차는 5시 정각에 떠났다.
She always keeps appointments **to the minute**.
그녀는 늘 약속 시간을 정확히 지킨다.

amount to (총계) …가 되다, …에 달하다, …에 해당하다

When his father died, the debt of the family **amounted to** $10,000.
그의 아버지가 돌아가셨을 때 가족의 부채는 만 달러에 이르렀다.
His debts **amount to** a considerable sum.
그가 빚진 돈은 상당한 액수에 달한다.

SYN. total; correspond to; add up to

at leisure 한가한, 시간이 있는, 일이 없는

If you are **at leisure**, would you help me with the mathematics?
시간이 있으면 수학 좀 도와 주겠니?
There is no need to rush that report, so you can write it **at leisure**.
그 보고서는 급히 서두르지 않아도 되는 것이니까 한가한 시간에 써도 된다.

SYN. not at work; not busy

in one's presence 면전에서

Don't talk about it **in Mike's presence**.
마이크 앞에서 그것에 관해 말하지 마라.
The accident happened **in my presence**.
그 사고는 내 면전에서 일어났다.

SYN. in the presence of
cf. to one's face …의 면전에서, 노골적으로 (= frankly; openly)
behind one's back 등뒤에서 (= at the back of)

suffer from 1. …을 앓다, (병 등에) 걸리다, 병들다 2. 괴로워 하다, 고민하다

She has **suffered from** arthritis for many years.
그녀는 여러 해 동안 관절염을 앓고 있다.
The residents of the apartment complex are **suffering from** lack of water.
그 아파트 단지 주민들은 물 부족으로 고생하고 있다.

SYN. 1. be ill with something usually over a long period of time 2. feel pain; be in agony

hold up 1. 위로 쳐들다, 올리다 2. 지탱하다, 버티다

The pupil **held up** his hand to ask a question.
학생이 질문하기 위해 손을 들었다.
The tiny chair can't **hold up** your grandmother.
그 조그만 의자는 할머니를 지탱할 수 없다.

SYN. 1. raise; lift up; send up; put up 2. support; bear up; stand out

amuse oneself with [by] (…을 하며) 즐기다

On Sundays, I **amuse myself with** watching TV.
일요일이면 나는 TV를 보면서 즐긴다.
I **amuse myself with** reading all day long.
나는 온종일 독서를 낙으로 삼고 있다.

SYN. enjoy oneself with

short of ···이 부족한
We are **short of** both food and water.
우리는 식량과 물 모두 부족하다.
We are **short of** hands.
일손이 모자란다.

[SYN] insufficient; deficient; short; wanting

attend on〔upon〕 시중들다, 간호하다, 섬기다, 수행하다
He has only one servant to **attend on** him.
그는 자신을 시중들 하인을 한 명만 데리고 있다.
There's no sign of recovering, I must **attend on** my mother day and night.
회복할 기미가 보이지 않으므로 나는 어머니를 밤낮으로 간호해야 한다.

[SYN] serve; wait on; take care of

here and now 1. (부사적) 지금 당장에, 즉시, 곧 2. (명사적) 지금 당장, 오늘
I want my book and I want it **here and now**.
내 책을 당장 줘.
I enjoy the pleasures of the **here and now**, and never think about tomorrow.
나는 당장의 즐거움에 빠져 있으며 내일 생각은 절대로 하지 않는다.

[SYN] 1. at this very time and place; right now; immediately 2. the present time and place; today
cf. then and there 그 자리에서, 즉시 (= here and then; at that moment)

vote against ···에 반대 투표하다
If you **vote against** me, I won't see you again.
나에게 반대 투표를 하면 다시는 너를 보지 않겠다.
Most members **voted against** the new membership rule.
대부분 회원들은 새로운 회원 규칙에 반대표를 던졌다.

[SYN] ballot against

kill oneself 자살하다
The girl tried to **kill herself** again.
소녀는 또 다시 자살을 기도했다.
The man who lost his job finally **killed himself** by jumping into the river.
직장을 잃은 남자는 마침내 강물에 뛰어 들어 자살했다.

[SYN] do away with oneself; put an end to one's own life

day in and day out 계속해서, 날이면 날마다, 언제나, 오늘도 내일도
He plays tennis **day in and day out**.
그는 날마다 테니스를 친다.
I go to the library **day in and day out**.

[SYN] continuously; every day; always; day after day

나는 날이면 날마다 도서관에 간다.

essential to …에 필수불가결한, …에 없어서는 안 되는
Impartiality is absolutely **essential to** a judge.
법관에게는 공평무사가 절대 필요하다.
Tolerance is absolutely **essential to** the success of democracy.
관용은 민주주의의 성공에 절대적인 요소이다.

[SYN] indispensable; requisite; necessary; all-important

come of age 성년이 되다, 법적으로 성년이 되다
When Max **comes of age**, he will run the company.
성년이 되면 맥스는 그 회사를 경영하게 될 것이다.
When you **come of age**, your parents won't be able to oppose to your marriage with him.
네가 성년이 되면 부모들도 네가 그와 결혼하는 것을 반대하지 못할 것이다.

[SYN] become an adult

pass on [upon] 1. 다음으로 넘어가다, 주다 2. 죽다
Read the paper and **pass** it **on**.
서류를 읽고 다음 페이지로 넘기세요.
The poor old lady **passed on** alone at her home.
가엾은 노부인은 집에서 혼자 숨을 거두었다.

[SYN] 1. allot; assign; give 2. die; lose one's life

one …, the other ~ 한쪽[편]은 …, 다른 쪽[편]은 ~
Both my sisters went abroad, **one** is in America, **the other** in England.
누이 둘 다 외국으로 갔는데 한 명은 미국에 있고 다른 한 명은 영국에 있다.
There are two doctors among his friends; **one** is a surgeon, and **the other** an eye doctor.
그의 친구 중에는 의사가 둘 있는데 한 사람은 외과 의사이고 다른 사람은 안과 의사이다.

[SYN] on the one hand …, on the other hand ~

opposed to …에 반대하는, 대립하는
Most population are **opposed to** the death penalty system.
대부분 국민들은 사형제도에 반대한다.
Love is **opposed to** hate.
사랑은 미움의 반대이다.

[SYN] object to; taking an active position against

correspond with …과 일치하다, 서신교환하다

[SYN] agree; communicate

Your actions do not **correspond with** your words.
너의 행동은 너의 말과 일치하지 않는다.
He earnestly wishes to **correspond with** her.
그는 그녀와의 서신왕래를 열렬히 바라고 있다.

cf. correspond to …에 상당하다 (=answer to)

gaze at 빤히 쳐다보다, 응시하다
In the darkness, John was **gazing at** someone approaching him.
어둠 속에서 존은 그를 향해 다가오는 사람을 빤히 쳐다보고 있었다.
Mary was sitting on a bench, **gazing at** the horizon.
메리는 벤치에 앉아서 수평선을 응시하고 있었다.

SYN fix on; fix upon

go for 1. 가지러 가다, 부르러 가다 2. 얻으려고 애쓰다
We should have **gone for** a doctor.
우리는 의사를 부르러 갔어야 했다.
These days many young people are **going for** a job.
요즘 많은 젊은이들이 취업하려고 애쓰고 있다.

SYN 1. bring for; send for 2. try to obtain; aim for; try for

major in …을 전공하다
Despite my parents' opposition, I decided to **major in** theology.
부모님의 반대에도 불구하고 나는 신학을 전공하기로 결정했다.
Those who **majored in** English tend to get a job easily.
영어 전공자들은 취직하기가 쉽다.

SYN specialize in

keep company 사귀다, 동석하다
You should not **keep company** with such a bad guy.
그런 나쁜 사람과 사귀면 안 된다.
My daughter **keeps company** with a promising, young lawyer.
내 딸은 장래성 있고 젊은 법률가와 교제한다.

SYN make friends; become acquainted; associate; have relations

mind one's own business 자기 일에만 신경 쓰다
You **mind your own business** and stay out of mine!
넌 네 일에나 신경 쓰고 나에게 상관하지 마!
Mind your own business.

SYN not interfere in the lives of others

네 일이나 잘 해.
(=Don't interfere in the affairs of others.
=That's not your business.
=What business is that of yours?
=You have no business to interfere in the matter.)

go against …을 거스르다

His suggestion **went against** the party's rule.
그의 제안은 당의 규칙에 어긋나는 것이었다.
The idea of deceiving other people **goes against** her principle to live honestly.
다른 사람들을 속이는 것은 정직하게 살려는 그녀의 원칙에 위배된다.

[SYN] be contrary to; be out of harmony with

fall to 1. (식사·싸움·일 등을) 시작하다 2. …하기 시작하다

They **fell to** and the fight lasted for hours.
그들은 싸우기 시작했으며 싸움은 몇 시간 동안 계속되었다.
The two parties **fell to** negotiation.
양측은 협상을 시작했다.

[SYN] 1. begin to work; begin to eat; begin to fight 2. begin to

on duty 당번의, 근무 중인

I have to be **on duty** once a week.
나는 매주 한 번씩 당번을 한다.
A police officer usually wears a uniform when **on duty**.
경찰관은 근무 중일 때 대개 제복을 입는다.

[SYN] working in a position of responsibility

keep to (시간·규정 등을) 굳게 지키다

All of the students should **keep to** the rules of the school.
모든 학생들은 학칙을 지켜야 한다.
Everybody must **keep to** the right on the road.
모두가 도로에서는 우측 통행을 지켜야 한다.
Keep to the left.
좌측 통행.

[SYN] adhere; conform to; follow a plan or an agreement

on guard 감시하여, 조심하여

While a thief robbed the shop, two men were **on guard** at the door.
도둑이 가게를 터는 동안 두 남자가 문에서 망을 보았다.
The bus driver warned the passenger to be **on guard** for pickpockets.

[SYN] watchful; watching

버스 운전기사는 승객들에게 소매치기를 조심하라고 경고했다.

go off 1. (일이) 되어가다, 행해지다 2. 가버리다, 떠나다 3. 발사되다, 폭발하다

The celebration party **went off** successfully.
축하 파티는 성공적으로 진행되었다.
If I **go off** now, I won't be back in a few months.
지금 떠나면 몇 달 동안 돌아오지 않을 것이다.
The bomb **went off** and wounded several people.
폭탄이 터져서 몇 사람에게 부상을 입혔다.

[SYN] 1. happen; go on; progress; advance 2. leave; depart 3. be fired; explode

have one's day 전성시대가 있다

Every dog **has his day**.
쥐구멍에도 볕들 날이 있다.

[SYN] be in one's best days
cf. have had one's day 전성시대가 지났다

eager to …하려고 열심인, …하려고 열망하는

Richard was **eager to** be a painter.
리차드는 화가가 되기를 열망했다.
Jean is **eager to** pass the audition to be a musical actress.
진은 뮤지컬 여배우가 되려고 오디션에 합격하기 위해 열심이다.

[SYN] enthusiastic about; anxious to do; longing for

off duty 비번의

When I'm **off duty**, I play golf.
내가 비번일 때는, 골프를 친다.
John is **off duty** on Mondays.
존은 월요일은 비번이다.

[SYN] not working; off guard
[OPP] on duty 당번인, 근무 중인 (= working in a position of responsibility)

get away 1. 도망가다, (악습·생각 등에서) 벗어나다, (현실에서) 도피하다 2. 출발하다, 떠나다

The thief wanted to **get away** but failed.
도둑은 도망가기를 원했지만 실패했다.
The family **got away** early in the morning on the first day.
그 가족은 첫날 아침 일찍 출발했다.

[SYN] 1. flee; escape; run away; fly 2. start; leave

제 3 장 시험에서 노리는 급소

제 3 장에서 공부할 것은
시험에서 노리는 급소!

출제자의 의도를 간파할 수 있다면
시험에서의 성공은 보장된 것이다.

이 장에는 바로
출제자의 의도가
나타나 있다.

철저한 반복 학습이
성공의 지름길이라는 사실을
기억하자!

제3장 시험에서 노리는 급소

be at the bottom of ···에 책임이 있다, ···의 주원인이다

There were mixed opinions about the accident, but brake failure **was at the bottom of** it.
사고에 대해 의견이 분분했지만 브레이크 고장이 주원인이었다.

I can guess who **is at the bottom of** the financial crisis of our company.
나는 우리 회사 재정난의 책임이 누구에게 있는지 추측할 수 있다.

SYN. be responsible for; be the real reason for

all but 거의, ···을 제외한 전부

When the rescue boat arrived there, he was **all but** drowned.
구조선이 도착했을 때 그는 거의 익사 지경에 있었다.

A picture of **all but** nudity does not appeal to me.
거의 나체인 그림은 내 마음에는 들지 않는다.

SYN. nearly; almost; all except

come into existence 태어나다, 성립하다, 생기다

This is the way how the new system **came into existence**.
이렇게 해서 새 제도가 생기게 되었다.

This is how that great empire **came into existence**.
이렇게 해서 그 위대한 제국이 탄생했다.

SYN. form; be created; come into being

come by 입수하다, 얻다

I was happy to **come by** this poster of my favorite singer.
나는 좋아하는 가수의 이 포스터를 손에 넣게 되어 기뻤다.

Money easily **come by** is often easily spent.
쉽게 번 돈은 쉽게 나간다.

SYN. get; acquire; obtain; secure; earn

on no account 결코 ···않아, 아무리 해도 ···않아

On no account must you leave the baby alone.
절대로 갓난아기를 혼자 두지 마라.

On no account should you buy the expensive necklace.
절대로 그 비싼 목걸이를 사면 안 된다.

SYN. never; in no way
cf. of no account 쓸데없는; 중요하지 않은

make sense (사물이) 이치에 맞다, (표현·행동 등이) 뜻을 이루다, 이해하다
The passage doesn't **make sense**.
이 구절은 이해가 가지 않는다.
Our staying here any longer doesn't **make sense**.
더 이상 이곳에 있어 봤자 소용 없다.

SYN be understandable; be intelligible

make up 1. (여러 가지 것으로) 구성하다, 이루다, 조성하다 2. 화해하다, 원만하게 해결하다
The Morse code is **made up** of dots and dashes.
모스 부호는 점과 선으로 되어 있다.
Let's shake hands and **make up**.
악수하고 화해합시다.

SYN 1. be made up of; be composed of 2. become friends again

second to none 누구〔무엇〕에게도 뒤지지 않는, 첫째가는
He is **second to none** in German writing in his class.
그는 독일어 작문에 있어서는 학급에서 누구에게도 뒤지지 않는다.
In intelligence he is **second to none**.
그는 지적인 면에 있어서 누구에게도 뒤지지 않는다.

SYN the best; yield to none

see to it that …하도록 하다〔돌보다, 조처하다〕
We **saw to it that** the electric bill was paid.
우리는 전기 요금이 납부되도록 조처했다.
I will **see to it that** you meet her at the party.
네가 파티에서 그녀를 만날 수 있도록 해 주겠다.

SYN make sure something is done

in〔on〕 behalf of 1. …을 대표하여, 대신하여 2. …을 위하여
The coach accepted the championship award **in behalf of** the team.
코치가 팀을 대신하여 우승상을 받았다.
The social worker spent most of his time **on behalf of** the poor.
그 사회사업가는 가난한 사람들을 위해서 대부분의 시간을 보냈다.

SYN 1. in place of; as a representative of 2. for the good of

in the light of 1. …에 비추어 2. …로서
History should be read **in the light of** these facts.
역사는 이같은 사실에 비추어 읽어야 한다.
I now view my action **in the light of** a crime.
나는 지금 나의 행위를 범죄로 보고 있다.

SYN 1. in view of; considering 2. as

there is nothing for it but to …하는 수밖에, 다른 도리가 없다

There is nothing for it but to do it this way.
이렇게 밖에는 달리 방법이 없다.
There was nothing for it but to give up.
포기할 수밖에 없었다.
There was nothing for it but to hold my tongue.
잠자코 있을 수밖에 다른 방법이 없었다.

[SYN] have no other choice; have no alternative

to a great extent [degree] 대부분은, 크게

Inflation has slowed **to a great extent**.
인플레가 크게 늦추어졌다.
Our work has been done **to a great degree**, with only finishing job left.
우리 일이 대부분 끝났고 마무리 작업만 남았다.

[SYN] mostly; largely; mainly

be convinced of 확신하다, 납득하다, 깨닫게 하다

Although he insists on his innocence, I **am convinced of** his guilty.
비록 그는 자신의 결백함을 주장하지만 나는 그가 유죄라고 확신한다.
I **am convinced of** her honesty. She couldn't have stolen that money.
나는 그녀가 정직하다고 확신한다. 그녀가 그 돈을 훔쳤을 리가 없다.

[SYN] believe firmly; be sure of

be entitled to …을 받을 자격이 있다

You **are entitled to** receive the prize.
당신은 그 상을 받을 자격이 있다.
All the people of the nation **are entitled to** an education.
우리 나라의 모든 국민들은 교육을 받을 권리가 있다.

[SYN] have qualification; have a right

at all costs 어떤 대가를 치르더라도, 무슨 수를 써서라도, 기어코

I must pass the exam **at all costs** to make my father happy.
무슨 수를 써서라도 시험에 합격해서 아버지를 행복하게 해 드려야 한다.
I must finish this report **at all costs**.
어떻게 해서든 이 보고서를 끝내야겠다.

[SYN] at all events; by all means; regardless of the results

persist in 고집하다, 고수하다, 주장하다

He always **persists in** his opinion.

[SYN] insist on; stick to; adhere to; hold fast to

그는 항상 자기 의견을 고집한다.
He **persisted in** denying his knowledge of it.
그는 끝까지 그것을 모른다고 우겼다.

come to 의식을 회복하다

Helen fainted but **came to** in a few minutes.
헬렌은 기절했지만 곧 깨어났다.
After the operation, she **came to** and looked around.
수술 후 그녀는 의식을 회복하고 주변을 둘러보았다.

SYN. come to one's senses

come to one's senses 1. 사태를 파악하다 2. 의식을 회복하다

Why don't you **come to your senses** and stop smoking?
정신 차리고 담배 좀 끊어.
Three hours after the serious operation, the patient **came to his senses**.
대수술을 받은 지 세 시간 후에 환자는 깨어났다.

SYN. 1. understand the situation 2. wake up

pull together 협력하여 일하다, (조직 등을) 다시 세우다

If a large business like this is to succeed, all of us must **pull together**.
이와 같은 대기업이 성공하려면 우리 모두가 협력해야 한다.
We can finish in time if we all **pull together**.
우리 모두 협력해서 하면 시간 내에 끝낼 수 있다.

SYN. work as a team

put aside (후일을 위해) 저축하다, 따로 떼어두다

You should **put aside** a certain sum every month.
매달 일정한 돈을 저축해야 한다.
Mother advised me to **put** money **aside** for my old age.
어머니는 노후를 위해 돈을 저축해 두라고 충고하셨다.

SYN. save; reserve; lay aside

go so far as to …할 정도까지 하다, …까지 하다

Did you **go so far as to** resign your post?
당신은 그 직책을 사임까지 했습니까?
He **went so far as to** call me a thief.
그는 나를 도둑놈이라고까지 극언했다.

SYN. so far as to do

get through with …을 완성하다, 끝내다

SYN. finish; complete

Have you **got through with** your work?
일을 끝마쳤습니까?
When you **get through with** this work, please bring it to me.
이 일이 마무리되면 제게 가져다 주세요.

take (it) for granted ···을 당연한 것으로 생각하다
I **took (it) for granted** that he was an American.
나는 그가 당연히 미국인일 것이라고 생각했다.
He **took it for granted** that the invitation included his wife.
그는 그 초대를 당연히 아내와 함께 오라는 것으로 여겼다.

SYN accept as a matter of course

to one's taste 기호에 맞춰서, 마음에 들어서
Abstract art is not **to my taste**.
추상 예술은 내 취향에 안 맞는다.
You may furnish your room **to your taste**.
네 방을 취향대로 꾸며도 된다.

SYN pleasing to someone; so as to please someone

with all one's heart 진심으로, 충심으로, 기꺼이
With all my heart, I hope you will succeed.
진심으로 당신이 성공하기를 바랍니다.
I say congratulations **with all my heart**.
진심으로 축하합니다.

SYN with complete sincerity; with pleasure

with might and main 전력을 다하여, 힘껏
The committee argued **with might and main**.
위원회는 전력을 다해 논쟁을 했다.
The fishers pulled the rope **with might and main** to save the sinking boat.
어부들은 침몰하고 있는 배를 구하기 위해 밧줄을 힘껏 잡아당겼다.

SYN with all one's effort; to the best of one's ability; with all one's might

year in, year out / year in and year out
1년 내내, 해마다 정해 놓고, 끊임없이
I am sick of doing same job **year in, year out**.
1년 내내 같은 일을 하는 데 질렸다.
Our family goes to the golf resort **year in and year out**.
우리 가족은 해마다 정기적으로 골프 리조트에 간다.

SYN regularly through years; continuously; all the year round

X out x표를 하여 지우다
The teacher told us to **X out** mistakes in the test

SYN cross out

paper.
선생님은 우리에게 시험지에서 잘못된 것을 지우라고 말씀하셨다.
Mother decided to **X out** some of the guests from the list.
어머니께서는 명단에서 손님 일부를 지우기로 하셨다.

suspect A of B A에게 B의 의심을 갖다

We began to **suspect** him **of** having a hand in her death.
우리는 그가 그녀의 죽음과 관계가 있다고 의심하기 시작했다.
Several people have been **suspected of** the murder.
몇 사람이 살인 혐의를 받고 있다.

[SYN] have suspicion; be suspicious; think that someone is guilty of something

subject to …의 지배를 받는, (피해·병 등에) 걸리기[입기] 쉬운, …을 필요로 하는

She is **subject to** colds.
그녀는 감기에 잘 걸린다.
The agricultural products are **subject to** sudden changes of weather.
농작물은 급격한 날씨 변화의 영향을 많이 받는다.

[SYN] controlled by; vulnerable to

on the contrary 그와는 반대로

On the contrary, I like this job from the bottom of my heart.
그와는 반대로, 나는 정말 이 일이 좋다.
"You look depressed." "**On the contrary** I feel good."
"기운이 없어 보이는데." "천만에 아주 좋아."

[SYN] in opposition to what has been stated
cf. to the contrary 그와 반대로, 그 반대의 (= to the opposite effect)

off and on / on and off 때때로, 하다 말다

The girl baby cried **off and on** all night.
갓난 딸이 밤새 울다 말다 했다.
Jane wrote to a friend in Korea **on and off** for many years.
제인은 한국에 있는 친구에게 여러 해 동안 가끔 편지를 썼다.

[SYN] occasionally; sometimes; not regularly

more than once 한 번뿐 아니라, 여러 번에 걸쳐, 몇 번이나

When young, I went to New York **more than once**.
젊었을 때 나는 여러 번 뉴욕에 갔었다.
A book worth reading at all is likely to be read

[SYN] several times; many times; often

more than once.
읽을 가치가 있는 책은 몇 번이고 되풀이하여 읽혀지는 것 같다.

make a long story short 간추려서 말하다, 짧게 말하다

[SYN] sum up; summarize

I don't have much time, so please **make a long story short**.
시간이 많지 않으니 요점만 말해.
To **make a long story short**, I want you to lend me some money.
간단히 말해서 나에게 돈을 좀 빌려 주었으면 좋겠다.

get [be] wet to the skin 흠뻑 젖다

[SYN] be wet through

On the way home I got caught in a shower and **got wet to the skin**.
집에 오는 길에 소나기를 만나서 흠뻑 젖었다.
The girl caught a cold after **getting wet to the skin** in the heavy rain.
소녀는 폭우에 흠뻑 젖은 후 감기에 걸렸다.

be on the point of 바야흐로 …하려고 하다, …하는 순간이다

[SYN] be at the point of; be in the act of; be about to

I **was on the point of** starting when she phoned.
내가 막 출발하려고 할 때 그녀가 전화를 했다.
John **was on the point of** winning the 200-meter race, but he fell down.
200미터 경주에서 우승을 할 순간에 존이 넘어져 버렸다.

in spite of oneself 저도 모르게, 무심코

[SYN] against one's will; unconsciously

I cried at the news **in spite of myself**.
그 소식을 듣고 나도 모르게 울음이 나왔다.
He burst out laughing **in spite of himself**.
그는 자기도 모르게 웃음을 터뜨렸다.

be in charge of …을 담당하다, 돌보고 있다

[SYN] undertake; take in hand
cf. take charge of …을 맡다, …을 담당하다 (=look after)

If you like it or not, I will **be in charge of** the new project.
당신이 좋아하든 아니든 나는 새 프로젝트를 맡을 것이다.
She **is in charge of** the third year class.
그녀는 3학년 학급을 맡고 있다.

admit of (의심·변명 등의) 여지가 있다, …을 넣을 자리

[SYN] have room for

가 있다

You must hurry up. This matter **admits of** no delay.

서둘러. 이것은 시간을 다투는 문제야.

His statement **admits of** no doubt, so you can take it as an evidence.

그의 말은 의심의 여지가 없으므로 증거로 채택해도 된다.

against one's will 본의 아니게, 억지로

They made me start learning how to use a computer **against my will**.

내 의지와는 달리, 그들은 나로 하여금 컴퓨터의 사용법을 배우게 했다.

It was **against his will** that Jake went to the medical college.

제이크가 의과 대학에 간 것은 본의가 아니었다.

[SYN] contrary to one's desires or wishes
[OPP] at will 마음대로, 뜻대로, 좋을 대로 (=at one's will; freely; as one likes)
cf. with a will 단호히, 진심으로 (=heartily; firmly; resolutely)

break into 1. 침입하다 2. 갑자기 …하기 시작하다

Someone **broke into** my room and stole all the money.

누군가가 내 방에 늘어와 돈을 모두 훔쳐 갔다.

When people watched the movie seriously, a boy **broke into** laughter.

사람들이 심각하게 영화를 보고 있을 때 한 소년이 갑자기 웃음을 터뜨렸다.

[SYN] 1. break in; force an entrance into 2. suddenly begin to do something
cf. break in 침입하다, 끼어들다
break out 발발하다 (=occur suddenly)
break off 갑자기 그만두다 (=stop suddenly)

be impatient of+일 …에 참을 수 없다

I **am impatient of** sitting still.

나는 가만히 앉아 있지 못한다.

He **was impatient of** the views which did not agree with his own.

그는 자기의 의견과 다른 의견에는 견딜 수 없었다.

[SYN] be unbearable
cf. be impatient with+사람 (사람)에 참지 못하다
be impatient for 간절히 바라다 (=be eager for)

deprive A of B A로부터 B를 빼앗다

The hot sun **deprived** the flowers **of** water.

뜨거운 태양이 꽃으로부터 수분을 앗아 갔다.

The tall building **deprived** us **of** sunlight.

그 높은 건물 때문에 우리에게 햇빛이 닿지 않았다.

[SYN] rob A of B; steal B from A; take away B from A

dispose of …을 처분(양도)하다, 팔아 버리다, 버리다

After enjoying your picnic, please **dispose of** the trash.

[SYN] sell; throw away

소풍을 즐긴 후에는 쓰레기를 버리시오.
He wants to **dispose of** this painting.
그는 이 그림을 처분하기를 원한다.

make amends for 보상하다, 벌충하다

Work hard to **make amends for** lost time.
낭비한 시간을 벌충하기 위해 열심히 공부해라.
I apologized to my friend to **make amends for** criticizing him too much.
나는 내 친구를 너무 많이 비판한 것을 보상하기 위해 그에게 사과했다.

[SYN] make good; make up for; compensate for

meet with 1. 맞닥뜨리다, 마주치다 2. (불행·친절 등을) 경험하다, 당하다

The girl **met with** two strange men in the darkness.
소녀는 어둠 속에서 낯선 남자 둘과 마주쳤다.
The tourist **met with** an accident on a highway.
여행자는 간선 도로에서 사고를 당했다.

[SYN] 1. meet somebody, usually by accident 2. experience; suffer

with the exception of …을 제외하고, …외에는, …은 예외로 하고

I like all the subjects **with the exception of** English.
나는 영어를 제외하고는 모든 과목을 다 좋아한다.
With the exception of John, the family are all tall.
존만 빼고 그 가족은 모두 키가 크다.

[SYN] except; but; excepted; exclusive of

in respect of [to] …에 관하여, …에 대해서

The enemy surpassed us **in respect of** weapon.
적은 무기에 있어서 우리를 능가했다.
In respect to artistic skill, he is the best.
예술적인 기교에 있어서는 그가 최고이다.

[SYN] concerning; about

suggest itself to …의 마음(염두)에 떠오르다

A good idea **suggested itself to** me.
좋은 생각이 떠올랐다.
A few new ideas **suggested themselves to** him.
몇 가지 새로운 착상이 그에게 떠올랐다.

[SYN] occur to; come to mind; come across one's mind

strive for [after] 얻으려고 애쓰다

They are **striving for** victory.

[SYN] endeavor; make great efforts; try very hard

그들은 승리하려고 애쓰고 있다.
Mistakes are inevitable, but **strive for** accuracy.
실수는 부득이한 일이지만 정확성을 기하라.

put forth 1. (초목의 싹 등이) 나오다 2. 말을 꺼내다, 제안하다

Plants **put forth** buds in March.
3월에는 식물의 싹이 돋아 나온다.
No one has **put forth** a workable solution.
아무도 실현성 있는 해결책을 내놓지 않았다.

[SYN] 1. bring out; bear; grow 2. offer for

put off 연기하다, 미루다

The outdoor event was **put off** because of heavy rain.
폭우 때문에 야외 행사가 연기되었다.
Never **put off** till tomorrow what you can do today.
오늘 할 수 있는 것을 내일로 미루지 마라.

[SYN] postpone; delay; defer; adjourn

take over 1. 이어받다, 인계하다, 인수하다, 접수하다 2. 점거하다, 우세하게 되다

She **took over** the business after her husband died.
남편이 죽은 후 그녀가 사업을 물려받았다.
They say that the conservatives are **taking over** in Europe.
유럽에서는 보수 세력이 우세하다고들 한다.

[SYN] 1. assume control of; take charge of; answer for; undertake; accept 2. gain control

take account of …을 고려에 넣다, 참작하다, …에 주의하다, …을 계산에 넣다

When you **take account of** his age, you cannot punish him.
그의 나이를 고려한다면 그에게 벌을 줄 수 없다.
We must **take account of** all possibilities.
우리는 모든 가능성을 고려해야 한다.

[SYN] consider; take into consideration
cf. take advantage of …을 이용하다, …의 틈을 타다

lose one's heart 사랑에 빠지다

Nancy **lost her heart** to the hero who was featured in the movie.
낸시는 영화에 나온 주인공을 사랑하게 되었다.
Little Fred **lost his heart** to the kitty the first time he saw it.
어린 프레드는 고양이를 처음 본 순간부터 좋아하기 시작했다.

[SYN] fall in love

lose one's mind 1. 발광하다, 미치다 2. 좋아하다, 몹시 원하다

He **lost his mind** and is in a mental hospital now.
그는 미쳐서 현재 정신 병원에 있다.
He has **lost his mind** over his new girlfriend.
그는 새로운 여자 친구에게 빠져 있다.

[SYN] 1. go insane; become crazy 2. like or desire greatly

have seen (known) better days 이전에는 세월이 좋았었다

He **has seen better days**.
그에게는 잘 나가던 때가 있었다.
He once **has seen better days**.
그는 한때 잘 살던 사람이었다.

[SYN] experienced better or more affluent time

have trouble with (병·곤란 등으로) 난처해 있다, 어려움에 처해 있다

I am sure you will **have trouble with** the work.
당신은 분명 그 일로 곤란을 당할 것이다.
She is **having trouble with** her teeth now.
그녀는 지금 이빨 때문에 고생하고 있다.

[SYN] be embarrassed by (with); be at a loss

make one's way (애써) 나아가다, 번창(번영)하다, 출세하다

He **made his way** through difficulties.
그는 역경을 헤치고 전진했다.
His only ambition is to **make his way** in the world.
그의 유일한 야심은 성공하는 것이다.

[SYN] go forward; flourish; be successful
cf. make one's own way 자력으로 출세하다, 생계를 세우서 나가다
feel one's way 더듬어 나아가다
have (get) one's (own) way 제멋대로 하다

make a clean breast of (마음에 걸리는 일들을) 남김 없이 털어놓다

The thieves **made a clean breast of** their past crimes.
도둑들은 자신들이 과거에 저지른 범행을 다 털어놓았다.
If you **make a clean breast of** cheating in the test, I will forgive you.
시험에서 부정 행위를 한 것을 다 이야기하면 용서하겠다.

[SYN] tell all about; confess everything

spell out 자세히 설명하다

He does not understand the process; you will have to **spell** it **out** for him.
그는 그 과정을 이해하지 못하니까 네가 자세히 설명해 주어야 할 것이다.

[SYN] explain in detail; give a full explanation

I'd like you to **spell out** your reasons of moving to other company.
다른 회사로 옮기는 이유를 설명해 주기 바란다.

see much of 자주 만나다

I **see much of** him at the bus station.
그와는 버스 정류장에서 자주 만난다.
I haven't **seen much of** him recently.
최근에는 그를 별로 만나지 못했다.

SYN. see a great deal of

come to a conclusion 결론에 도달하다, 결말이 나다

It took almost three hours for him to **come to a conclusion**.
그가 결론을 얻기까지는 거의 세 시간이 걸렸다.
We finally have **come to a conclusion** that we cannot give up here.
우리는 마침내 여기에서 포기할 수 없다는 결론에 도달했다.

SYN. arrive at a conclusion; draw a conclusion

come to light 알려지다, 드러나다

Some facts **came to light** when we investigated the phenomenon.
그 현상을 조사해 보았더니 몇 가지 사실들이 드러났다.
If too many bad things **come to light**, he may lose the election.
너무 많은 나쁜 것들이 드러나면 그는 선거에서 패할 수도 있다.

SYN. become known; appear; be discovered

get through 1. 합격하다 2. ···을 끝내다

If you **get through** the test, you will be able to get a job more easily.
시험에 합격한다면 좀더 쉽게 취업할 수 있을 것이다.
Today I **got through** two novels.
오늘 나는 소설 두 권을 다 읽었다.

SYN. 1. pass 2. complete; finish
cf. get through with ···을 끝내다

give oneself up to ···에 몰두하다, ···에 빠지다, ···에 맡기다

My husband **gave himself up to** the theater.
남편은 연극에 몰두했다.
When you become sick, you should **give yourself up to** the hands of the doctor.
병이 날 때에는 의사의 손에 맡겨야 한다.

SYN. be absorbed in; leave someone in the care of

all the more 그만큼 더, 도리어, 오히려 더
I want to help him **all the more**, because he is in trouble.
나는 그가 곤경에 처해 있기 때문에 더욱 돕고 싶은 것이다.
You don't believe me, but I love her **all the more** for her faults.
당신은 믿지 않겠지만 나는 그녀의 결점들 때문에 그녀를 더욱 사랑한다.

[SYN] rather; still (much) more

approve of …을 찬성하다, 시인하다
Mother will never **approve of** my marriage.
어머니는 내 결혼을 결코 찬성하지 않을 것이다.
His parents didn't **approve of** it.
그의 부모들은 그것을 찬성하지 않았다.

[SYN] consent; agree with; support; endorse

sell on 설득하다, 납득시키다
I **sold** my wife **on** the idea of moving to New York.
나는 아내에게 뉴욕으로 이사할 생각을 설득시켰다.
"Is your father always stubborn?" "Yes, it's hard to **sell** him **on** anything."
"너의 아버지는 항상 완고하시니?" "그래. 무엇이든 납득시키기가 힘이 들어."

[SYN] persuade; bring around

show into (in) 안내하다, …를 불러(맞아)들이다
We were **shown into** the exhibit hall.
우리는 전시실로 안내되었다.
If Mr. James comes, **show** him **in** immediately.
제임스 씨가 오면 곧 안으로 안내해 주세요.

[SYN] usher into a given place; escort into

on the strength of …의 도움으로, …에 힘입어, …의 덕분에
I will employ new persons **on the strength of** the results of the test and interview.
시험과 면접 결과로 신입 사원을 채용할 것이다.
I opened a shop **on the strength of** his help.
나는 그의 도움에 힘입어 가게를 열었다.

[SYN] encouraged by; relying upon; thanks to; make an effort

one and all 누구나(아무것이나) 다, 모두, 모조리
Welcome, **one and all**!
여러분, 모두 잘 오셨습니다!
Thank you, **one and all**!
여러분 모두에게 감사드립니다!

[SYN] everyone; all those involved

in detail 상세하게, 자세히, 세부에 걸쳐서
I will explain it **in detail**.
그것을 상세히 설명하겠습니다.
The paper gives an account of the demonstration in opposition to the race discrimination **in detail**.
신문은 인종차별 반대 시위에 관한 기사를 상세하게 보도하고 있다.

[SYN] at length; at large; minutely

impose on 1. 부과하다 2. 속이다
The king **imposed** heavy taxes **on** his people.
왕은 국민에게 무거운 세금을 부과했다.
I won't be **imposed on**(**upon**) anymore.
더 이상은 속지 않겠다.

[SYN] 1. levy on 2. deceive; cheat; fool

be of (the) opinion that …라고 믿다, 생각하다, …이라는 의견이다
I **am of the opinion that** his plan is unrealistic.
나의 의견으로는 그의 계획에는 현실성이 없다.
I **am of** (**the**) **opinion that** drunken driving is a challenge to our community.
음주운전은 우리 사회에 대한 도전이라는 것이 내 의견이다.

[SYN] in one's opinion

be hard up for …이 바닥나다, …이 결핍되다
George **is hard up for** money for his planned travel.
조지는 예정된 여행을 할 돈이 없다.
The parents **are hard up for** money to pay for their son's school tuition.
그 부모들은 아들의 수업료를 낼 돈이 없다.

[SYN] be all gone; be short of; be drained

apply to …에 적용되다, …을 충당하다, …에 관계되다
Unfortunately, the universal rule didn't **apply to** our case.
불행히도 보편적인 법칙이 우리 경우에는 적용되지 않았다.
You chose a wrong book. This doesn't **apply to** beginners like you.
당신은 책을 잘못 골랐다. 이 책은 당신과 같은 초보자들과는 관계가 없다.

[SYN] apply (a rule to a case); be linked to

apart from …은 별개로 하고, …은 제쳐놓고
Apart from its cost, the tour plan is very good.
비용은 별도로 치고, 그 여행 계획은 정말 좋다.
Apart from joking, what do you mean to do?

[SYN] aside from; besides; in addition to

농담은 그만하고, 너는 무엇을 할 생각이니?

come what may 어떤 일이 일어나더라도

Charley has decided to marry Jane, **come what may**.
찰리는 어떤 일이 있더라도 제인과 결혼하기로 결심했다.
The head of the company promised to the workers that he would protect it, **come what may**.
회사 사장은 어떤 상황이 일어나더라도 회사를 지키겠다고 근로자들에게 약속했다.

[SYN] whatever may happen; even if troubles come; no matter what happens

come to terms (with) 화해하다, 타협하다

If we don't **come to terms** about the cost, this whole project will fail.
만약 우리가 경비에 대해 타협하지 못하면 이 프로젝트는 완전히 무산될 것이다.
She hasn't **come to terms with** her landlord about the rent.
그녀는 방세 건으로 집주인과 타협을 못하고 있다.

[SYN] settle an agreement; come to an agreement

true to life 실물 그대로의, 정확한

This portrait is **true to life**.
이 초상화는 실물과 똑같다.
The autobiographic movie is **true to life**.
그 자서전적인 영화는 정확하다.

[SYN] lifelike; accurate

take the trouble to 수고하다, 노고를 아끼지 않고 …하다

They **take the trouble to** consult the idiom dictionary.
그들은 수고를 아끼지 않고 숙어 사전을 찾아본다.
It was kind of you to **take the trouble to** meet us.
일부러 저희를 마중 나와 주셔서 감사했습니다.

[SYN] spare no pains to do something

read between the lines 언외의 뜻을 헤아리다, 말속에 담긴 속 뜻을 파악하다

Diplomatic messages have to be **read between the lines**.
외교 문서는 글 뒤에 숨어 있는 의미를 파악하지 않으면 안 된다.
To understand the essay, you have to **read between the lines**.
그 에세이를 이해하려면 속에 담긴 뜻을 파악해야 한다.

[SYN] find meaning although it is not stated clearly

read into ···의 뜻으로 해석하다 (흔히 곡해를 하여), ···의 뜻이라고 잘못 해석하다

He tends to **read** something negative **into** everything I write.
그는 내가 쓰는 것은 무엇이든지 부정적으로 해석하는 경향이 있다.
He **read into** her words that she didn't like him.
그는 그녀가 그를 좋아하지 않는 것으로 그녀의 말을 곡해했다.

[SYN] give something it doesn't have

want for nothing 부족한 것이 없다, 불편한 데가 없다

You shall **want for nothing** (that money can buy).
(돈으로 살 수 있는 것이라면) 너를 옹색하게 만들진 않겠다.
You shall **want for nothing** as long as I live.
내가 살아 있는 동안에는 당신이 불편하지 않도록 하겠습니다.

[SYN] lack nothing
cf. want for ···이 부족하다, 모자라다 (=lack; need; insufficient; short)

without (any) delay 지체없이, 곧

I recommend you to set about your business **without delay**.
곧 사업을 시작하도록 권유한다.
I hope you carry out the good plan **without delay**.
그 좋은 계획을 곧 실천하기를 바란다.

[SYN] at once; promptly; immediately

be endowed with (재능을) 타고나다, 선천적으로 가지고 있다

John **was** highly **endowed** by nature **with** artistic talent.
존은 높은 예술적 재능을 천성적으로 타고났다.
Her daughters **are** all **endowed with** remarkable beauty and grace just like her.
그녀의 딸들은 그녀와 마찬가지로 뛰어난 아름다움과 우아함을 가지고 태어났다.

[SYN] be gifted with; be born with

be up and doing [coming] 활동적이다, 적극적이다, 크게 활약하고 있다

You must **be up and doing**.
너는 크게 활약해야 한다.
Young as he is, he **is up and doing** now.
비록 그는 나이는 어리지만 지금 크게 활동하고 있다.

[SYN] be in full activity; be full of activities

all in all 1. 전부하여, 모두 해서, 대체로 2. 둘도 없이 소중한 것, 전부

All in all his presentation of the new product was a

[SYN] 1. in total; in general; in summary; generally 2. the person or thing that you love

success.
그의 신제품 발표는 대체로 성공적이었다.
Children became her **all in all** after her husband's death.
남편이 죽은 후 그녀에게는 아이들이 전부가 되었다.

appeal to …에 호소하다, 간청하다

This picture does not **appeal to** me at all.
이 그림은 내게는 조금도 호소력이 없다.
The human rights group **appealed to** the world leaders to help the refugees.
인권 단체는 난민들을 도와 달라고 세계 지도자들에게 호소했다.

[SYN] ask to; beg to

on the move 항상 움직이고 있는, 활동하고 있는, 이동 중의, 진행 중의

In vacation season, all the roads are full of families **on the move**.
휴가철이 되면 모든 도로에는 이동 중인 가족들로 가득하다.
If he won the election, he would get the country **on the move**.
그는 선거에서 당선될 경우 국가를 더욱 발전시키겠다고 약속했다.

[SYN] busy; active; going from one place to another

(be) on the brink of 바야흐로 …하려고 하는

He **was on the brink of** death.
그는 죽음 직면에 있었다.
He **was on the brink of** tears.
그는 금방 울음을 터뜨릴 것 같았다.

[SYN] be about to; on the verge of
cf. of the moment 목하의, 현재의 (=of the present time)

within one's means …의 신분에 어울리게, 분수에 맞게

The father advised his sons to live **within their means**.
아버지는 아들들에게 분수에 맞게 살라고 충고했다.
At the present time, he lives **within his means**.
요즈음 그는 분수에 맞게 살고 있다.

[SYN] according to one's means
[OPP] beyond one's means

without so much as …조차 아니하고〔없이〕

He went out **without so much as** saying goodbye.
그는 인사도 없이 나가버렸다.
She walked past me **without so much as** looking at me.
그녀는 나를 쳐다보지도 않고 내 곁을 지나갔다.

[SYN] without even

sit in on ···을 방청(참관·청강·견학)하다

I **sat in on** the philosophy class, but didn't understand a thing.
나는 철학을 청강했지만 도무지 이해할 수가 없었다.
Would you mind if I **sit in on** your 10 o'clock class?
선생님의 10시 수업에 참관해도 괜찮겠습니까?

SYN. attend; be there; be present

single out 뽑아내다, 선발하다, 하나만 고르다

Why did you **single out** my child to stay after school?
어째서 우리 아이만 방과 후에 남게 된 것입니까?
We have **singled** you **out** from all the candidates.
우리는 모든 지원자 가운데 당신을 선발했다.

SYN. choose or indicate one person from a group

provide against 대비하다, 준비하다 (불의의 사고에 대해)

It is wise and good to **provide against** the rainy days.
만약의 경우에 대비하는 것이 현명한 처사이다.
The farmers should **provide against** a poor harvest.
농민들은 흉년에 대비해야 한다.

SYN. make preparations against

prevail on (upon) ···을 설득하다, 설복하다

I **prevailed on** her to accept my mother's invitation to the dinner.
나는 어머니의 저녁 초대에 응하도록 그녀를 설득했다.
I was **prevailed upon** to stay all night at Nancy's house.
나는 설득당하여 낸시 집에서 하룻밤 묵었다.

SYN. influence or persuade someone

keep body and soul together 겨우 살아가다 (생계를 유지하다)

My first year in Seoul, I earned just enough to **keep body and soul together**.
서울에서의 첫 해, 나는 겨우 살아갈 수 있을 정도밖에는 벌지 못했다.
She is so poor that it's all she can do to **keep body and soul together**.
그녀는 너무 가난해서 겨우 생계를 유지할 수 있을 뿐이다.

SYN. support oneself; maintain life

keep to oneself ···을 독점하다, (사물·정보 등을) 마음에 간직해 두다

SYN. keep secret

She is very shy and **keeps to herself** most of the time.
그녀는 매우 수줍어해서 대개 혼자 있는다.
She often **keeps** creative ideas **to herself**.
그녀는 종종 창의적인 생각을 남에게 이야기하지 않는다.

back up 후원하다, 지지하다
Don't worry! I'll **back** you **up** at the meeting.
걱정하지 마! 그 회의에서 자네를 지지하겠네.
You should have **backed** him **up**.
당신은 그를 응원했어야 했는데.

[SYN] support; help

be akin to …와 유사하다
Pity **is akin to** love.
동정은 사랑에 가깝다. (속담)
They **are akin to** each other in their thinking.
그들은 서로 사고방식이 비슷하다.

[SYN] be similar to

picture to oneself 상상하다, 마음에 그리다
He **pictured** the scene **to himself**.
그는 그 장면을 마음에 그려 보았다.
He couldn't **picture to himself** her asking him that favor.
그는 그녀가 자기에게 그런 부탁을 하리라고는 상상도 못했다.

[SYN] imagine; suppose; fancy; conjecture; speculate

persuade oneself of〔that〕…을 확신하다, …을 믿다
I could not **persuade myself of** its truth.
나는 그것이 사실이라고는 믿을 수가 없었다.
I **persuaded myself that** he would leave me forever.
그가 영원히 내 곁을 떠나가는 것이라고 확신했다.

[SYN] believe firmly; be convinced of

compete with 경쟁하다, 겨루다
If you want to **compete with** me, you must work harder.
나하고 경쟁하고 싶으면 더 열심히 노력해야 한다.
They **competed with** each other for the prize.
그들은 상을 타려고 서로 겨루었다.

[SYN] contend with; rival; cope with; contest

compensate for 보상하다, 배상하다
The company **compensated** her **for** extra work.

[SYN] make up for; recompense; make amends for

회사는 그녀의 초과 근무에 대해서 보상했다.
I must **compensate** you **for** your services.
나는 당신의 수고에 대하여 보상해야 한다.

act on (upon) …에 따라 행동하다, …에 영향을 주다, …에 작용하다

He would not **act on** his teacher's advice.
그는 그의 선생님의 충고에 따르지 않았다.
Acids **act upon** metals.
산은 금속에 작용한다.

[SYN] act according to; proceed in accordance with; influence on

accuse A of B B의 일로 A(사람)를 비난(고소)하다

He **accused** me **of** having neglected my duty.
그는 내가 직무를 게을리한 것을 책망했다.
He was **accused of** betraying his country.
그는 조국을 배신했다고 비난받았다.

[SYN] lay blame on; charge

contrast with 대비하다, 대조를 이루다

His behaviors **contrast with** his words.
그의 행동은 말과는 딴판이다.
His Indian clothes **contrasted** oddly **with** his fluent English.
그의 인디언 복장은 유창한 영어와 묘한 대조를 이루었다.

[SYN] compare with

contrary to …에 반해서, …와 대조적으로

His behavior was **contrary to** the national law.
그의 행동은 국법에 어긋난 것이었다.
He failed to get elected **contrary to** our expectation.
그는 우리의 예측과는 반대로 낙선했다.

[SYN] against; in opposition to

out of sorts 기분이 나쁜, 의기소침한

The boy is **out of sorts** because his mother won't take him to the cinema.
소년은 어머니가 영화관에 데리고 가지 않을 것이라고 시무룩해 있다.
She is feeling **out of sorts** after having a big quarrel with her boyfriend.
그녀는 남자 친구와 크게 싸우고 나서 지금 기분이 좋지 않다.

[SYN] feeling bad or angry; in a bad mood

only too 1. (glad, happy, pleased 등과 to do로 이어지는 꼴로) 매우, 아주, 더없이, 이를 데 없이 2. 유감스럽지만, 유감이나

I shall be **only too** pleased to come.

[SYN] 1. very; exceedingly; willing to do something 2. really, much to one's regret

기꺼이 가 뵙겠습니다.
It is **only too** true.
유감스럽지만 사실이다.

pull up 멈춰 서다, 세우다

The driver **pulled up** when the traffic lights changed.
신호가 바뀌자 운전자는 차를 세웠다.
Nick **pulled up** his car at the corner.
닉은 길모퉁이에 차를 세웠다.

[SYN] stop; cease

play up to …에게 아첨 떨다, 환심을 사려고 노력하다

He **plays up to** his boss because he wants a raise in salary.
그는 임금 인상을 원하기 때문에 사장의 환심을 사려고 노력한다.
He has **played up to** people all his life.
그는 지금까지 남의 비위나 맞추면서 살아왔다.

[SYN] seek favor with; flatter; try to please by flattery

to the full 최대한으로, 마음껏, 충분히

I appreciate your kindness **to the full**.
당신의 친절에 정말 감사드립니다.
He should be punished **to the full**.
그는 충분히 벌을 받아야 한다.

[SYN] to the utmost extent
cf. in full (성명 등을) 생략하지 않고, 자세히 (= in detail; at length; fully), (자금 등의) 전부, 전액

take a fancy [liking] to [for] …을 좋아하다[하게 되다], …을 사랑하다, …이 마음에 들다

My daughter **took a fancy to** a doll.
내 딸은 인형을 좋아했다.
He seems to have **taken a fancy to** the pretty girl.
그는 그 예쁜 아가씨를 연모하는 것처럼 보인다.

[SYN] become fond of; have a liking for

lay aside [by] 저축하다, 간직하다, 따로 두다, 불행에 대비해 두다

Ants **lay aside** food for winter.
개미는 겨울을 위해 식량을 비축한다.
She **laid by** a dollar every day to buy a guitar.
그녀는 기타를 사기 위해 매일 1달러씩 저축했다.

[SYN] lay by; lay up; set aside; make a fortune

lose no time (in) -ing 지체없이 …하다

I shall **lose no time in** send**ing** you an answer.
즉시 당신에게 회답을 보내겠습니다.
I shall **lose no time in** beginn**ing** work.

[SYN] without delay; promptly

즉시 일에 착수하겠습니다.

be devoid of / be destitute of ···이 없다, ···이 부족하다

John is an able scientist but he **is devoid of** common sense.
존은 능력 있는 과학자이지만 상식이 없다.
There are some politicians who seem to **be destitute of** any sense of right or wrong.
옳고 그름에 대한 감각이 전혀 없는 듯한 정치인들이 일부 있다.

[SYN] be without; want; lack

(be) bent on ···에 열중하고 있다, ···을 몹시 하고 싶어 하다

Only a week ago, he **was bent on** swimming, but now it's baseball.
불과 일주일 전만 해도 그는 수영에 열중하더니 지금은 야구이다.
She **is bent on** leaving right now.
그녀는 당장 출발하고 싶어 안달이다.

[SYN] be indulged to; eager to do

abstain from ···을 삼가다, 자제하다

We must **abstain from** speaking ill of others.
우리는 다른 사람들을 욕하는 것을 삼가야 한다.
The teacher decided to **abstain from** smoking.
그 선생님은 금연하기로 결심했다.

[SYN] refrain from; give up

attach A to B A를 B에 붙이다

He bought a trailer and **attached** it **to** his car.
그는 트레일러를 사서 자동차에 부착시켰다.
He **attached** the label **to** his trunk.
그는 트렁크에 명찰을 붙였다.

[SYN] fasten; fix; add
cf. be attached to ···에 애착(애정)을 가지다, ···을 귀여워하다 (= become attached (to); from attachment to(for))

consent to 동의하다, 찬성하다, 승인하다, 허가하다

Her father reluctantly **consented to** her marrying the prisoner.
그녀의 아버지는 마지못해 딸이 재소자와 결혼하는 것을 허락했다.
He **consented to** make a speech suited for the use of the general public.
그는 대중에게 알맞은 연설을 할 것에 동의했다.

[SYN] agree; approve; assent to; comply with

convert into ···로 바꾸다, 개조하다

During the war, we couldn't **convert** our property **into** cash.

[SYN] remodel; refashion; reconstruct; modify; renew; change

전시에는 재산을 현금으로 바꿀 수 없었다.
They **converted** their living house **into** a bar.
그들은 살림집을 술집으로 개조했다.

to the effect that …라는 취지로[뜻으로]

The medical doctor wrote a letter **to the effect that** his daughter would soon get better.
의사는 그의 딸이 곧 회복될 것이라는 취지의 편지를 썼다.
He has made an announcement **to the effect that** more people will lose their jobs.
그는 실직자가 더 많이 생길 것이라는 취지를 공표했다.

[SYN] with the purport or meaning

to the best of one's ability 힘 자라는 데까지, 힘껏

He struggled against the reform **to the best of his ability**.
그는 힘자라는 데까지 개혁에 대항했다.
(=He made great efforts to stop the reform as best he could.)
I will solve the problems with ease **to the best of my ability**.
나는 최선을 다해서 문제들을 쉽게 해결할 것이다.

[SYN] with all one's might; to the utmost of one's power

next[second] to none 최고의, 어느 누구에게도 뒤지지 않는, 제일 …인

Among friends, John is **next to none** in swimming.
친구들 중에서 존이 수영을 제일 잘 한다.
In mathematics he is **next to none** in his class though weak in English.
영어는 잘 하지 못한다고 해도 수학은 그가 그의 학급에서 제일이다.

[SYN] the best; the highest; supreme
cf. next to nothing 거의 아무것도 아닌, 거의 없는 (=almost nothing)

phase out 단계적으로 폐지[제거]하다

The old machines will be **phased out**.
낡은 기계들은 단계적으로 제거될 것이다.
The authorities decided to **phase out** the current tax system.
당국은 현 세제를 단계적으로 폐지하기로 결정했다.

[SYN] reduce or remove in stages

put to death 처형하다

Anyone who are caught appearing in the streets after curfew will be **put to death**.
누구든 통금 후에 거리에 나타나다가 적발되는 사람은 처형될 것이다.

[SYN] inflict punishment on; punish

The authorities **put** the murderer of his mother **to death**.
당국은 그의 어머니의 살인범을 처형했다.

take back 1. 되찾다 2. 철회하다, 취소하다

He **took back** the tools that he loaned me.
그는 나에게 빌려 준 도구들을 찾아갔다.
I'll **take back** all I said about her conduct.
그녀의 행실에 대해 한 말을 전부 취소하겠다.

[SYN] 1. repossess something; recover 2. retract; apologize for saying something

to a (high) degree 대단히, 매우, 약간

In common sense, I am ignorant **to a degree**.
나는 상식에는 매우 무지하다.
He is scrupulous **to a degree**.
그는 상당히 신중하다.

[SYN] to a great extent; somewhat
cf. to some degree 얼마간, 다소 (=more or less; somewhat)

cut out 제거하다, 베어내다

I **cut** the article **out** of the newspaper and sent it to Bill.
나는 신문에서 그 기사를 잘라 빌에게 보냈다.
You'll have to **cut out** the special budget for overseas trips.
해외 여행을 위한 특별 예산을 삭제하는 수밖에 없다.

[SYN] remove; take off; weed out; get rid of

count for much 중요하다, 상당히 쓸모가 있다

In modern times, such virtues may not **count for much**.
현대에는 그러한 미덕들이 중요하지 않을지도 모른다.
For a job interview, clean clothes and tidy appearance **count for much**.
취업 면접에서는 깨끗한 의복과 단정한 외모가 중요하다.

[SYN] be important; very useful
cf. count for nothing 하찮것없다, 중요치 않다 (=be trivial; be worthless)
count for something 어느 정도 중요하다

What ... is to, ~ is to …에 대한 관계는 (마치) ~에 대한 관계와 같다

What reading **is to** the mind, exercise **is to** the body.
독서가 정신에 미치는 영향은 운동이 신체에 미치는 영향과 같다.
(=Reading is to the mind what exercise is to the body.)

[SYN] A is to B as C is to D; (Just) as C is to D, so A is to B

watch out (for) 조심하다, 주의하다

Watch out for children crossing the street.

[SYN] take precautions; take care of

길을 건너는 아이들을 조심해라.
I told my son to **watch out for** ice on the road.
나는 아들에게 길에 있는 얼음을 조심하라고 말했다.

cut it fine [close] (시간·돈 등이) 얼마 남지 않다

[SYN] do not leave much time or money

We are **cutting it fine**, so please hurry up.
시간이 얼마 없으니 좀 서둘러.
They **cut it close**, and they barely had enough money to return.
그들은 돈을 너무 빠듯하게 계산해서 돌아올 돈도 거의 없었다.

come from 1. ··· 출신이다 2. ···에서 나오다(생기다)

[SYN] 1. be a native or resident of 2. be produced by; originate

The president of our company **comes from** peasant stock.
우리 회사 사장은 농민 출신이다.
The weather in other countries often **comes from** Antarctica.
다른 나라의 기후는 종종 남극에서 생겨난다.

send out 1. 발송하다, (초대장·주문품 등을) 내다, 보내다, 파견하다 2. (나무가 싹 등을) 내다 3. (빛·향기를) 발산하다

[SYN] 1. distribute; dispatch forward; mail out 2. bud out; sprout; spring up 3. emit; send forth; give out

They **sent out** their fall catalogue.
그들은 가을 상품 카탈로그를 발송했다.
In spring most trees **send out** new leaves.
봄이 되면 대부분 나무에서 새 잎이 난다.
The sun **sends out** heat and light.
태양은 열과 빛을 발한다.

seek out 찾아내다, ···을 열심히 찾다

[SYN] find out; discover; hunt out

These rockets are designed to **seek out** and destroy enemy bombers.
이 로켓들은 적의 폭격기를 찾아내도록 되어 있다.
The intervention of the government made the issue of **seeking out** an industrial spy complicated.
정부의 개입은 산업 스파이를 색출하는 문제를 복잡하게 만들었다.

be lost to 1. 이미 ···의 것이 아니다, ···에서 제거되다, 거부되다 2. ···에게 무감각하다, 거부되다

[SYN] 1. be refused to 2. be senseless; not feeling

Since my husband's death, happiness has **been lost to** me.
남편이 죽은 후 내게 행복이란 없었다.

Bill **is lost to** sense of humor.
빌에게 유머 감각이란 없다.

bring to light 폭로하다, 햇볕을 보게 하다, 세상에 드러내다, 밝히다

[SYN] reveal; show to the world

Many ancient things in the tombs have been **brought to light** by archaeologists.
무덤 속에 있는 많은 고대의 물건들이 고고학자들에 의해 세상에 모습을 드러냈다.
After three years' study, the scientists **brought** their findings **to light**.
3년간의 연구 끝에 과학자들은 연구 결과를 발표했다.

at short notice 즉시, 급히

[SYN] right after; immediately; quickly

He had to fly to New York **at short notice**.
그는 즉시 뉴욕으로 가야 했다.
He appeared **at short notice** around the corner of the street.
그는 그 거리 바로 어귀에서 예고 없이 나타났다.

at stake 관련이 되어, 위험에 처한, 내기에 걸려 있는

[SYN] depending; like a bet, on the outcome of something uncertain

My honor is **at stake**.
내 명예가 걸려 있는 문제이다.
We can't persuade him to do the job because his life is **at stake**.
그의 목숨이 걸려 있는 문제이므로 우리는 그에게 그 일을 하라고 설득할 수 없다.

by leaps and bounds 일사천리로, 급속하게, 일취월장하여

[SYN] making rapid progress; improving very fast

My English has improved **by leaps and bounds** since I started to speak with foreigners.
내가 외국인들과 말하기 시작한 이후 영어가 급속히 향상되고 있다.
The deadline is tomorrow so we must push the work **by leaps and bounds**.
마감이 내일이므로 우리는 그 일을 일사천리로 밀어붙여야 한다.

(be) characteristic of …의 특징을 나타내는, …에 특유한

[SYN] typical; characterize; peculiar; unique; unusual

It **is characteristic of** him to positive things.
그의 특징은 긍정적으로 말하는 것이다.
Sympathy **is** the feeling **characteristic of** mankind.

동정은 인간 특유의 감정이다.

call it a day 1. 일을 마치다, 하루를 마치다 2. 자다
All of the players are exhausted from hard training. Let's **call it a day**.
모든 선수들이 힘든 훈련으로 지쳤다. 오늘은 그만 하자.
I am so tired and I think I'll have to **call it a day**.
너무 피곤해서 이만 자야 할 것 같다.

SYN 1. finish work of the day 2. sleep; have sleep; roll in

cover up 감추다, 숨기다
The bank clerk couldn't **cover up** his error.
은행원은 자기 잘못을 감추어 둘 수가 없었다.
He was accused of **covering up** a big scandal.
그는 큰 스캔들을 은폐했다고 비난을 받았다.

SYN hide; conceal; cover one's mistake; bury one's wrongdoing

tell from 구별(식별)하다
Can you **tell** Tom **from** his twin brother?
톰을 그의 쌍둥이 형제와 구별할 수 있니?
It is not easy to **tell** cultured pearls **from** genuine pearls.
양식 진주와 진짜 진주를 구별하는 것은 쉽지 않다.

SYN distinguish between; make a distinction between

take it easy 마음을 느긋하게 먹다, 쉬엄쉬엄하다
If you don't **take it easy**, you will finally damage your health.
쉬엄쉬엄하지 않으면 결국 건강을 해치게 될 것이다.
The doctor advised Sam to **take it easy** for a while after the operation.
의사는 샘에게 수술 후에는 한동안 무리하지 말아야 한다고 충고했다.

SYN relax; refrain from anger, violence, hate, etc.; refrain from hard work

push around [about] (사람을) 매정하게 다루다, 혹사하다, 들볶다, 못살게 굴다
She tries to **push** the other committee members **around**.
그녀는 다른 위원들을 못살게 군다.
The big boy always **pushes** the smaller kids **about**.
그 큰 소년은 항상 어린 아이들을 괴롭힌다.

SYN treat someone roughly or unfairly

pull one's leg 남을 놀리다, 속이다
His remarks hurt you? Forget them, because he was **pulling your leg**.
그의 말에 상처를 입었다고? 잊어버려. 그가 너를 놀리려고 한 말이

SYN kid; fool; trick somebody

니까.
Someday he will **pull your leg**, so don't trust him so much.
언젠가는 그가 너를 속이려 들 테니까 그를 너무 믿지 마.

seek after (for) …을 찾다, 추구하다, 탐내다

He is **seeking after** wealth and power and position.
그는 부와 권력을 추구하고 있다.
Everyone **seeks for** happiness and so do I.
누구나 행복을 갈구하며 나도 마찬가지이다.

[SYN.] pursue; look for; search for; desire eagerly; try to find

see to 신경 쓰다, 유의하다, …을 보다, 살피다

As your face look pale, you must **see to** your health.
얼굴이 창백해 보이니 건강에 유의해야겠다.
I will **see to** the patient, so take some rest.
그 환자는 내가 돌볼 테니 좀 쉬어라.

[SYN.] be careful; care about; keep in mind; take care of; care for

at one's wit's (wits') end 어찌할 바를 몰라, 생각다 못해

The authorities are **at their wits' end** about juvenile delinquency.
당국은 청소년 비행에 대해 어찌할 바를 몰랐다.
He was completely **at his wits' end**.
그는 도무지 어찌할 줄을 몰랐다.

[SYN.] not knowing what to do; at a loss

at one's disposal 자유롭게, 마음대로

The house is my own property, so it is **at my disposal**.
그 집은 내 재산이니까 내 마음대로 해도 된다.
You are my guest so my yacht is **at your disposal**.
당신은 내 손님이므로 내 요트를 마음대로 써도 좋다.

[SYN.] at will; freely

to the life 실물 그대로, 생생하게, 조금도 틀림없이

This picture is not beautiful, but seems to be drawn **to the life**.
이 그림은 그다지 예쁘진 않지만 실물 그대로 그려진 것 같다.
This picture of an apple is exact **to the life**.
이 사과 그림은 꼭 실물 같다.

[SYN.] like the living original; exactly

to say the least (of it) 줄잡아 말하더라도, 관대히

[SYN.] to put it very mildly

봐주더라도
It's a boring novel, **to say the least**.
아무리 잘 봐준다 해도 이 소설은 따분하다.
To say the least of it, it is dangerous to smoke so much.
아무리 봐줘서 말해도 담배를 그렇게 많이 피우는 것은 위험하다.

rain cats and dogs 비가 억수같이 내리다

In the middle of the baseball game, it started to **rain cats and dogs**.
야구 경기 중간에 비가 억수같이 내리기 시작했다.
As it started to **rain cats and dogs**, we had to cancel the picnic.
비가 억수같이 내리기 시작하여 우리는 야유회를 취소해야 했다.

[SYN] rain very heavily

rub it in 싫은 것을 집요하게 말하다

Don't **rub it in**.
그렇게 자꾸 잔소리하지 마.
They **rubbed it in** that he had made a mistake.
그들은 그가 실수했다고 듣기 싫게 되풀이했다.

[SYN] remind one of his/her failures

at heart 마음속은, 본심은, 실제로

My father has welfare of our family **at heart**.
아버지는 가족의 행복을 항상 마음에 두고 계신다.
Although he looks perverse, he's good-natured **at heart**.
그는 괴팍해 보이지만 천성은 착하다.

[SYN] at bottom; in reality; basically

at a glance 한눈에, 언뜻 보면

She saw **at a glance** that her daughter had been crying.
그녀는 한눈에 딸이 울고 있었음을 알았다.
At a glance he looks very competent, but the truth is not so.
언뜻 보면 그는 매우 유능해 보이지만 사실은 그렇지 않다.

[SYN] at the first blush

come over 일어나다, 엄습하다

A sudden fit of anger **came over** him.
갑자기 분노가 그를 사로잡았다.
A great tenderness **came over** her and John fell in love with her at the first sight.
그 여자에게서 대단한 부드러움이 풍겼으며 존은 첫눈에 그녀를 사랑

[SYN] happen; seize; take by surprise

하게 되었다.

come to pass 일어나다, 생기다
An unbelievable accident **came to pass**.
믿지 못할 사고가 일어났다.
When did all of this **come to pass**?
언제 이 모든 일이 일어났느냐?

[SYN] happen; occur; take place

in one's company …와 함께 있으면
I feel comfortable **in his company**.
그와 함께라면 마음이 편하다.

[SYN] together with; along with

in one's line 성미에 맞는, 장기인, …의 전문인, 잘 하는
To lie is not **in his line**.
그는 거짓말하는 것에 서투르다.
John may not look so, but poetry is **in his line**.
그렇게 보이지 않겠지만 존은 시가 전문이다.

[SYN] good at; proficient in; congenial to

mix up 혼동하다
Students of English often **mix up** the words 'lie' and 'lay'.
영어를 공부하는 학생들은 lie와 lay를 잘 혼동한다.
She often **mixes up** fancies with realities.
그녀는 종종 공상과 현실을 혼동한다.

[SYN] confuse
cf. mix A with B A와 B를 혼합하다

make good 1. 성공하다 2. (입장·지위를) 유지하다, 약속을 지키다
She **made good** at banking career.
그녀는 금융 분야에서 성공했다.
You must **make good** your promise to me.
당신은 내게 한 약속을 지켜야 한다.

[SYN] 1. succeed; make a go of; be successful 2. do what one promises to do

take part[sides] with / take part of … (쪽을) 편들다
America **took part with** England in World War II.
미국은 2차 세계대전에서 영국 편을 들었다.
He always **takes sides with** the poor.
그는 항상 가난한 사람들 편을 든다.

[SYN] range oneself; side with; take up for

tide over 헤쳐나가다, 극복하다
Will the money **tide** you **over** until you get your

[SYN] overcome; get over; surmount

wages?
급료를 받을 때까지 그 돈으로 꾸려 나갈 수 있겠는가?
My father lost his job last year, but he had saved enough money to **tide** us **over** for some time.
아버지는 지난 해 실직하셨지만 당분간 견딜 수 있을 만큼 돈을 충분히 저축하셨다.

all ears 귀를 기울여서, 경청하여

Why do you stop? Go ahead. Don't you see that we are **all ears** like this?
왜 그만두는 거야? 계속해. 우리가 이렇게 귀를 기울이고 있는 것이 안 보여?
When the teacher started to talk about dinosaur, the students were **all ears**.
선생님이 공룡 이야기를 시작하자 학생들은 모두 경청했다.

[SYN] listening carefully; listen attentively to; strain one's ears to

ascribe A to B A에 대해 B 탓으로 돌리다

He **ascribed** his failure **to** his mother.
그는 자신의 실패를 어머니의 탓으로 돌렸다.
He **ascribed** his success **to** luck.
그는 성공을 행운의 탓으로 돌렸다.

[SYN] attribute; blame somebody for something

hang around 하는 일도 없이 시간을 보내다, 빈둥거리다

The final examination is just around the corner and you are **hanging around**.
기말 시험이 바로 코앞에 닥쳤는데 빈둥거리고 있구나.
The teacher warned the students not to **hang around** on the street after school.
선생님은 학생들에게 방과 후에 거리에서 어슬렁거리지 말라고 경고했다.

[SYN] loaf near or in

hold out 1. (희망·가능성 등을) 주다, 제공하다 2. 계속 남아 있다

The shop keeper **held out** a dress for the customer to try on.
점원은 손님에게 옷을 주고 입어 보라고 했다.
I think my socks will **hold out** till Christmas.
내 양말은 크리스마스 때까지는 남아 있을 것이다.

[SYN] 1. put forward; reach out; extend; offer 2. remain; last

bring in 1. (이익·수입을) 초래하다, 생기게 하다 2. 도입하다, 가지고 들어오다, 소개하다

[SYN] 1. earn a particular amount of money; produce a

If he works for our institute, his research will **bring in** $60 a week.
만약 그가 우리 연구소에서 일한다면 그의 연구는 일주일에 60달러의 수입을 발생시킬 것이다.
The government have **brought in** a new law on dangerous dogs.
정부는 위험한 개에 대한 새로운 법을 도입했다.

profit 2. introduce; induce; import

by the light of …의 도움으로

At night, the old man read the letter again and again **by the light of** a candle.
밤에 노인은 촛불로 편지를 읽고 또 읽었다.
Even the children can tell right from wrong **by the light of** nature.
어린이들은 (가르치지 않아도) 직감으로 선과 악을 구분할 수 있다.

[SYN] with the help of

think a great deal of / think a lot of / think much of 매우 중요하게 여기다

The company **thought a great deal of** Bill's plan to save money.
회사는 빌의 절약 안을 매우 중요하게 여겼다.
The politicians must **think a lot of** the people.
정치인들은 국민을 중히 여겨야 한다.
The movie was good generally, though I didn't **think much of** the ending.
결말 부분은 별로 좋지 않았지만 영화는 대체로 좋았다.

[SYN] consider to be very worthy, valuable, or important; esteem highly

to make a long story short 간단히 말하면

To make a long story short, I don't want to go there.
간단히 말해서 나는 거기 가고 싶지 않다.
To make a long story short, she cannot swim across the river.
한 마디로 그녀는 그 강을 헤엄쳐 건널 수 없다.

[SYN] in short; in a word

give vent to 표출하다, 나타내다

The crowd **gave vent to** their anger by throwing stones.
군중들은 돌을 던져서 분노심을 표현했다.
Why don't you **give vent to** your feelings?
왜 자네 감정을 나타내지 않는가?

[SYN] express; show; represent

go in for 1. (경기 등에) 참가하다, (시험을) 치르다 2. …을 좋아하다, 취미로 하다

Mary **went in for** violin contest and won the third prize.
메리는 바이올린 대회에 참가하여 3등을 했다.
I **went in for** a test which was important for my future.
나는 나의 미래를 위해 중요한 시험을 치렀다.
I like skiing, but I don't **go in** much **for** golf.
나는 스키는 좋아하지만 골프는 별로 좋아하지 않는다.

[SYN] 1. take part in; participate in 2. do as a hobby; like

to one's heart's content 마음껏, 만족할 때까지, 실컷

When left alone after the funeral, she cried **to her heart's content**.
장례식이 끝나고 혼자가 되자 그녀는 실컷 울었다.
She revenged herself **to her heart's content**.
그녀는 마음껏 한을 풀었다.

[SYN] as much as one likes; to one's satisfaction; to the full

take one's time 천천히 하다, 서두르지 않다

Not to make mistakes, you should **take your time** than hurry.
실수를 하지 않으려면 서두르기보다는 천천히 해야 한다.
There is much time left, so **take your time**.
아직 시간이 많이 남았으니 서두르지 마라.

[SYN] be slow or unhurried; delay; act slowly

beside the point 요점에서 벗어나, 예상을 빗나가, 부적절하여

The professor's remarks were **beside the point**.
교수의 의견은 요점에서 빗나갔다.
I was sure that Sally would like the birthday present, but that is **beside the point**.
나는 샐리가 생일 선물을 좋아할 것이라고 확신했는데 예상이 빗나갔다.

[SYN] out of point, not appropriate; off the subject

beneath one's dignity 체면이 손상되는

He seems to consider it to be **beneath his dignity** to discuss such a matter openly.
그는 그런 문제를 공개적으로 논의하는 것을 체면에 손상되는 일로 생각하는 것 같다.
It is **beneath my dignity** to answer such a question.

[SYN] hurt one's honor

그런 질문에 대답한다는 것은 체면 문제다.

reflect on [upon] 1. 곰곰이 생각하다, 회고하다 2. …의 체면을 손상하다, 나쁜 영향을 미치다

An old man **reflected on** what he had done in his lifetime.
노인은 평생 무슨 일을 했는지 곰곰이 생각했다.
Your conduct **reflects on** your parents.
너의 행동은 부모님의 체면을 손상시키는 것이다.

SYN 1. think deeply about; ponder on; think on; consider 2. cast blame or discredit

result from 1. …에서 생기다, 유래하다 2. …을 일으키다

To my regret nothing has **resulted from** my efforts.
유감스럽게도 내 노력이 수포로 돌아갔다.
The war **resulted from** a mistaken policy.
그 전쟁은 잘못된 정책 때문에 일어났다.

SYN 1. be caused by 2. bring about
cf. result in …로 끝나다, …에 귀결하다 (=cause; have a result)

to one's honor …의 명예가 되어

Greatly **to his honor**, he passed the examination first on the list.
대단히 명예스럽게도 그는 일등으로 합격했다.

SYN to one's credit

to one's cost 자신의 부담으로, 피해[손해]를 입고, 쓰라린 경험을 하여

I know it **to my cost**.
나는 그것을 쓰라린 경험을 통해 알고 있다.
I learned that **to my cost**.
이제 그 일에는 넌더리가 난다.

SYN according to one's bitter experience; as one knows to one's cost

seeing (that) …인 관점에서 보면, …이라는 점에 비추어, …인 셈치고는, …이므로

The salary was not a bad one, **seeing that** he was still young.
그가 아직 젊은 점을 감안하면 그 봉급은 적은 편이 아니었다.
Seeing (that) it is nine o'clock, we will wait for him no longer.
아홉 시니 그를 더 이상 기다리지 않겠다.

SYN since; as; because; considering; in view of the fact

say to oneself 마음 속으로 생각하다, 혼잣말하다, 다짐하다

She often **says to herself**, Study hard.

SYN talk or mutter to oneself; think

그 여자는 종종 "열심히 공부해"라고 혼잣말을 한다.
Jimmy woke up early and **said to himself**, Shall I get up?
지미는 아침 일찍 잠에서 깨어서 "일어나 볼까?"라고 혼잣말을 했다.

make no difference 차이가 없다, 중요하지 않다, 조금도 문제가 안 된다

It **makes no difference** whether you go today or tomorrow.
오늘 가도 좋고 내일 가도 좋다.
It **makes no difference** to Kathy whether her son marries or not.
그녀의 아들이 결혼을 하든 안 하든 케이시는 상관 없다.

[SYN] not matter; be not important

bring home to …에게 명심시키다, 절실히 느끼게 하다, 깨닫게 하다

My father wants to **bring home to** me the value of money.
아버지는 내가 돈의 가치를 깨우치길 원하신다.
Grown-ups should **bring home to** children the significance of human rights.
어른들은 아이들에게 인권의 중요성을 절실히 깨닫게 해야 한다.

[SYN] make someone remember; show clearly; make realize

by a hair's breadth 가까스로, 간발의 차이로, 아슬아슬하게

The bullet passed the deer **by a hair's breadth** and it ran away.
총알이 아슬아슬하게 사슴을 스쳐 지나가서 사슴은 도망가 버렸다.
I escaped death **by a hair's breadth**.
나는 위기일발로 살아났다.

[SYN] by the skin of one's teeth; barely; narrowly; with difficulty

to a man 예외 없이, 만장일치로, 최후의 한 사람까지

The unionists voted **to a man** to struggle until the company met their demands.
노조원들은 투표를 통해 회사가 그들의 요구를 수용할 때까지 투쟁하는 데 만장일치로 찬성했다.
When John was in a trouble, his friends stood by him **to a man**.
존이 곤경에 처해 있을 때 친구들은 한 사람도 빠짐없이 그를 지지했다.

[SYN] without exception; unanimously; without a single dissenting voice

the minute (that) …하자마자, …하는 즉시, 동시에

[SYN] as soon as; no sooner ~

I knew her **the minute that** I heard the sound of footsteps.
발자국 소리를 듣는 순간 그녀임을 알았다.
I will give him your message **the minute that** he arrives.
그가 도착하는 즉시 당신 전갈을 전해 주겠다.

SYN. than; directly; the moment

(be) assured of ⋯을 확신하고 있다
As you have tried so hard, I **am assured of** your success as a car salesman.
당신이 그렇게 노력을 해왔으니 틀림없이 자동차 영업사원으로 성공할 거야.
I **am assured of** his plan will go well.
그의 계획이 잘 될 것이라고 믿는다.

SYN. be convinced of; be sure of

ask a favor of ⋯에게 부탁하다
Can I **ask a favor of** you?
부탁 하나 해도 될까요?
I want to **ask a favor of** you; will you lend me your book?
한 가지 부탁이 있는데 자네 책 좀 빌려 주겠어?

SYN. ask; beg; make a request

live up to 1. ⋯에 맞게 살아가다, ⋯에 따라 행동하다 2. 기대에 부응하다
He **lives up to** his income.
그는 그의 수입에 맞게 살아간다.
You must **live up to** your father's expectation.
아버지의 기대에 어긋나지 않도록 해야 한다.

SYN. 1. behave according to 2. come to one's expectation

look to A for B A에게 B를 기대하다
He **looked to** his uncle **for** advice.
그는 아저씨에게 조언을 바랐다.
You should not **look to** others **for** help so easily.
남의 도움을 그렇게 쉽게 바래서는 안 된다.

SYN. depend on A for B

as much as to say ... ⋯라고 말하기라도 하듯이
He looked **as much as to say** I told you so.
그는 마치 "내가 그랬지"라고 하는 듯한 표정이었다.
She gave me a look **as much as to say** she hated me.
그녀는 나를 미워하고 있는 듯한 눈초리로 바라보았다.

SYN. as if to say ...

as ... as ever …에 못지 않게, 변함 없이, 여전히

As far as I know, he is **as** great a novelist **as ever** lived.
내가 알고 있는 한 그는 보기 드문 훌륭한 소설가이다.
Mr. Kim is **as** diligent **as ever**.
김 군은 언제 봐도 변함 없이 부지런하다.

[SYN] constantly; still, (as) yet; as (it was) before; as usual; as always
cf. as ... as any …못지 않게 ~하다 (최상급의 뜻)

but that …이 없다면 (뒤에 절이 옴)

But that my parents supported me, my company would certainly have closed the door.
부모님들이 도와 주지 않았다면 회사는 분명 문을 닫았을 것이다.
But that I saw it, I could not have believed it.
그것을 보지 않았더라면 나는 그것을 믿을 수가 없었을 것이다.

[SYN] but for the fact that

beyond one's means 능력 이상으로

They are living **beyond their means**.
그들은 분수에 넘치게 살고 있다.
I am afraid that this car is **beyond our means**.
이 자동차는 우리 분수에 맞지 않는 것 같다.

[SYN] beyond one's ability

out of breath 숨이 차서, 헐떡이며

He ran so fast that he is **out of breath**.
그는 너무 빨리 뛰어서 숨이 차다.
My grandmother gets **out of breath** when she goes up the stairs.
할머니는 계단을 올라갈 때 숨을 헐떡이신다.

[SYN] needing air; breathless

out of season 철이 지난, 한물 간

I am sorry, but because oysters are **out of season**, they are very expensive.
죄송하지만 굴이 제철이 아니어서 무척 비쌉니다.
Now apples are **out of season**, so you'd better eat some other fruit.
지금 사과는 제철이 아니니까 다른 과일을 먹는 것이 좋겠다.

[SYN] not in season; not at the right time

make a fool of …을 놀리다, 우롱하다, 바보로 만들다, 속이다

You had better not **make a fool of** anyone for the purpose of success.
성공을 위해 남을 바보로 만드는 짓은 하지 않는 것이 좋다.
If you continue to **make a fool of** me, I will never meet you again.

[SYN] play a joke on; jeer; poke fun at; deceive

나를 계속 속이면 다시는 너를 만나지 않겠다.

make nothing of ⋯을 아무렇지도 않게 여기다, ⋯을 우습게 여기다

He **makes nothing of** walking 30 miles a day.
그는 하루에 30마일 걷는 것쯤은 아무렇지도 않게 여긴다.
He **made nothing of** hardship.
그는 고생 따위는 아무렇지도 않았다.

[SYN] minimize the importance of something; downplay

leave out 삭제하다, 제외하다, 생략하다

You **left out** the important part in your report.
너는 보고서에서 중요한 부분을 빼먹었다.
See that no one is **left out** at the party.
파티에 한 사람도 빠지지 않도록 주의하여라.

[SYN] omit; eliminate; cross out

let go of ⋯을 놓다

When I **let go of** the ball, it rolled down the hill.
공을 놓자, 공은 언덕 아래도 굴러갔다.
A monkey **let go of** a branch and dropped to the ground.
원숭이는 가지에서 손을 놓고 땅으로 떨어졌다.

[SYN] release one's hold on; release

run away with 1. 훔치어 도망치다 2. ⋯와 함께 도망치다

Susan's teenage son **ran away with** her jewels last night.
수잔의 십대 아들이 어젯밤 그녀의 보석을 가지고 도망쳤다.
She **ran away with** her baby so that no one would take him.
그녀는 누구도 아기를 빼앗아 가지 못하게 아기를 데리고 도망쳤다.

[SYN] 1. depart and take with one; steal something 2. escape with someone

resort to 1. (수단 등에) 호소하다, 도움을 청하다 2. 잘 가다(다니다), 가다

If other means fail, we shall **resort to** force.
다른 방법들이 실패하면 무력에 호소할 것이다.
Young people **resort to** the seaside or the mountains in summer.
젊은이들은 여름에 바닷가나 산으로 잘 간다.

[SYN] 1. do or use something extreme, often dishonest; appeal to 2. frequently visit

come home to 가슴에 사무치다

If you read the letter carefully, its meaning will **come home to** you.

[SYN] become gradually clear to

편지를 주의 깊게 읽으면 그 의미가 분명해질 것이다.
None of these **come home to** me so truly.
이들 중 어느 것도 나에게는 그렇게 진실로 와 닿지 않는다.

come close to 거의 …할 뻔하다, 하마터면 …할 뻔하다

[SYN] come near to

The national football team **came close to** losing the game.
국가 대표 축구팀은 거의 시합에서 질 뻔했다.
When the rescuer arrived, I **came close to** drowning.
구조대원이 도착했을 때 나는 하마터면 익사할 뻔했다.

quiet down 조용해지다

[SYN] become quiet

They'll **quiet down** as soon as you begin speaking.
당신이 연설을 시작하면 곧 조용해질 거요.
If you don't **quiet down**, I'll call the police.
당신이 조용하지 않으면, 경찰을 부르겠소.

not that ..., but that ~ …때문이 아니라 ~ 때문에

[SYN] not because ... but because ~

Not that he is lazy, **but that** he is a dull fellow.
그가 게으른 게 아니라 미련한 놈이라는 것이다.
Not that I loved Caesar less, **but that** I loved Rome more.
내가 시저를 덜 사랑해서가 아니라 로마를 더 사랑했기 때문이다.

keep one's temper 참다, 화를 억누르다

[SYN] control of one's anger; be patient; endure

People should learn to **keep their temper** when they are children.
사람들은 어렸을 때 참는 것을 배워야 한다.
Bill got thrown off the club, because he couldn't **keep his temper**.
빌은 성질을 억제하지 못해 클럽에서 쫓겨났다.

know by heart 암기하고 있다 (배운 것을 이미 암기하고 있는 상태를 말함)

[SYN] have by heart
cf. learn by heart …을 암기하다, 외우다 (=get by heart; commit to memory; memorize)

Little as the girl is, she **knows** those old songs **by heart**.
그 소녀는 어린데도 그 옛날 노래들을 다 알고 있다.
My brother **knows** a lot of English poems **by heart**.
내 남동생은 영어시를 많이 외우고 있다.

fall short 부족하다, 모자라다, 미달이다, 목표를 달성하지 못하다

They died of hunger, and it was because provisions **fell short**.
그들은 굶어 죽었으며 그것은 식량 부족 때문이었다.
The rope **fell short**, so we failed to save the victim.
밧줄이 짧아서 조난자를 구하지 못했다.

[SYN] be lacking; be insufficient; be in want (of); be in need (of); be wanting (in); fail to reach
cf. fall short of 뜻은 위와 동일하지만 다음에 명사나 동명사가 옴.

fight it out 싸움을 해결하다

You want me to **fight it out**, but it's none of my business.
당신은 내가 해결하기를 바라지만 그건 나하고는 전혀 상관 없는 문제다.
Let them **fight it out** alone.
그들끼리 해결하도록 냐둬.

[SYN] settle the argument

in earnest 진정으로, 진지하게, 본격적으로

Are you **in earnest**?
정말이야 (농담은 아니겠지)?
It started to rain **in earnest**.
비가 본격적으로 내리기 시작했다.

[SYN] seriously; in a determined way

apply oneself to …에 전념하다, …에 몰두하다

You will always **apply yourself to** your study.
너는 항상 학문에 전념하겠지.
He **applied himself to** the study of medicine.
그는 의학 연구에 전념했다.

[SYN] devote(give) oneself to; be absorbed in; concentrate on

as regards …에 관해서, …에 대해

He is always secretive **as regards** what he did during the war.
전쟁 동안 한 일에 대해서 그는 항상 비밀로 한다.
You don't have to worry **as regards** the cost of the event, because we have many patrons.
행사 비용에 대해서는 걱정하지 않아도 된다. 우리에게는 후원자가 많이 있어.

[SYN] regarding; concerning; about

play along with 적당히 얼버무리다

Don't worry, I'll **play along with** him as usual.
염려하지 마, 늘 하듯이 얼버무릴 테니.
I'll **play along with** whatever he says.
그가 하는 말에는 적당히 넘어가려고 해.

[SYN] pretend to agree with someone

under (the) cover of (어둠 등을) 틈타, …의 엄호를 받아, …을 이용하여, …을 빙자하여

He stole a watermelon **under cover of** darkness.
그는 어둠을 틈타 수박을 훔쳤다.
Some prisoners escaped **under cover of** the loose guard.
경비가 소홀한 틈을 타서 죄수 몇 명이 도망쳤다.

[SYN] taking advantage of; on pretence of

set down 1. 적다, 적어두다 2. 아래에 놓다, 내려놓다 3. 탈 것에서 내리다

The writer **set down** her thoughts in a journal.
작가는 잡지에 자신의 생각을 기술했다.
He **set down** the heavy box at the corner.
그는 무거운 상자를 구석에 내려놓았다.
I will **set** you **down** at the subway station.
지하철역에서 내려 드리겠습니다.

[SYN] 1. put in writing 2. put down; unload 3. set a passenger down; drop; discharge

scrape together (자금·선수 등을) 긁어모으다, 마련하다, 고생하여 모으다

See if you can **scrape together** enough boys for a soccer game.
축구 시합을 할 수 있을 정도의 아이들을 모아 봐.
I finally **scraped together** enough money for a flight home.
마침내 집으로 갈 항공료를 마련했다.

[SYN] accumulate with difficulty

vote down 투표로 부결시키다

There are rumors that the council may **vote down** the pay raise for city employees.
시 직원의 봉급 인상을 시의회가 부결시킨다는 소문이 있다.
The senate **voted down** the proposed budget.
상원은 예산안을 부결했다.

[SYN] defeat by voting

draw on 1. …에 가까워지다, …이 다가오다 2. (근원을) …에 의존하다, …을 이용하다 3. (장갑·양말 등을) 신다, 끼다

With the examination **drawing on**, there are many students in the library.
시험이 다가오니 도서관에 학생들이 많다.
They could **draw on** the company for expenses of the picnic.
그들은 야유회 경비를 회사에 의존할 수 있었다.

[SYN] 1. come near; approach 2. depend on 3. wear; put on

It's cold outside, so you should **draw on** your wool socks.
밖이 추우니까 모 양말을 신어라.

disapprove of 불찬성을 주장하다
The mother **disapproved of** her child's going on a trip.
그 엄마는 아이가 여행가는 것에 찬성하지 않았다.
My father strongly **disapproves of** girls' drinking and smoking.
아버지는 소녀들이 술 마시고 담배 피우는 것에 대해 절대 반대하신다.

[SYN] have or express a low opinion of

without the knowledge of …에게 알리지도 않고
They married **without the knowledge of** their parents.
그들은 부모님들에게 알리지도 않고 결혼했다.
He left for Paris **without the knowledge of** his wife.
그는 아내 모르게 파리로 떠났다.

[SYN] without informing

with reason 사리에 맞아, 당연하여, 이유가 있어
He complains **with reason**.
그가 불평하는 것도 당연하다.
She stopped talking to him **with reason**; he made her very angry.
그가 그녀를 매우 화나게 했기 때문에 그녀가 그에게 말을 하지 않는 것도 당연하다.

[SYN] rightly; justifiably

through thick and thin 시종여일하게, 온갖 고난을 무릅쓰고, 물불 가리지 않고
The two friends were faithful **through thick and thin**.
그 두 친구는 좋을 때나 나쁠 때나 우애가 좋았다.
We decided to be together **through thick and thin** until we die.
우리는 죽을 때까지 항상 함께 하기로 결심했다.

[SYN] in good times and bad times; in every eventuality

to do + 사람[사물] + justice …을 공정하게 평가하자면
To do her justice, she was not a kind woman.
그 여자를 공정하게 평가하자면 친절한 여자는 아니었다.

[SYN] to be fair; in fairness to

To do him justice, he is a talented musician.
공평하게 평하면 그는 재능 있는 음악가다.

give off 내다, 방출하다, 발하다

[SYN] emit; send out; release

Cheap perfume **gives off** bad smell.
싸구려 향수는 악취가 난다.
When water boils, it **gives off** steam.
물이 끓으면 김이 난다.

every inch [nook, corner] 어디까지나, 완전히, 철두철미, 구석구석까지

[SYN] completely; entirely; through and through

I know **every inch** of this town.
나는 이 마을의 구석구석까지 알고 있다.
Educated in England, John is **every inch** a gentleman.
영국에서 교육받은 존은 어느 모로 보나 신사이다.

have done with …을 중단하다

[SYN] stop doing or using something

When you **have done with** the copy machine, I would like to use it.
네가 복사기를 다 쓰고 나면 내가 쓰고 싶다.
I wish you would **have done with** your complaint.
불평을 좀 그만 했으면 좋겠다.

judge by …으로 판단[비평, 평가]하다

[SYN] from a judgment; decide; estimate

One is often **judged by** the company one keeps.
사람은 종종 교제하는 친구에 의해 평가된다.
Judging by reports, he seems to be a great man.
보고서로 판단하건대 그는 아주 훌륭한 사람인 것 같다.

one and the same 동일한

[SYN] same

The man whom you are mentioning and Bill are **one and the same**.
당신이 말하고 있는 남자와 빌은 같은 사람이다.
I thought your husband and the generous businessman were **one and the same**.
나는 당신 남편과 그 관대한 사업가가 동일 인물인 줄 알았다.

out of one's mind 제 정신이 아닌, 미친

[SYN] mad; insane

She is beautiful and attractive, but seems to be **out of her mind**.
그녀는 아름답고 매력적이지만 제 정신이 아닌 것 같다.

When I met her, she was **out of her mind** because of her husband's death.
내가 그녀를 만났을 때 그녀는 남편의 죽음으로 제 정신이 아니었다.

break with 관계를 끊다, 그만두다, 거부하다

He **broke with** all his relatives.
그는 모든 친척들과 절교했다.
You had better **break with** such a bad habit.
그런 나쁜 버릇은 끊는 것이 좋겠다.

[SYN.] have done with; break off

be too much for …에게 벅차다, …의 힘에 겹다

This book **was too much for** me, so I decided to give it up.
이 책은 나에게 너무 어려워서 포기하기로 했다.
The boy **is too much for** the teacher.
그 선생님은 그 아이를 감당할 수가 없다.

[SYN.] be beyond someone's power; be above someone's ability

without leave 무단으로, 허가 없이

In the dormitory, you must not do as you like **without leave**.
기숙사에서는 허가 없이 하고 싶은 대로 해서는 안 된다.
They are mine, so don't take any of them **without leave**.
그것들은 내 것이니까 무엇이든 허락 없이 가지고 가지 마라.

[SYN.] without permission; without notice

work out 1. 풀다, 잘 해결하다 2. 잘 되어가다, 좋은 결과가 되다

Bill tried to **work out** the math problems all by himself.
빌은 수학 문제를 혼자 힘으로 풀려고 애썼다.
Don't worry, because everything will **work out** all right in the end.
결국 모든 것이 잘 될 테니까 걱정하지 마.

[SYN.] 1. find an answer to; solve; bring to settlement 2. get results; be efficient

come off 1. 일어나다 2. …의 결과가 되다, 성공하다

Everybody in the company worried but the general strike didn't **come off**.
회사 사람 모두가 걱정했지만 총파업은 일어나지 않았다.
The peace talk finally **came off** though there were some obstacles.
장애물이 좀 있었지만 평화 회담은 결국 성사되었다.

[SYN.] 1. happen; take place; occur 2. succeed; do well; come about

come up to 접근하다, 필적하다, 맞다
Your work doesn't **come up to** what I expect of you.
네 일은 내가 기대하는 만큼 좋지 않다.
The work ability of new employees has not **come up to** that of their seniors.
신입 사원들의 업무 능력은 그들 선배에 미치지 못했다.

[SYN] reach; get to; be equal; match; approach

pride oneself on …을 자랑하다, …을 자만하다
He **prides himself on** having a son who is a famed scientist.
그는 유명한 과학자 아들을 둔 것을 자랑스럽게 생각한다.
Neil **prides himself on** his talent as a comedy writer.
닐은 코미디 작가로서의 재능을 자랑스럽게 여긴다.

[SYN] be proud of; take pride in

pat on the back [shoulder etc.] 등을 두드려 격려하다
The coach **patted** the runners **on the back** before the race.
시합 전에 코치는 선수들의 등을 두드려 격려했다.
He **patted** me **on the shoulder**.
그는 가볍게 내 어깨를 쳤다.

[SYN] clap lightly on the back in encouragement, or praise

date from [back to] …로 거슬러가다
This university **dates from** the early 17th century.
이 대학은 17세기 초기에 시작됐다.
I can **date back to** when I was five years old.
내 기억은 내가 다섯 살이었을 때까지 거슬러 올라간다.

[SYN] go back to; lead back to; originate in

take in 1. …을 이해하다 2. …을 속이다
He spoke too fast for me to **take in**.
그는 말을 너무 빨리 해서 이해할 수가 없었다.
The teacher was **taken in** by the boy's innocent manner.
선생님은 소년의 순진한 태도에 속았다.

[SYN] 1. understand; make out 2. deceive; trick; cheat
cf. take to 1. …에 몰두하다 (= be absorbed in; devote oneself to) 2. …을 좋아하게 되다 (= care for; become fond of)

take down 적어 놓다, 써 두다
Please **take down** my telephone number in case you should forget it.
잊으면 안 되니까 제 전화번호를 적어 두세요.
I will tell you the best way to get there, so you had

[SYN] write down; put down; record; note

better **take down**.
그 곳에 가는 가장 좋은 방법을 일러 줄 테니까 적어 둬라.

so [as] far as ... (be) concerned ···에 관한 한은

[SYN] to the extent that

So far as I **am concerned**, forget the whole thing.
나에 관한 한 전부 잊어라.
So far as grammar **is concerned**, this composition leaves nothing to be desired.
문법에 관한 한 이 작문은 더 바랄 것이 없다.

shrink from 꽁무니를 빼다, 피하다, 주눅들다

[SYN] move away from something horrible or frightening

A shy man **shrinks from** meeting strangers.
내성적인 사람은 모르는 사람들과 만나는 것을 피한다.
She **shrinks from** meeting people and always stays at home.
그녀는 사람들과 만나는 것을 피하고 집에만 있는다.

without exaggeration 과장 없이

[SYN] without overstatement; without magnification

It may be said **without exaggeration** that he is a genius.
그는 천재라고 해도 과언이 아니다.
(=It is no exaggeration to say that he is a genius.)

go through with 끝마치다, 계획한 대로 실행하다

[SYN] complete, finish

I don't think Bill will **go through with** his plan.
빌이 그의 계획을 실천하리라고 생각지 않는다.
However hard the plan may be, we are resolved to **go through with** it.
아무리 그 계획이 어렵다 할지라도 우리는 그것을 수행하기로 결심했다.

have something to oneself ···을 혼자 차지하다

[SYN] possess exclusively; monopolize; engross

The man **had** a two-person seat **to himself** on the crowded bus.
그 남자는 복잡한 버스에서 2인용 좌석을 혼자 차지하고 있었다.
Why do you **have** such a big desk **to yourself**?
왜 혼자서 그 큰 책상을 차지하고 있는 거야?

establish oneself as ···로서 입신하다, 명성을 얻다

[SYN] succeed in life; get on in life

She **established herself as** a great lawyer of the day.

그녀는 당대의 훌륭한 변호사가 되었다.

vouch for ⋯ 보증을 서다

I can personally **vouch for** his ability.
개인적으로 제가 그의 능력을 보증할 수 있습니다.
I can **vouch for** his financial integrity.
그가 재정 면에서 문제가 없다는 것은 제가 보증합니다.

[SYN] give assurance about someone

indulge (oneself) in 빠지다, 탐닉하다

It is a bad habit to **indulge in** smoking when young.
젊어서 흡연에 빠지는 것은 나쁜 습관이다.
She sometimes **indulges herself in** drinking.
그녀는 가끔 술에 탐닉한다.

[SYN] allow oneself to enjoy; abandon oneself to
cf. indulgent to (with) 관대한, 눈감아 주는 (=generous; broad-minded)

It is doubtful whether ⋯인지 의문이다

It is doubtful whether he will execute the work properly.
그가 그 일을 제대로 수행할지 의문이다.
(=I doubt whether he will execute the work properly.)

[SYN] We doubt whether (if)

again and again 여러 번, 되풀이하여, 재삼

I hate that song because he played the same record **again and again**.
그가 같은 음반을 몇 번이고 틀었기 때문에 나는 그 노래가 싫다.
I've told you **again and again** to save money to buy the computer.
컴퓨터 살 돈을 모으라고 몇 번이나 말했잖아.

[SYN] repeatedly; over and over again; more than once; often
cf. ever and again 때때로 (=now and again)

as far as ... goes / as far as ... is concerned ⋯에 관해 말하자면, 실제로

I didn't enjoy the book, and **as far as** that **goes**, I never like mystery novels.
그 책은 재미가 없었어. 그리고 사실 말이지 나는 추리소설이 정말 싫어.
As far as swimming **is concerned**, Jim is pretty good at that.
수영에 관한 한 짐은 상당히 잘 해.

[SYN] while we are talking about it; also; actually

none too 조금도 ⋯아니다, 조금도 ⋯않다

You arrived **none too** late, so you don't have to

[SYN] not at all

feel sorry.
조금도 늦게 오지 않았으니 미안하게 느낄 필요 없다.
Your new clothes are **none too** fashionable.
너의 새 옷은 전혀 멋지지 않다.

not ... because ~ ~이라고 해서 …하면 안 되는

We should **not** look down on the man **because** he is poor.
우리는 그가 가난하다고 해서 그를 업신여겨서는 안 된다.
You must **not** be absent from school just **because** you are busy.
그저 바쁘다고 해서 학교를 결석해서는 안 된다.

no better than …에 불과한, …에 지나지 않는, …나 다름이 없는

He is **no better than** a beggar.
그는 거지나 다름없다.
With that kind of inflation their money is **no better than** mere paper.
그러한 인플레이션 하에서 그들의 돈은 단지 종이에 불과하다.

[SYN] nothing but; much the same; all the same
cf. not better than …보다 낫지 않아, 기껏해야 …에 불과하여 (= not so good as)

flatter oneself 자만하다

Tom **flatters himself** that he is the best swimmer in his class.
톰은 자기가 반에서 수영을 가장 잘 한다고 자만하고 있다.
Mary **flatters herself** that she is beautiful and smart.
메리는 자기 딴에는 예쁘고 똑똑하다고 생각한다.

[SYN] be conceited; fancy oneself

for fear that ... may [might] / lest ... should …하지 않을까 하고, …하지 않도록

The clerk had told a lie **for fear that** she **might** be scolded.
점원은 야단을 맞을까 두려워 거짓말을 했다.
You had better take your raincoat **lest** it **should** rain.
비가 올지 모르니까 우비를 가지고 가는 것이 좋겠다.
I fear **lest** he **should** die.
그가 죽지나 않을까 걱정이다.

[SYN] for fear of; so that ... not

keep one's [an] eye on [upon] …에 주의하다, …을 주목하다, 지켜보다

[SYN] keep watch; look out
cf. keep out off 방심하다, …로부

Keep your eye on my dog while I am out.
내가 없는 동안 우리 개에게 신경을 좀 써 줘.
As he is a dishonest fellow, we must **keep an eye on** him.
그는 정직하지 못한 놈이므로 그를 감시해야 한다.

터 눈을 떼다

keep good time 시간이 정확하다 (보통 시계에 사용)

The watch is very old and not good-looking, but it **keeps good time**.
그 시계는 매우 오래 되었고 보기도 좋지 않지만 시간은 정확하다.
My watch **keeps** very **good time**.
내 시계는 시간이 아주 잘 맞는다.

[SYN] be punctual; be accurate
cf. keep bad time (시계가) 잘 안 맞다

under the circumstances 그러한 사정에서는, 현 상황에서, 현재의 조건에서

Under the circumstances, that is the best (that) I can do.
현 상태로는 내가 할 수 있는 것은 그것이 고작이다.
Under the circumstances, I can't join the strike risking my job.
현 상황에서는 직장을 잃을 각오를 하면서 파업에 동참할 수 없다.

[SYN] conditions being what they are or were

rest on [upon] 1. (눈·시선이) 멈추다, 쏠리다 2. …에 의거하다, …에 기초를 두고 있다 3. (짐·책임이) 지워져 있다

His eyes **rested on** a lace cap she had been making.
그의 시선은 그녀가 만들고 있던 레이스 모자에 쏠렸다.
He **rests** his theory **on** three basic premises.
그의 이론은 세 가지 기본 전제에 의거한다.
No responsibility **rests on** you.
당신에게는 아무런 책임이 없소.

[SYN] 1. look at quietly 2. depend on; use for support; be based on 3. be imposed on

lead astray 길을 잃게 하다, 타락시키다

John will **lead** you **astray**, so you should not keep company with him.
존은 너를 나쁜 길로 들게 할 것이니 그와 어울리지 않는 것이 좋다.
I heard that he **led** every friend he met **astray**.
나는 그가 만나는 친구마다 타락시킨다고 들었다.

[SYN] tempt somebody to do wrong

make a point of -ing 1. 항상(반드시) …하다, …하는 것을 결코 잊지 않다 2. …을 주장(강조, 중요시)하다

[SYN] 1. never fail to do something 2. emphasize;

He **made a point of** tak**ing** a walk before breakfast.

그는 아침식사 전에 반드시 산책을 한다.

Father **made** a great **point of** our return**ing** home on time.

아버지는 우리에게 정시에 귀가하라고 매우 강조하셨다.

stress

come up with 1. …을 따라잡다 2. 제안하다

Her car easily **came up with** my car.

그녀의 차는 쉽게 내 차를 따라잡았다.

Janet **came up with** nice ideas for improving on her previous plans.

재닛은 이전의 계획을 개선할 좋은 생각을 내 놓았다.

[SYN] 1. catch up; overtake 2. suggest; offer

cf. come up to 접근하다, 필적하다 (=reach; get to; be equal; match; approach)

pull oneself together 기운을 차리다, 회복하다, 원기를 회복하다, 재기하다

After his mother's funeral, he **pulled himself together**.

어머니의 장례식을 치른 후 그는 기운을 차렸다.

She was really depressed because of her test, but she **pulled herself together**.

그녀는 시험 때문에 정말 기분이 엉망이었지만 기운을 차렸다.

[SYN] regain one's power, courage; collect one's facilities

out of sight 보이지 않는

Until the train was **out of sight**, mother stood on the platform.

기차가 보이지 않을 때까지 어머니는 플랫폼에 서 있었다.

While the guests are in the house, stay **out of sight**.

손님들이 집에 계시는 동안 보이지 않게 있어라.

[SYN] not visible

on the one hand …, on the other hand 한편으로는 …, 또 한편으로는

On the one hand I have to work, **on the other hand** I have many visitors to see.

한편으로는 나는 일을 해야 하며 다른 한편으로는 만나야 할 손님들이 많다.

On the one hand he is intelligent, but **on the other hand** he is lazy.

한편으로 그는 똑똑하지만 또 한편으로는 게으르다.

[SYN] viewed one way, then another way

replace A by (with) B A와 B를 바꾸다, 교체하

[SYN] exchange A for B

다, 갈다
They have **replaced** their sedan **by** a coupe.
그들은 세단형 차를 쿠페형으로 바꾸었다.
The old bridge was **replaced by** a new one.
낡은 다리는 새 것으로 교체되었다.

reluctant to ⋯하기 싫어하는, 마지못해 하는, 마음 내키지 않는

She was **reluctant to** marry him.
그녀는 그와의 결혼에 마음이 내키지 않았다.
He was very **reluctant to** help our group.
그는 우리를 돕는 것을 아주 싫어했다.

[SYN] unwilling to

know better than to ⋯할 만큼 바보는 아니다, 더 현명하다, 한층 분별이 있다

He **knows better than to** do such a thing.
그는 그런 일을 할 만큼 어리석지 않다.
(=He is not so foolish as to do such a thing.
 =He is not such a fool as to do such a thing.
 =He is too wise to do such a thing.
 =He is wise enough not to do such a thing.
 =He is so wise that he cannot do such a thing.)

[SYN] be not so foolish as to; be not such a fool as to; be too wise to; be wise enough not to; so wise that ... cannot)

follow up on 철저히 추구하다

I want you to **follow up on** that story about the fire.
그 화재 사건을 추적 취재해 주기 바랍니다.
A good salesman always **follows up on** potential customers.
훌륭한 세일즈맨은 항상 잠재 고객을 철저히 추구한다.

[SYN] act further on; carry out fully

for the life of one (보통 부정문에서) 도저히, 아무리 해도 (⋯않다)

I couldn't, **for the life of me**, remember where I had left my bag.
어디다 가방을 두었는지 도저히 생각나지 않았다.
I cannot, **for the life of me**, remember when John's birthday is.
존의 생일이 언제인지 아무리 해도 기억이 나지 않는다.

[SYN] even with the utmost effort; by any means
cf. for dear life; for one's life 목숨을 걸고, 필사적으로, 열심히 (= desperately)

at will 마음대로, 뜻대로, 좋을 대로

The manager controls his men **at will**.

[SYN] at one's will; freely; as one likes

경영자는 그의 사원들을 마음대로 부리고 있다.
When you have done with the job assigned to you, you may go home **at will**.
주어진 일을 다 하면 마음대로 집에 가도 좋다.

cf. with a will 단호히, 진심으로, 열심히 (= heartily; firmly; resolutely)

attribute A to B A를 B의 탓으로 돌리다, A를 B의 것이라고 생각하다

He **attributed** his success **to** good luck.
그는 자신의 성공을 행운의 탓으로 돌렸다.
They **attributed** the recently discovered manuscript **to** Shakespeare.
사람들은 최근에 발견된 원고가 셰익스피어의 것이라고 생각했다.

[SYN.] ascribe A to B; impute A to B

come near -ing 거의 …하게끔 되다, 자칫 …할 뻔하다

At the department store, I **came near** buy**ing** an expensive bag.
백화점에서 나는 비싼 핸드백을 살 뻔했다.
I was so angry last night at my wife's rude words that I **came near** hitt**ing** her.
지난밤에는 아내의 무례한 말에 너무 화가 나서 자칫하면 아내를 때릴 뻔했다.

[SYN.] almost do; nearly do

cope with 대처하다, 극복하다

At present we have various difficulties to **cope with**.
현재 대처해야할 난관들이 여러 가지 있다.
My mother hired a babysitter to **cope with** the new baby.
어머니는 새로 태어난 아기를 돌봐 줄 사람을 구했다.

[SYN.] deal effectively; manage adequately

As …, so ~ …와 마찬가지로 ~도 그러한

As food nourishes our body, **so** books nourish our mind.
음식이 몸에 영양이 되는 것처럼 책은 마음의 영양이 된다.
As the desert is like a sea, **so** is the camel like a ship.
사막이 바다라면 낙타는 배다.

[SYN.] equally; as well; likewise; as well as

as the case may be 경우에 따라서, 사정에 맞게

We can meet later at one of those places **as the case may be**.

[SYN.] as facts or circumstances direct, or are applicable

우리는 나중에 형편에 맞게 그 장소들 중 한 곳에서 만나면 돼.
This report has no deadline, so you can finish it **as the case may be**.
이 보고서는 기한이 없는 것이니까 상황에 따라 끝내도 된다.

stand out 눈에 잘 띄다, 두드러지다

Since he is so tall, he **stands out** in the crowd.
그는 키가 너무 커서 많은 사람들 중에서 두드러진다.
There are a number of qualified people, but Baker **stands out** as the best candidate.
자격이 되는 사람이 다수 있지만 베이커가 최적임자로 보인다.

[SYN] be easily seen; be noticeable

set forth 1. 발표하다, 밝히다, 말하다, 설명하다 2. 출발하다, 여행을 떠나다

He **set forth** his view upon the new doctrine.
그는 새 이론에 대하여 견해를 밝혔다.
The troop **set forth** on their 10-mile hike early in the morning.
군대는 10마일 구보를 하기 위해 아침 일찍 출발했다.

[SYN] 1. express formally; publish; express in words; state 2. set out; start; depart; shove off
cf. set forward 촉진하다, 나아가게 하다; 제출(제언)하다; 진술하다

be persuaded of (that) …을 확신하다

I **was persuaded of** his innocence.
나는 그의 무죄를 확신했다.
(= I was persuaded that he was innocent.)

[SYN] believe firmly; be convinced of; be sure of

between ourselves 우리들끼리 만의 이야기인데, 이것은 비밀인데

Between ourselves, I know that John loves Mary.
이것은 비밀인데 존이 메리를 사랑한다는 걸 난 알아.
Between ourselves, she is not honest.
우리끼리 이야기인데 그녀는 정직하지 않다.
(= Between you and me, she is not honest.)

[SYN] between you, me, and the gatepost; between you and me, in confidence

can (can't) afford to …할 여유가 있다(없다)

I **can't afford to** buy the book.
나는 그 책을 살 여유가 없다.
I **can't afford to** let a chance like this go by.
이런 기회를 그냥 놓칠 수는 없다.

[SYN] be (not) able to pay for something without difficulty

leave off 1. 그만두다 2. …을 벗다

Leave off biting your nails.
손톱 깨무는 것을 그만두어라.

[SYN] 1. stop; cease; abandon 2. take off; peel off

I hope you will **leave off** both drinking and smoking.
네가 술도 담배도 다 끊기를 바란다.
Leave off your wet coat.
젖은 코트를 벗으세요.

keep away from 가까이 하지 않다, 접근시키지 않다, 피하다

I told the children to **keep away from** the stray dogs.
나는 아이들에게 떠돌아다니는 개들을 멀리 하라고 일렀다.
Keep away from the water edge.
물가에 가까이 가지 말아라.

[SYN] stay at a distance from; not go near somebody or something

persuade ... of …을 납득시키다, 권하여 …하게 하다

The teacher **persuaded** his students **of** their mistakes.
선생님은 학생들에게 그들의 잘못을 납득시켰다.
I couldn't **persuade** him **of** my honesty.
나는 그에게 나의 정직함을 납득시키지 못했다.

[SYN] make somebody consent; convince

pass over 1. …을 무시하다 2. 제외하다, 빼놓다

He **passed** Jane **over** in favor of her prettier sister.
그는 제인을 무시하고 더 예쁜 동생에게 눈을 돌렸다.
A few items in the program were **passed over** for a lack of time.
시간이 모자라서 프로그램에서 몇 개 항목이 빠졌다.

[SYN] 1. ignore; disregard; pay no attention 2. eliminate from consideration; leave out; omit

spring from 1. 발원하다 2. 싹트다 3. 나타나다 4. …출신이다

The river **springs from** the southern side of the mountain.
그 강은 산의 남쪽에서 발원한다.
Every plant **springs from** its seed.
모든 식물은 씨에서 싹이 튼다.
Where have you **sprung from**?
어디 출신입니까?
He **sprung from** one of the noble families in the kingdom.
그는 왕국의 귀족 출신이었다.

[SYN] 1. flow, rise, or come from; spring up; originate in 2. sprout; bud 3. appear; show up; come out 4. come from

stand in need of / be in need of …을 필요로

[SYN] need; call for; require;

하다 | want
The ship **stands in need of** repairs.
그 배는 수리할 필요가 있다.
He **is in need of** rest.
그에게는 휴식이 필요하다.

rid oneself of ···을 면하다, 제거하다

She **rid herself of** bad habits, like smoking cigarettes.
그녀는 흡연과 같은 나쁜 버릇들을 없앴다.
My father was never able to **rid himself of** the debts.
아버지는 결코 빚에서 헤어날 수 없었다.

[SYN] be free from; relieve

rise in the world 출세하다

I want to **rise in the world** as a graphic artist.
나는 그래픽 예술가로 출세하기를 원한다.
He came up to a big city in search of an opportunity to **rise in the world**.
그는 출세 길을 찾아 대도시로 왔다.

[SYN] succeed in life; get on in life; rise in life

talk+사람+into -ing ···을 설득해서 ~하게 하다

Father **talked** mother **into buying** a new car.
아버지는 어머니를 설득해서 새 차를 사게 했다.
I couldn't **talk** him **into going** fishing with me.
나와 함께 낚시 가도록 그를 설득하지 못했다.

[SYN] persuade; convince; persuade somebody to do
[OPP] talk+사람+out of -ing ···을 설득해서 ~ 못하게 하다

tell on 1. ···을 고자질하다, 일러바치다, 비밀을 폭로하다 2. 지치게 하다

A student stole pencils and another student **told on** him to the teacher.
한 학생이 연필을 훔쳤고 다른 학생은 선생님에게 고자질했다.
His heavy schedule has begun to **tell on** him.
그의 바쁜 스케줄이 그를 지치게 하기 시작했다.

[SYN] 1. reveal; tattle on; split on 2. tire; wear out

for a change 기분 전환으로, 변화를 위해

She went to the country **for a change**.
그녀는 기분 전환을 위해 시골에 갔다.
Let's go to a restaurant **for a change**.
기분 전환으로 레스토랑에 갑시다.

[SYN] as diversion; as relaxation
cf. for a change of air 전지요양으로

frown on (upon) ···에 눈살을 찌푸리다

[SYN] disapprove of; hesitate

I've heard that Korean companies **frown upon** divorce of their employees.
한국 기업들은 자사 직원들의 이혼을 못마땅하게 여긴다고 들었다.
Our professor **frowns on** students coming to class late.
우리 교수님은 학생들이 수업시간에 늦게 오면 눈살을 찌푸린다.

[SYN] to

move up 승진하다

He's really **moving up** in the company.
사실 그는 회사 내에서 출세가도를 달리고 있다.
This song is **moving up** the popularity charts.
이 노래는 인기 차트에서 상승 중이다.

[SYN] advance to a higher rank or level

as ... as any + 단수명사 누구(무엇)보다도 못하지 않는

He is **as** hard working **as any** student.
그는 누구에게도 뒤지지 않게 열심히 공부한다.
I know **as** much about dogs **as any** man alive.
나는 개에 대해서라면 누구 못지 않게 잘 알고 있다.

[SYN] not inferior (to); no less (than)

as best one can (may) 할 수 있는 한, 될 수 있는 대로, 힘이 닿는 데까지

Do it **as best you can**.
힘껏 해 보아라.
I comforted her **as best I could**.
나는 그녀를 힘껏 위로했다.

[SYN] as well as one can; by whatever means are available

cut a (fine) figure 눈에 띄다, 두각을 나타내다

She **cuts a figure** in that skiwear.
그녀는 그 스키복을 입으면 눈에 잘 띈다.
The actor **cuts a fine figure** since he bought too many new clothes.
그 배우는 지나치게 많은 옷을 구입하였기 때문에 유명해졌다.

[SYN] cut a conspicuous figure

confuse A with B A와 B를 혼동하다, 혼란시키다

People often tend to **confuse** liberty **with** license.
사람들은 종종 자유와 방종을 혼동하는 경향이 있다.
He **confused** me **with** a deluge of polite words.
그는 계속 정중한 말을 하여 나를 혼란시켰다.

[SYN] mix up; puzzle; embarrass; bewilder

be absorbed in ···에 열중하다, ···에 몰두하다

He **was absorbed in** reading the novel.
그는 그 소설을 읽는 데 열중했다.

[SYN] be engaged in; be fascinated with

Don **was absorbed in** watching TV.
돈은 TV 보는 데 열중해 있었다.

joking apart〔aside〕 농담은 그만두고, 과장 없이

Joking apart, what are you going to do after graduation next year?
농담은 그만두고 내년에 졸업하면 무엇을 할 거니?
Joking apart, the number of people who attended the ceremony was over a thousand.
조금도 과장 없이 의식에 참가한 사람 수는 천 명이 넘었다.

[SYN] apart from joking; without exaggeration

(be) all smiles 희색이 만면하다

She **was all smiles**.
그녀는 희색이 만면했다.

[SYN] brighten up with joy; beam with joy

speak for itself 자명하다

Five thousand years of Korean art **speaks for itself**.
한국 미술의 5천 년 역사는 자명하다.
The truth **speaks for itself**.
진리는 자명하다.

[SYN] be self-evident

specialize in 1. …을 전문으로 하다 2. …을 전공하다

For a long time, the scientist has **specialized in** AIDS research.
오랫동안 그 과학자는 AIDS를 전문적으로 연구해왔다.
The study which he **specializes in** is economics.
그의 전공 과목은 경제학이다.

[SYN] 1. make a specialty of 2. make a special study of

narrow down 제한하다

The number of contestants has been **narrowed down** to six.
경쟁자의 수는 6명으로 좁혀졌다.
"Have you chosen a name for your new brand of cigarettes?" "Well, we've **narrowed** it **down** to two choices."
"새로 내놓을 담배의 이름을 골랐습니까?" "둘 중 하나까지 좁혔어요."

[SYN] restrict; limit; restrain

keep early〔good〕hours 일찍 자고 일찍 일어나다

Those who **keep early hours** will live long.

[OPP] keep late〔bad〕hours 늦게 자고 늦게 일어나다

일찍 자고 일찍 일어나는 사람이 장수한다.

have an eye for 정확하게 판단할 수 있다, 심미안이 있다, …에 대한 안목이 있다

She **has an eye for** hairstyle.
그녀는 헤어스타일을 보는 눈이 있다.
Though he is young, he **has an eye for** the fair and beautiful.
그는 어리지만 심미안을 가지고 있다.

[SYN.] have the seeing eyes; have a keen appreciation; can judge precisely
cf. have an ear for 이해하다 (= make out; understand)

pull out 1. 떠나다, 출발하다 2. 손을 떼다 3. 빼내다, 꺼내다, 뽑아내다

When I arrived at the station, the train was **pulling out**.
내가 역에 도착했을 때 기차는 출발하고 있었다.
I don't like the final stage of our project, so I have decided to **pull out**.
우리 프로젝트의 마지막 단계가 마음에 들지 않아서 나는 손을 떼기로 결정했다.
He **pulled out** a knife and opened the box with it.
그는 칼을 꺼내서 그것으로 상자를 열었다.

[SYN.] 1. depart; set out; leave; take leave of 2. withdraw; stop participating; finish with 3. take out

pass through 1. …을 지나가다 2. 경험하다

We **passed through** several small villages.
우리는 작은 마을 몇 곳을 지나왔다.
He **passed through** many difficulties in his life.
그는 지금까지 많은 곤란을 경험했다.

[SYN.] 1. pass by; go past 2. experience; go through; undergo

something like 1. 얼마간 … 같은, 다소 …와 비슷한, 거의, 대략 2. 굉장한, 훌륭한

They walked **something like** three miles.
그들은 약 3마일을 걸었다.
This is **something like** a present.
이건 굉장한 선물이다.

[SYN.] 1. all but; around; as good as 2. splendid; excellent

keep aloof from …에서 멀리 떨어져 있다, 초연해 있다

The new student **kept aloof from** other students.
새로 온 학생은 다른 학생들에게서 멀리 떨어져 있었다.
In any case he **kept aloof from** making money.
어떤 경우에도 그는 돈 버는 일에 초연하다.

[SYN.] keep away from; be indifferent; be disinterested

preferable to ···보다 바람직한, 더 나은
She found life in the city **preferable to** her quiet life in the country.
그녀는 도시 생활이 조용한 시골 생활보다 더 낫다는 것을 알았다.
Poverty is **preferable to** ill health.
가난이 병보다 낫다.

[SYN] better or suitable; preferred

bring oneself to do ···하고 싶은 생각이 나다
Somehow I could not **bring myself to** join the party.
왠지 나는 그 일행에 끼고 싶은 생각이 들지 않았다.
But I could hardly **bring myself to** go to work the next day.
하지만 그 다음날도 어쩐지 출근하고 싶지가 않았다.

[SYN] feel like -ing; feel inclined to do

of one's own accord [free will] 자발적으로, 자연히, 저절로
He did it **of his own accord**.
그는 자발적으로 그것을 했다.
John doesn't do anything **of his own free will**.
존은 무엇이든 결코 자발적으로 하는 법이 없다.

[SYN] voluntarily; willingly

on the verge of (파멸 등에) 직면하여, 바야흐로 ···하려고 하여
The nation seemed to be **on the verge of** a civil war.
그 나라는 내란의 고비에 있는 것 같았다.
She is **on the verge of** making a decision.
그녀는 이제 결정을 해야 한다.

[SYN] in the face of; on the brink of

just as soon ···하기보다는 차라리
If you ask my opinion, I'd **just as soon** stop the project.
내 의견을 묻는다면 나는 프로젝트를 중단하는 것이 좋겠다.

[SYN] rather than doing something

substitute A for B B 대신에 A를 사용하다, 바꾸다, 대용하다
We can **substitute** margarine **for** butter.
버터 대신 마가린을 사용할 수 있다.
New computers are being **substituted for** the old one.
낡은 컴퓨터를 새 것으로 교체하고 있다.

[SYN] put or use in place of another

such as it is 이렇게 보잘것없는 것이지만, 변변치 못하지만

You may use my car tomorrow, **such as it is**.
변변치는 못하지만 내일 내 차를 써도 좋습니다.
You may use my computer, **such as it is**.
썩 좋은 것은 아니지만 내 컴퓨터를 사용해도 좋습니다.

[SYN] being the kind it is (used in referring to something in either an apologetic or a derogatory way)

trifle with …을 아무렇게나[소홀히] 다루다

It's your fault because she is not a person to be **trifled with**.
그녀는 소홀히 다루어질 그런 사람이 아니므로 당신 잘못이다.
John is **trifling with** Nancy's feelings.
존은 낸시의 감정을 우롱하고 있다.

[SYN] treat someone or their feelings without respect

tear down 헐다, 부수다

They're going to **tear down** the old Palace Theater.
낡은 팰리스 극장이 헐릴 것이다.
The city plans to **tear down** all the old apartment buildings.
시는 오래된 아파트를 모두 헐어 버릴 계획을 하고 있다.

[SYN] wreck; demolish; destroy

in all likelihood 아마, 십중팔구

In all likelihood we shall be away for a week.
아마 우리는 1주일간 집을 비우게 될 것이다.
In all likelihood she will be found innocent.
아마 그 여자에겐 무죄판결이 내려질 것이다.

[SYN] perhaps; possibly; ten to one

in no way 결코[조금도] …않다

They are **in no way** satisfied with the results of their researches.
그들은 연구 결과에 결코 만족하지 않는다.
In no way am I a politically effective person.
나는 결코 정치적으로 영향력 있는 사람이 아니다.

[SYN] not ... at all

leave nothing to be desired 더할 나위 없이 좋다, 흠 잡을 데 없다

It **leaves nothing to be desired**.
그것은 더할 나위 없이 만족스럽다.
All of us are satisfied because the plans **leave nothing to be desired**.
계획들이 조금도 아쉬운 점이 없어서 우리는 모두 만족스럽다.

[OPP] leave much to be desired
아쉬운 점이 많다

without a break 쉬지 않고, 끊임없이

It has been raining **without a break** since early morning.
이른 아침부터 쉬지 않고 비가 내리고 있다.
He's worked for 27 hours **without a break**.
그는 쉬지 않고 27시간 일했다.

SYN without rest; continuously; without stopping

waste away 점점 야위고 쇠약해지다

She has some rare disease and is just **wasting away**.
그녀는 희귀병에 걸려서 점점 쇠약해지고 있다.
She has cancer and is slowly **wasting away**.
그녀는 암에 걸려서 서서히 허약해지고 있다.

SYN become more thin and weak every day

from one's point of view ···의 입장에서 보면

From a teacher's point of view, such students who do nothing but study have no appeal.
교사의 입장에서 보면 공부밖에 모르는 학생은 아무런 매력이 없다.
(=To teachers, students who keep studying all the time are of no interest.)

SYN to somebody; from somebody's view point
cf. from a point of view ···라는 견지에서

for nothing 1. 무료로 2. 무익하게, 헛되이

I cannot give instruction **for nothing**.
나는 무료로 가르칠 수는 없다.
Our trip had to be canceled; we spent all that time planning it **for nothing**.
우리는 여행을 계획하느라 시간을 헛되이 다 써버렸기 때문에 우리 여행은 취소되어야 했다.

SYN 1. without payment; free of charge 2. without achieving anything

by twos and threes 두세 사람씩, 삼삼오오 (떼를 지어서)

They went home **by twos and threes**.
그들은 삼삼오오 떼를 지어 집으로 갔다.
The students gathered **by twos and threes**.
학생들은 삼삼오오 집합했다.

SYN in knots

wear off 1. 점차로 사라지다, 서서히 없어지다 2. 점점 줄어들다, 작아지다

The novelty of living in Rome **wore off** in a few weeks.
로마에서 사는 신기함도 몇 주 지나자 사라져 버렸다.
Her lipstick **wore off** by noon.

SYN 1. pass away or diminish by degrees; lose effect gradually; disappear slowly 2. lose color, shine, etc. by rubbing, time, etc.

정오 무렵 그녀의 립스틱이 다 지워졌다.

without reserve 거리낌없이, 무조건으로

Everybody expressed his opinions **without reserve**.
모두들 자신의 의견을 거리낌없이 발표했다.
I accept your offer **without reserve**.
무조건 당신의 제의를 받아들이겠다.

[SYN] without hesitation; frankly; confidently; unconditionally

get on in the world 직업에서 성공하다, 사회적(경제적) 지위를 향상시키다

Deborah really **got on in the world** as a management of consultant.
데보라는 경영 고문으로 정말 성공했다.
My brother wanted to **get on in the world**, but he seemed to lack a little confidence.
동생은 성공하기 원했지만 자신감이 약간 부족해 보였다.

[SYN] succeed in the business world; improve social or economic status

give back 되돌려주다, 원상태로 회복하다

I want you to **give back** the book.
책을 돌려주세요.
Even the best doctors can't **give** me **back** the use of my arms.
가장 훌륭한 의사들도 내 팔을 원상태로 회복시킬 수 없다.

[SYN] return to its owner
cf. turn back 되돌아가다

stop short 1. 갑자기 서다 2. …하기까지에는 이르지 않다

The car in front of me **stopped short** and I almost hit it.
앞차가 갑자기 서서 내가 그 차를 받을 뻔했다.
The factory director **stopped short** of firing Jack.
공장장은 잭을 해고하지는 않았다.

[SYN] 1. stop suddenly 2. not go too much

presence of mind 침착

John always has the **presence of mind** and is never embarrassed.
존은 항상 침착하여 절대로 당황하는 법이 없다.
She had the **presence of mind** and reported to the police.
그녀는 침착하게 경찰에 신고했다.

[SYN] self-possession; composure

keep up with 뒤떨어지지 않다

[SYN] keep pace with; keep

It is rather difficult for an old man to **keep up with** the times.
노인이 시대에 뒤떨어지지 않고 따라가기는 좀 어려운 일이다.
He could not **keep up with** his class.
그는 수업을 따라갈 수가 없었다.

<small>abreast of</small>

in good〔high, great〕spirits 원기 왕성하게, 기분이 (썩) 좋아
We are **in high spirits**.
우리들은 매우 원기가 좋다.
She was **in high spirits** after receiving the prize.
그녀는 상을 받아서 기분이 매우 좋았다.

<small>[SYN] in a good mood
[OPP] in low spirits 기분이 좋지 않아</small>

make allowance(s) for …을 참작하다, …을 고려하다, 여유를 잡아두다
We will **make allowance for** the circumstances.
사정을 고려하겠습니다.
The judge should have **made allowances for** her illness.
재판관은 그녀가 병에 걸렸다는 점을 고려했어야 했다.

<small>[SYN] take into consideration; allow for</small>

be given to …에 빠지다, …에 열중하다
He **is** much **given to** tennis.
그는 테니스에 아주 열중하고 있다.
He **is given to** drink.
그는 술에 빠져 있다.

<small>[SYN] be bent on; be absorbed in</small>

owe A to B 1. B(다른 사람)에게 A(돈 등)를 빚지고 있다 2. A는 B 덕분이다
I still **owe** ten dollars **to** him.
나는 아직 그에게 10달러의 빚이 있다.
He **owes** his success **to** good luck.
그의 성공은 행운 덕분이다.

<small>[SYN] be indebted to</small>

walk out on …을 버리다, 돌보지 않다
I detest people who **walk out on** their responsibilities.
책임을 회피하는 사람은 질색이다.
The husband **walked out on** his family one day and never returned.
남편은 어느 날 갑자기 가족을 버리더니 다시는 돌아오지 않았다.

<small>[SYN] desert; leave suddenly; abandon</small>

cut in 방해하다, 끼어 들다, 엿듣다

I wish big trucks wouldn't **cut in** like that.
대형 트럭들이 저런 식으로 끼어 들지 않았으면 좋겠다.
Don't **cut in** while I'm talking.
내가 말하고 있을 때 끼어 들지 마라.

[SYN.] interfere; interrupt; chip into; break into

under the influence (of) 1. …의 영향으로, …에 좌우되어, …의 힘으로 2. (마약이나 술에) 취해

He behaved rudely **under the influence of** drink.
그는 취기로 무례하게 행동했다.
He was caught driving **under the influence**.
그는 음주운전을 하다가 적발됐다.

[SYN.] 1. affected by the influence of; owing to influence 2. drunk; intoxicated

put an end to 그만두게 하다, 폐지하다, 파괴하다, 죽이다

I **put an end to** her complaints by simply telling her to stop.
나는 그녀에게 그만 하라고 말하여 불평을 중단했다.
The democratic movement **put an end to** the dictatorial regime that lasted for 20 years.
민주 운동이 20년 동안 지속되어온 독재 정권을 종식시켰다.

[SYN.] stop; finish; do away with; abolish

turn over a new leaf 마음을 고치다(돌리다), 새 생활을 시작하다

After failing school, he decided to **turn over a new leaf**.
학교에서 낙제를 한 후 그는 마음을 가다듬을 결심을 했다.
If you try to **turn over a new leaf**, I will help you.
새롭게 출발하려고 노력하면 내가 도와 주겠다.

[SYN.] make a new start; change mind

look over 검토하다, 바라보다, 대충 훑어보다, …을 조사하다

The manager wants to **look over** the applications.
부장은 신청서를 조사해 보기를 바라고 있다.
Please **look over** this will and see if it reflects your wishes.
이 유언장을 잘 살펴보시고 당신의 희망 사항이 잘 반영되어 있는지 보세요.

[SYN.] run over; look through; inspect carefully; examine

look out for 1. …에 주의하다 2. …을 찾다

If you go to the festival, **look out for** pickpockets.
축제에 가면 소매치기를 조심하라.

[SYN.] 1. give attention to 2. look for; search for

I am **looking out for** a house to rent.
나는 셋집을 찾고 있다.

queue up 줄서다
It was raining and I didn't want to **queue up** for an hour.
비가 오고 있었고 나는 한 시간이나 줄서는 게 싫었다.
Please **queue up** here for the local bus.
시내 버스 이용자는 여기서 줄을 서시오.

[SYN] stand in line

have a good mind to 대단히 …하고 싶어하다
I **had a good mind to** see the movie but I didn't have any money.
나는 그 영화가 정말 보고 싶었지만 돈이 없었다.
I **have a good mind to** help you but I am too busy because of the new research.
정말 당신을 돕고 싶지만 새 연구 때문에 너무 바쁘군요.

[SYN] want to do something greatly

veer off 급히 방향을 바꾸다
That car suddenly **veered off** the road and hit the tree.
저 차가 갑자기 길을 벗어나 나무에 충돌했다.
The plane **veered off** course to avoid the thunderstorm.
비행기는 뇌우를 피하기 위해 코스를 변경했다.

[SYN] change direction suddenly

not better than …보다 낫지 않아, 기껏 해봐야 …에 불과하여
He is **not better than** an engineer.
그는 기술자에 불과하다.
He is**n't better than** a beggar.
그는 거지보다 나을 게 없다.

[SYN] inferior to; not so good as

(be) all eyes 열심히 주시하다, 눈을 크게 떠서 보다
At the circus which was rare in the remote village, children **were all eyes**.
외딴 마을에서는 보기 드문 서커스 장에서 아이들은 눈을 크게 뜨고 열심히 보았다.
When the colorful street parade marched on, almost all the passers-by stopped and **were all eyes**.
화려한 시가 행진 대열이 행진할 때 거의 모든 행인들은 걸음을 멈추고 열심히 바라보았다.

[SYN] watch very closely; watch with wide eyes

in defiance of ⋯을 불구하고, 무릅쓰고, 무시하고

The girl kept on sleeping in class **in defiance of** her teacher's warning.
그 여학생은 선생님의 경고에도 불구하고 수업시간에 계속 잠을 잤다.
In defiance of the coach's orders, two players didn't participate in the practice.
코치의 지시를 무시하고 두 선수가 연습에 불참했다.

[SYN] acting against; in disobedience to

for all the world 1. (부정을 강조하여) 절대로, 결코
2. 모든 점에서, 전적으로

I would never divorce with my wife **for all the world**.
나는 절대로 아내와 이혼하지 않겠다.
Mary looks **for all the world** like her mother.
메리는 그녀의 어머니를 꼭 닮았다.

[SYN] 1. for anything; for any price 2. entirely; all aspects

fall (a) victim to ⋯의 피해를 입다

My second son **fell a victim to** the dictator's vengeance.
둘째 아들이 독재자의 복수의 희생자가 되었다.
John **fell victim to** his own ambition to succeed in the political world.
존은 정계에서 성공하려는 그의 야심의 포로가 되었다.

[SYN] be harmed or destroyed by, either physically or in one's career

stay away from 결석하다, 집을 비우다, 부재중이다

He has **stayed away from** school for a week because of illness.
그는 아파서 일주일째 결석하고 있다.
I have **stayed away from** my house on vacation for two weeks.
나는 휴가로 2주간 집에 없었다.

[SYN] be absent from; be away from; be not in

keep at a distance / keep at arm's length 소원하게 대하다, 가까이 하지 않다

You'd better **keep** those rough boys **at a distance**.
저렇게 거친 아이들은 가까이 하지 않는 것이 좋다.
She has **kept** him **at arm's length**.
그녀는 그를 멀리하고 있다.

[SYN] avoid someone's company

in consequence of ⋯의 결과, ⋯ 때문에

He could not attend school **in consequence of** flood.

[SYN] as a result of; owing to

그는 홍수 때문에 학교에 출석할 수가 없었다.
She got thoroughly wet, and **in consequence of** it, she has got a bad cold.
그녀는 전신이 흠뻑 젖어 심한 감기에 걸렸다.

destined to ···하도록 운명지어져 있는, 운명이 지어진

She was **destined to** be a famous singer from childhood.
그녀는 어릴 때부터 유명한 가수가 될 운명이었다.
The adventurers were **destined to** meet a storm in the open sea.
그 모험가들은 넓은 바다에서 폭풍을 만나도록 운명지어졌다.

[SYN] intended by fortune or heavenly forces; fated

go out of one's way 특별히 노력하다, 평소보다 더 노력하다

I want all the employees to **go out of their way**.
종업원 모두가 평소보다 더 잘하기 바란다.
Students **went out of their way** to be nice to their new teacher.
학생들은 새로 오신 선생님을 잘 대해 주기 위해 특별히 노력했다.

[SYN] make an extra effort; do more than usual

get out of 1. (습관 등을) 버리다 2. 피하다, 면하다

He **got out of** the habit of smoking.
그는 담배 피우는 습관을 버렸다.
I **got out of** washing the car by saying I had things to do.
나는 할 일이 있다고 말해 세차를 하지 않아도 되었다.

[SYN] 1. give up; forsake 2. avoid; escape from the responsibility or obligation

exert oneself 노력하다, 진력하다

He **exerted himself** to improve education.
그는 교육의 개선을 위해 노력했다.
Mary **exerted herself** all year to get the scholarship.
메리는 장학금을 타기 위해 일년 내내 노력했다.

[SYN] make efforts(an effort); take pains; endeavor

read over 1. 재빨리 훑어보다 2. 다시 읽다

Take a couple of minutes to **read** it **over**. I'd like your impressions.
몇 분 시간을 내어 그것을 훑어봐. 네 감상을 듣고 싶어.
Read over the questions a few times before answering them.
해답을 쓰기 전에 문제를 두세 번 되풀이해서 읽어 봐.

[SYN] 1. read quickly 2. re-read; read again

relieve A of B 1. A(사람)에게서 B(짐·걱정·부담·책임 등)를 제거하다, 덜어주다 2. …을 훔치다, 빼앗다

A cup of coffee **relieved** me **of** a headache.
커피를 마셨더니 두통이 사라졌다.
The pickpocket **relieved** him **of** his purse.
소매치기가 그의 지갑을 훔쳤다.

[SYN] exclude; get rid of; remove

watch one's step 발 조심하다, 신중히 행동하다

Watch your step, it's very muddy.
발 조심해, 진흙투성이니까.
Mr. Graham told me to **watch my step** or I might repeat the same year.
그레이엄 선생님은 나에게 정신차리지 않으면 유급하게 될지도 모른다고 말했다.

[SYN] act with prudence
cf. watch one's tongue(language) 말조심하다

be lost in 1. …에 잠겨 있다 2. …에 휩쓸려서 보이지 않게 되다

He **was lost in** thought.
그는 생각에 잠겨 있었다.
He **was** quite **lost in** the crowd.
그는 인파에 파묻혀 보이지 않게 되었다.

[SYN] 1. be absorbed in; devote oneself to 2. be swept along in the crowd

lay out 돈을 쓰다

They **laid out** $37,000 for a foreign sports car.
그들은 외제 스포츠카를 구입하는 데 37,000달러를 썼다.
I hear that she **laid out** a fortune for her wedding.
그 여자가 자기 결혼식에 돈 좀 썼다고 들었어요.

[SYN] spend

catch up 1. (뒤진 것을) 만회하다 2. 따라잡다

Production is finally **catching up** with demand.
생산이 마침내 수요를 따라가고 있다.
The second runner is **catching up** with the first runner.
두 번째 주자가 첫 번째 주자를 따라잡고 있다.

[SYN] 1. retrieve; recover; restore 2. overtake; come even; go
cf. keep up with (사람·생각·유행 등에) 뒤떨어지지 않고 따라가다, (소식·사건 등에 대해서) 알고 있다

hand out 배포하다

Stand by the door and **hand out** these programs.
문 옆에 서서 이 프로그램을 나눠 줘.
The waiter **handed out** the menus to the guests.
웨이터는 손님들에게 메뉴를 나눠 주었다.

[SYN] distribute; deal out

can't make head(s) or tail(s) of 뭐가 뭔지

[SYN] can't understand at all;

알 수가 없다, 무슨 뜻인지 전혀 알 수가 없다 — can't know the meaning of

I **couldn't make heads or tails of** what she was saying.

나는 그녀가 무슨 말을 하는지 통 알 수가 없었다.

I **can't make heads or tails of** this sentence.

이 문장은 도무지 뭐가 뭔지 알 수가 없다.

under no circumstances 여하한 일이 있어도 … 않다

[SYN] never; in no way

I will **under no circumstances** let you go there.

어떤 일이 있어도 너를 거기 보내지 않겠다.

Under no circumstances should you take responsibility for that.

어떤 경우에도 당신이 그 일에 책임을 져서는 안 된다.

envious of …을 부러워하는, …을 질투하는

[SYN] wanting to have what someone else has

He is **envious of** my new car and wants one like it.

그는 내가 산 차를 부러워하며 그와 같은 것을 원한다.

John is **envious of** my good fortune at the horse race.

존은 나의 경마 행운을 부러워한다.

in store (for) 1. 비축하여, 준비하여, 갖추어져 2. 일어나려 하여, 박두하여, 대기하여

[SYN] 1. saved up in case of need 2. ready to happen; waiting

In case of electricity going off, we should have candles **in store** in the house.

전기가 나갈 경우에 대비하여 우리는 집에 양초를 갖추어 놓아야 한다.

Nobody knows what is **in store for** us, but we should do our best.

우리 앞길에 무슨 일이 일어날지는 아무도 모르지만 우리는 최선을 다해야 한다.

hand back 임자에게 돌려주다

[SYN] return to the owner

The teacher **handed back** the test papers.

선생님은 답안지를 돌려주셨다.

All right, but **hand** it **back** as soon as you're finished.

좋아, 보고 나서 바로 돌려주어야 해.

read up on 읽고 조사 연구하다

[SYN] research; learn a lot about a subject by reading

I've been **reading up on** the Civil War.

나는 남북전쟁에 관해 연구를 하고 있다.
I'm **reading up on** the history of Greece before I go there on vacation.
나는 휴가 때 그리스에 가기 전에 그리스 역사를 조사하고 있다.

about it

grow out of 성장해서 …이 맞지 않게 되다
It's not my fault. I'm **growing out of** all my clothes.
제 탓이 아닙니다. 그새 커서 맞는 옷이 하나도 없다고요.
Children **grow out of** their clothes very quickly.
아이들은 빨리 자라기 때문에 옷이 작아서 못 입게 된다.

[SYN] become too big for

dying to 간절히 …하고 싶어하는, …을 애타게 그리는
She is **dying to** see him.
그녀는 그를 몹시 만나고 싶어한다.
I am just **dying to** drink a cool beer.
지금 시원한 맥주가 무척 마시고 싶다.

[SYN] very anxious to do something; yearning for someone

keep abreast of …에 뒤지지 않다, …의 수준에 달해 있다
You should **keep abreast of** the time.
너는 시대에 뒤떨어지지 않도록 해야 한다.
We can't **keep abreast of** him in mathematics.
우리는 수학에서 그를 따라갈 수 없다.

[SYN] stay level with
cf. keep pace with …에 보조를 맞추어나가다 (=go at the same rate)

for all I know 아마 …일 것이다, …일지도 모른다
He may be a good man **for all I know**.
그는 아마 좋은 사람일지도 모른다.
He may be dead **for all I know**.
그는 아마 죽을지도 모른다.

[SYN] ten to one; presumably; maybe; in all likelihood; probably; possibly
cf. for all the word like; as if 아주 …와 똑 같은, 아주 꼭 닮은

stand on ceremony 격식을 차리다, 형식을 차리다
There is no need to **stand on ceremony** with us.
우리에게 격식을 차릴 필요는 없습니다.
Please don't **stand on ceremony**.
마음 편히 계십시오.

[SYN] behave in a formal or ceremonious manner; become formal

(as) compared with …와 비교해서
I have done very little this month **(as) compared with** what I did last month.
지난달에 한 것과 비교하면 이번 달에는 거의 한 것이 없다.
The earning of this year shows decrease of one

[SYN] in comparison with; in contrast to(with)

million won (**as**) **compared with** last year.
금년도의 수익은 작년도와 비교하면 백만 원이 줄었다.

vote in ···을 선출하다

The members **voted** John **in** as the president of the club.
회원들은 존을 클럽 회장으로 선출했다.
Most people expected that the influential candidate would be **voted in**.
대부분 사람들은 그 유력한 후보가 선출될 것으로 예상했다.

[SYN] choose someone; elect someone

not [little] ... still less 하물며[더구나] ···은 아닌

We know **little** about the body, **still less** about the mind.
우리는 육체에 대해 아는 것이 거의 없다. 더구나 마음에 대해서는 더욱 모른다.
I do **not** suggest that he is negligent, **still less** that he is dishonest.
그가 태만하다고 말하는 것이 아니며 더구나 그가 부정직하다는 것은 더욱 아니다.

[SYN] much less

take offense (at) ···에 불쾌해 하다

He must have **taken offense at** my rude remarks.
그는 무례한 내 발언에 불쾌했던 것이 분명하다.
If she **takes offense at** whatever he says, they can't work together.
만약 그녀가 그가 하는 모든 말에 기분이 상한다면 그들은 함께 일할 수 없다.

[SYN] be offended

part with 1. 내주다, 내놓다 2. 떠나다

A good advertisement will make a person decide to **part with** his money.
좋은 광고를 보면 사람들은 돈을 내놓으려고 하는 마음이 생긴다.
John **parted with** us on the way home from the trip.
존은 여행에서 집으로 돌아오는 길에 우리를 떠났다.

[SYN] 1. hand over; give away; deliver 2. take leave of; go away; leave

hold one's tongue 말을 삼가다, 잠자코 있다, 입을 다물고 있다 (보통 명령문으로 쓰임)

John, it's not your turn, so please **hold your tongue**.
존, 네 차례가 아니니 제발 입 좀 다물어라.

[SYN] keep silence; refrain from talking

You had better **hold your tongue**.
당신은 잠자코 있는 게 좋아.

clear up 1. 깨끗이 치우다 2. 해결하다

I told you to **clear up** the mess yourself.
어질러진 것을 치우라고 말했지.

This mystery will not be **cleared up** until we find who stole the key.
누가 열쇠를 훔쳤는지 판명될 때까지 이 문제는 해결되지 않을 것이다.

[SYN] 1. put in order; tidy up 2. solve

leave no stone unturned 가능한 모든 수단을 동원하다, 가능한 곳을 다 뒤지다

Mother **left no stone unturned** to look for a ring.
어머니는 반지를 찾으려고 사방을 다 뒤졌다.

Tom **left no stone unturned** to recover the relationships with his ex-wife.
톰은 전부인과의 관계를 회복시키기 위해 온갖 노력을 다했다.

[SYN] try all the possible means

It is not too much to say that …라고 말해도 과언은 아니다

It is not too much to say that he is a typical gentleman.
그는 전형적인 신사라고 해도 과언은 아니다.

It is not too much to say that he is a genius.
그가 천재라고 말해도 과언은 아니다.

[SYN] It is no exaggeration to say that …; It may fairly be said that …

write up 자세히 쓰다

The reporter **wrote up** the event for his paper.
그 기자는 자기 신문에 사건을 자세히 보도했다.

A reporter **wrote up** our baseball team's victory in the newspaper.
한 기자가 우리 야구팀의 승리를 신문에 상세히 보도했다.

[SYN] write in detail

break the ice 1. 문제해결의 실마리를 잡다 2. 딱딱한 분위기를 누그러뜨리다

Mike tried to **break the ice** by making a good joke.
마이크는 재미있는 농담을 하여 분위기를 누그러뜨리려고 했다.

To **break the ice**, the lecturer talked about how he had loved a girl onesidedly.
어색한 침묵을 깨기 위해서 연사는 한 소녀를 짝사랑했던 이야기를 했다.

[SYN] 1. find the clue 2. ease formal environment

on second thought(s) 곰곰이 생각한 뒤에, 다시 생각하여

SYN after much thought; after due consideration

I said it would rain today, but **on second thought**, I think it won't.

나는 오늘 비가 오겠다고 말했지만 다시 생각해 보니 비가 오지 않을 것 같다.

On second thought, we'd better not go out tonight.

다시 생각해 보니 오늘밤에는 외출하지 않는 게 좋겠다.

make [pull] faces [a face] 얼굴을 찌푸리다, 묘한[싫은] 표정을 짓다

SYN frown; wrinkle up

Tom **made a face** at his rival, Jim, when he saw him in the street.

톰은 길에서 연적인 짐을 보았을 때 얼굴을 찌푸렸다.

My son **pulls a face** when I tell him to eat the vegetables.

내가 채소를 먹으라고 말하면 아들은 인상을 쓴다.

go a long way 크게 도움이 되다

SYN help greatly

The new secretary **goes a long way** for the president.

새 비서는 사장에게 크게 도움이 된다.

This book will **go a long way** to help people understand Korea.

이 책은 사람들이 한국을 이해하는 데 큰 도움이 될 것이다.

dispense with …을 필요 없게 하다, …할 수고[절차]를 덜다, …없이 때우다

SYN do away with; do without

As you know I cannot **dispense with** this dictionary.

너도 알다시피 나는 이 사전 없이는 해낼 수 없다.

The new technique **dispense with** much human labor.

신기술은 일손을 크게 덜어 준다.

lay by 저축하다

SYN save, especially a little at a time

The farmers **lay by** some of their best corn to use next year for seed.

농부들은 다음 해에 씨앗으로 쓰기 위해 가장 좋은 옥수수 일부를 보관해 둔다.

Our friends agreed to **lay** a little money **by** every

month.
우리 친구들은 매달 돈을 조금씩 모으기로 약속했다.

take out 1. 제거하다, 없애다, 빼다 2. (면허 등을) 얻다, 따다

The dentist **took out** my wisdom tooth.
치과의사는 내 사랑니를 뺐다.
He **took out** a patent on his new invention.
그는 신발명품에 대한 특허를 얻었다.

SYN 1. remove; get rid of; subtract; extract 2. get; obtain; gain

win over 설득하다, …을 자기편으로 끌어들이다

Perhaps the new projects will **win** him **over**.
어쩌면 새 계획들로 그를 설득할 수 있을 것이다.
His solid arguments **won over** the opposition.
그의 확고한 주장은 반대파를 설복했다.

SYN persuade; change someone's mind; gain the support of

associate with 1. …와 교제하다 2. …를 연상시키다

Many decades ago, Korea began to **associate with** the rest of the world.
수십 년 전에 한국은 세계의 다른 여러 나라들과 교류를 시작했다.
In many parts of the world, people **associate** war **with** misery.
세계의 많은 지역에 있어서 사람들은 전쟁하면 비참함을 연상한다.

SYN 1. be friendly with 2. remind of
cf. (be) associated with 어떤 사물이나 사람과 연관되다 (= be connected with something or someone)

describe as …으로 평하다, 묘사하다

He is **described as** the greatest scholar ever lived.
그는 지금까지 없었던 가장 위대한 학자라는 평을 듣고 있다.
George **described** himself **as** a great painter.
조지는 훌륭한 화가라고 자칭한다.

SYN give an account or representation of in words

submit to 1. 복종하다, 굴복하다, 감수하다 2. 제출하다, 제시하다

She was too proud to **submit to** such treatment.
그녀는 자존심이 너무 강해서 그런 취급을 감수하지 않았다.
The motion was **submitted to** the city council.
동의서는 시의회에 제출되었다.

SYN 1. obey; yield 2. present; submit

it's high time 이제 …할 시간(때)이다

It's high time the two girls made friends with each other.
그 두 소녀는 이제 서로 잘 사귀어야할 때이다.
It's high time that he got recognition for what he

SYN it is past time; something is overdue

had accomplished for the nation.
그는 국가를 위해 이룩한 것에 대해 이제 인정을 받아야 할 때이다.

on the ground that [of] ···의 이유로, ···을 구실로 [핑계로]

[SYN] by reason; on account of; because; on the pretext of

I recommend him **on the ground that** he is an honest man.
나는 그가 정직한 사람이라는 이유로 그를 추천한다.
She was dismissed **on the ground of** being unpunctual.
그녀는 시간을 지키지 않는다는 이유로 해고되었다.

furnish A with B A에게 B를 공급하다

[SYN] provide; give something

He **furnished** the hungry **with** food.
그는 굶주린 자에게 먹을 것을 주었다.
(=He furnished food to the hungry.)

verge on ···가 되려 하고 있다

[SYN] be close to

Tell him to take a vacation. I think he's **verging on** a nervous breakdown.
휴가를 갖도록 말해 주시오. 노이로제에 걸려 있지 않나 여겨지는데.
That company is **verging on** bankruptcy.
그 회사는 도산 직전에 있다.

round up 모으다, 집합시키다

[SYN] gather; bring together; call together

Please **round** them **up** and tell them to wash their hands and faces.
모두 모아서 손과 얼굴을 씻으라고 말해 주세요.
Present-day cowboys **round up** cattle with helicopters.
현대의 카우보이는 헬리콥터로 소를 모아 집합시킨다.

none other than 다름 아닌 바로 그(것)

[SYN] not another person

The man was **none other than** the general himself.
그 남자야말로 바로 그 장군이었다.
The visitor was **none other than** the president in our company.
그 방문자는 다름 아닌 우리 회사 회장이었다.

in the interest of someone [something] ···을 위하여, ···에게 유익한

[SYN] for the sake of; in order to promote

In the interest of your health, I advise you to quit

smoking.
당신의 건강을 위해 담배를 끊으라고 충고합니다.
The company decided to build a fitness center **in the interest of** its employees.
회사는 종업원들을 위해 헬스클럽을 짓기로 했다.

clear out 떠나다, 도망쳐 버리다

The wife of the violent husband **cleared out** with the children.
폭력 남편의 아내는 아이들을 데리고 나가 버렸다.
We had better **clear out** of here as fast as we can.
가능하면 빨리 여기서 빠져나가는 것이 좋겠다.

SYN. leave; run away

partake of 1. (…의 성질을) 얼마간 띠다 2. 나누어 갖다, 함께 하다, (특히 남과 함께) 먹다

His attitude **partakes of** disrespect for his seniors.
그의 태도에는 선배들에 대해 불손함이 다소 있다.
All the people gathered here will **partake of** God's blessing.
이 곳에 모인 모든 사람들은 다같이 하나님의 축복을 받을 것이다.

SYN. 1. have the same qualities as; show the characteristics of 2. take some of; receive a share of

once and for all 1. 끝으로 한 번만 더, 이번뿐 2. 최종적으로, 딱 잘라

I will help you to pull out of the financial trouble **once and for all**.
마지막으로 한 번 더 너를 도와 재정난에서 벗어나도록 해 주겠다.
Let's settle the quarrel **once and for all**.
최종적으로 싸움에 결말을 짓자.

SYN. one time and never again; without any doubt; surely; definitely; finally

track down 1. 추적하다 2. 밝혀내다, 규명하다

The police **tracked down** the criminal.
경찰은 범인을 추적하여 잡았다.
The reporter **tracked down** the source of the rumor.
기자는 소문의 출처를 밝혀냈다.

SYN. 1. pursue until catch; search for 2. investigate fully or search for until find; find out

aside from …을 제외하고, …은 별도로 하고

Aside from the salary, the couple receive rent of a shopping center.
그 부부는 월급 외에 쇼핑센터 임대료를 받는다.
The children hardly study other subjects, **aside from** classical dance.

SYN. apart from; except for

그 아이들은 고전무용 외 다른 과목은 거의 공부하지 않는다.

farm out 하청을 주다

SYN. subcontract; sublet

Are you suggesting that we **farm out** some out of the work?
일부 하청을 주면 어떠냐는 말씀인가요?
That company **farms out** production of small parts.
그 회사는 부품의 생산을 하청주고 있다.

keep pace with …에 뒤떨어지지 않도록 따라가다, …과 보조를 맞추다

SYN. keep abreast of(with)

We must **keep pace with** the times.
우리는 시대에 뒤떨어지지 않도록 해야 한다.
Keep pace with the modern civilization.
현대 문명에 보조를 맞추어라.

draw up 1. (계획을) 입안하다, 작성하다 2. (차를) 세우다

SYN. 1. draft; write; put in writing; plan 2. stop; pull up; drag up

The lawyer **drew up** the document for the new case.
새 사건을 위해 변호사는 서류를 작성했다.
As a passer-by was crossing the road, I **drew** my car **up** short.
한 행인이 길을 건너고 있었으므로 나는 차를 급정지했다.

give way to …에 지다, 굴복하다, 길을 내주다

SYN. yield to
cf. give way 무너지다

You mustn't **give way to** their demands.
그들의 요구에 굴복해서는 안 된다.
I **gave way to** the bicycle.
나는 자전거에 길을 내 주었다.

be out of the question 문제가 되지 않다, 불가능한 일이다

SYN. impossible; impracticable
cf. out of question 의심 없이 (= beyond question)

His proposal **is out of the question**.
그의 제안은 실행 불가능하다.
Going out in this rain **is out of the question**.
이 빗속에 외출한다는 것은 불가능하다.

lay off 1. 일시 해고하다, 휴직시키다 2. 그만두다, 삼가다

SYN. 1. dismiss workers from their jobs, especially temporarily 2. stop; leave off

His company **laid off** about 300 employees due to the economic recession.
그의 회사는 불경기로 인해 종업원 300여 명을 해고했다.

I told you to **lay off** bothering my little brother.
내 동생을 그만 괴롭히라고 말했지.

tell off 1. (보통 수동태) (일을) 할당하다, 세어서 가르다 2. 꾸짖다, 잔소리하다

[SYN] 1. allot; count off 2. reprimand

Three students were **told off** to clean the classroom.
세 학생에게 교실 청소하는 일이 할당됐다.
Your naughty daughter needs to be **told off**.
버릇없는 네 딸은 야단을 좀 맞아야겠다.

side with …의 편을 들다, 지지(찬성)하다

[SYN] back up; agree with; support

He always **sides with** the strongest party.
그는 항상 가장 강한 쪽 편을 든다.
He **sides with** his wife even when she is wrong.
그는 그의 아내가 잘못 하고 있을 때도 아내 쪽 편을 든다.

refrain from 그만두다, 삼가다, 피하다, 자제하다

[SYN] not do something

Students **refrain from** smoking in the classroom.
학생들은 강의실에서 흡연을 삼간다.
Please **refrain from** speaking without permission.
허락 없이 말하는 것은 자제해 주세요.

next to nothing 거의 아무것도 아닌, 거의 없는

[SYN] almost nothing; very little

She has **next to nothing** in the bank.
그녀는 은행에 저축한 돈이 거의 없다.
In the lengthy meeting, I got **next to nothing**.
긴 회의에서 나는 얻은 것이 거의 없다.

point to …의 경향을 나타내다, 증거가 되다

[SYN] prohibit(show) a tendency to; testify; prove

The overall economic situation **points to** a serious recession.
전반적인 경제 상황은 심각한 불황을 나타내고 있다.
All the evidence has **pointed to** the criminal ring being involved in the drug dealing.
모든 증거는 범죄 조직이 마약 거래에 연루되었음을 보여 주었다.

look back on (upon) / look back to 회고하다, 돌아다보다

[SYN] recollect; retrospect; turn back

As the years went by, he often **looked back upon** his school days.
세월이 지남에 따라 그는 종종 학창 시절을 회상했다.
Generally speaking, there is none but **looks back**

on the days of his youth.
일반적으로 말해서 자신의 청년 시절을 회고하지 않는 사람은 없다.

in pursuit of …을 쫓아서, 추구하여

The ship cruised about **in pursuit of** whales.
그 배는 고래를 찾아 여기저기 항해하였다.
They work hard **in pursuit of** happiness.
그들은 행복을 추구하여 열심히 일한다.

[SYN] seek after; follow after

address oneself to 어떤 특정한 주제나 문제를 다루거나 토의하다, …에게 말을 걸다

He **addressed himself to** the task.
그는 그 일을 본격적으로 하기 시작했다.
I **addressed myself to** the chairman.
의장에게 발언을 요구하는 말을 했다.

[SYN] deal with or discuss a particular subject or problem

fool around with …을 가지고 놀다

How many times have I told you not to **fool around with** my tools?
내 연장을 가지고 장난하지 말라고 몇 번이나 말했어?
It's dangerous to **fool around with** electric wire.
전선을 가지고 장난하면 위험하다.

[SYN] toy with; play with; mess around with

do for 1. …의 대용이 되다 (진행형이 불가능함) 2. (신변을) 돌보다, 가정부 역할을 하다

We don't have enough chairs and the boxes will **do for** chairs.
의자가 충분치 않으며 그 상자들이 의자 대용이 될 것이다.
His grandmother is sick, so a nurse **does for** him.
그의 할머니가 아프기 때문에 간호사가 그를 돌볼 것이다.

[SYN] 1. substitute for; use for 2. care for; look after; take care of

go back on 약속을 어기다

If you **go back on** your word, no one will trust you.
약속을 어기면, 아무도 널 신용해 주지 않을 것이다.
If you **go back on** your promise, I'll never forgive you.
약속을 어기면 절대 용서 안 하겠다.

[SYN] break a promise

in token of …의 표시로서

This is a gift **in token of** my love.
이것은 내 사랑의 징표로서 주는 선물이다.
I sent her a present **in token of** gratitude.

[SYN] as evidence of; in proof of; in testimony of

감사의 표시로서 그녀에게 선물을 보냈다.

such being the case 이러한(그러한) 까닭으로 해서, 이렇기 때문에, 이러한 사정으로

Such being the case, I cannot meet her.
이러한 사정으로 나는 그녀를 만날 수 없다.

[SYN] under (in) these circumstances

look on (upon) A as B A를 B로 보다(간주하다)

Many people **look on** him **as** a true artist.
많은 사람들은 그를 진정한 예술가로 생각한다.
We **look upon** him **as** an imposter.
우리는 그를 협잡꾼으로 여긴다.

[SYN] regard A as B

on speaking terms with …와 말을 트고 지낼 정도로 친한

Andrew wanted to be **on speaking terms with** you, but you were too cold to him.
앤드류는 너와 친하게 지내고 싶어했는데 네가 그에게 너무 쌀쌀맞게 대했어.
We are not **on speaking terms with** each other, but I hope someday we will.
우리는 서로 친하지 않지만 언젠가는 그렇게 되기 바란다.

[SYN] friendly enough to exchange greetings or carry on conversation with someone

nail down 최종적으로 정하다

I want you to **nail** it **down** by the end of the week.
주말까지 최종적으로 정하도록 하시오.
The real estate agent **nailed down** the sale.
부동산 중개인은 매매계약을 정했다.

[SYN] establish; settle

write for (신문·잡지 등에) 기고하다

The fashion designer was asked to **write for** several magazines.
그 패션 디자이너는 여러 잡지에서 원고 청탁을 받았다.
I sometimes **write for** the newspaper.
나는 가끔 신문에 기고를 한다.

[SYN] contribute to a newspaper; write for a magazine

rule out (규정 등에 따라) 제외하다, 불가능하게 하다, 금지하다, 배제하다, 제거하다, 삭제하다

Don't **rule** him **out** as a candidate for the presidency.
그를 회장 후보에서 제외하지 말아요.
The present economic situation **rules out** such an

[SYN] decide something is not possible; eliminate; exclude

expenditure.
오늘날의 경제 사정으로는 그러한 세출 비용은 고려할 수 없습니다.

as follows 다음과 같이〔같은〕

His statement runs **as follows**.
그의 성명서는 다음과 같다.
The site of these sports events is **as follows**.
이들 경기를 할 장소는 다음과 같다.

[SYN] a list of things that come next; what is listed next

miss out on 기회를 놓치다

That's too bad. You **missed out on** a chance to hear some great music.
안됐군요. 훌륭한 음악을 들을 기회를 놓친 셈이군요.
I'm sorry I **missed out on** the farewell party for Mary.
메리의 송별회에 빠져 유감이다.

[SYN] lose an opportunity

talk out of 설득해서 …하지 못하게 하다, 말로써 모면하다

We tried to **talk** them **out of** getting a divorce.
우리는 그들을 설득해서 이혼을 단념케 하려고 했다.
Jack is good at **talking** his way **out of** troubles.
잭은 말로써 곤경을 피하는 데 능하다.

[SYN] discourage someone from doing something; dissuade

write off (빌려준 돈을) 장부에서 지우다, 탕감하다

The banks **wrote off** those debts as irrecoverable.
은행들은 그 빚을 회수 불능으로 장부에서 지웠다.
I'm reluctant to **write off** the project in Africa.
아프리카에서의 사업을 없었던 것으로 간주하는 것은 기분이 내키지 않는다.

[SYN] remove from a business record; cancel; accept as a loss

fall in with 1. 우연히 마주치다 2. …와 조화〔일치〕하다

On the road I **fell in with** an old friend.
길에서 우연히 옛 친구를 만났다.
To our regret, we couldn't **fall in with** their views.
유감스럽게도 우리는 그들과 의견이 일치하지 못했다.

[SYN] 1. meet by chance; come across 2. agree with

mull over 심사숙고하다

I need a few days to **mull** it **over**. It's a big decision.
몇 일 생각할 여유를 주세요. 중대한 결심이니까요.
Mull it **over** and give me an answer tomorrow.
잘 생각해서 내일 답을 주시오.

[SYN] consider carefully; give deep thought; ponder over

grow on 점점 더 좋아지다

After you've been in France for a while, it'll **grow on** you.
프랑스에 잠시 있어 보면, 그 사이 점점 더 좋아질 거야.
Living in the country **grows on** you after a while.
시골에서의 생활도 잠시 있으면 좋아지게 될 것이다.

SYN. grow gradually more pleasing to

dwell on (upon) 1. 곰곰이 생각하다 2. …에 대하여 상세하게 말하다, 길게 논하다

You tend to **dwell on** old wrongs.
너는 과거의 잘못을 자꾸 생각하는 경향이 있다.
The subject is too unpleasant to **dwell on**.
그 이야기는 불쾌해서 자세히 말하고 싶지 않다.

SYN. 1. think deeply; brood over; ponder on; think over
2. explain too long; speak in details about

one after the other (둘이) 교대로, 번갈아, 전후하여

Two dogs began to bark **one after the other** at a stranger.
개 두 마리가 번갈아 낯선 사람에게 짖기 시작했다.
He raised up and set down **one** of his feet **after the other**.
그는 두 발을 교대로 들었다 내렸다 했다.

SYN. by turns

call down 꾸짖다

The boss **called** us **down** for lateness.
사장은 우리가 지각한 것을 꾸짖었다.
Mother **called** John **down** for making his new clothes dirty.
어머니는 존이 새 옷을 더럽게 만들었다고 꾸짖었다.

SYN. rebuke; scold; reprimand; find fault with

not to speak of …은 말할 것도 없고, …은 제쳐놓고

She knows French and Spanish, **not to speak of** English.
그녀는 영어는 물론이고 프랑스 어와 스페인 어도 알고 있다.
Her friends will be very upset, **not to speak of** her parents.
그녀의 친구들이 매우 놀랄 것이다, 그녀의 부모는 말할 것도 없이.

SYN. not to mention; to say nothing of; let alone

do with 처리하다, 다루다

She does not know what to **do with**.
그녀는 그것을 어떻게 처리해야 좋을지 알지 못한다.
I don't know how to **do with** a dishonest guy like

SYN. cope with; deal with
cf. be done with …와 인연을 끊다 (=cut one's connections)
have done with …을 끝마치다

you.
너처럼 부정직한 친구는 어떻게 해야할지 모르겠다. | (=end; finish)

for [from] want of …이 부족해서, … 때문에, …이 없기 때문에

The tree died **for want of** water.
그 나무는 물이 부족해서 죽었다.
Many people died **for want of** food.
먹을 것이 없어서 많은 사람들이 죽었다.

[SYN] for lack of

on condition that …라는 조건으로, 만약 …이라면

I will go there **on condition that** you accompany me.
당신이 저와 함께 가 주신다면 거기 가겠습니다.
You may go out **on condition that** you return before sunset.
일몰 전에 돌아온다면 나가도 좋다.

[SYN] provided that; if

change one's mind 생각을 바꾸다, 생각을 고치다

I **changed my mind** about going shopping.
나는 쇼핑 가려는 생각을 바꿨다.
The manager **changed his mind** and decided not to hire her.
과장은 생각을 바꾸어서 그녀를 고용하지 않기로 결정했다.

[SYN] reconsider; think better of; change one's course

far from -ing …하기는 커녕, 결코 …가 아니다, …와 아주 딴판이다

His explanation was **far from (being)** satisfactory.
그의 설명은 결코 만족할 만한 것이 아니었다.
His English composition was **far from (being)** perfect.
그의 영작문은 완벽한 것과는 거리가 멀었다.

[SYN] not at all; not in the least (slightest)
cf. far from …로부터 멀리 떨어져서 (거리에 쓰임) / anything but 결코 …가 아닌

lose sight of 놓치다, 못보다

You mustn't **lose sight of** your main purpose.
본래의 목적을 잃어서는 안 된다.
I **lost sight of** Roy in the crowd.
나는 군중 속에서 로이를 놓쳤다.

[SYN] not be able to see any longer
[OPP] catch sight of …을 발견하다 (=discover; find)

what is more 그 위에, 더욱이, 게다가

He is hardworking, and, **what is more**, honest and punctual.

[SYN] in addition to; moreover; besides; into the bargain

그는 근면하며 게다가 정직하고 시간도 잘 지킨다.
He is a great politician, and, **what is more**, a good scholar.
그는 위대한 정치인일 뿐 아니라 게다가 훌륭한 학자이기도 하다.

give birth to 낳다

The bear at the zoo just **gave birth to** a baby cub.
동물원의 곰이 방금 새끼를 낳았다.
The effort of the scientists **gave birth to** the medicine.
과학자들의 노력으로 그 약이 생겨났다.

[SYN] bear; deliver; produce; bring forth

catch up with …을 만회하다, …을 따라잡다

Production is finally **catching up with** demand.
생산이 마침내 수요를 따라가고 있다.
The second runner is **catching up with** the first runner.
두 번째 주자가 첫 번째 주자를 따라잡고 있다.

[SYN] retrieve; restore
cf. catch on (with) …의 인기를 얻다, 유행하다 (=gain popularity)

fall on (upon) 1. …을 경험하다 2. 습격하다 3. …의 의무가 되다

The famous poet **fell on** unhappy days.
그 유명 시인은 불행한 시절을 경험했다.
The highwaymen **fell on** a party of traveling merchants.
노상강도들은 여행 중인 상인들을 습격했다.
It has **fallen on** me to support the family.
가족 부양의 책임은 나의 몫이 되었다.

[SYN] 1. experience; encounter 2. attack suddenly 3. be obligation of

go over 1. 넘다, 건너다 2. 잘 살펴보다, 검토하다 3. 복습하다, 되풀이하여 말하다

Many illegal immigrants tried to **go over** the border.
많은 불법 이주민들이 국경을 넘으려고 애썼다.
After I **go over** the report, we can discuss it further.
이 보고서를 검토한 후 더 상세하게 논의할 수 있다.
I don't want to **go over** it again, so ask John.
반복하여 말하고 싶지 않으니 존에게 물어 봐.

[SYN] 1. cross; pass over 2. examine; think about or look at carefully 3. repeat; do again

leave something to be desired 뭔가 아쉬운 점이 있다

[SYN] feel something wanting

I regret that our research **left something to be desired**.
우리 연구에 아쉬운 점이 있어서 유감스럽다.

come on 1. 진보하다, 차차 …이 되다 2. (비·폭풍이) 다가오다, 병들기 시작하다

[SYN] 1. improve; make advance 2. approach; become sick

Thanks to the employees' hard work, his business **came on** splendidly.
종업원들이 열심히 일한 덕분에 그의 회사는 눈부시게 발전했다.
When we started to climb down from the mountain, the rain **came on**.
우리가 하산을 시작했을 때 비가 오기 시작했다.
He felt a cold **coming on**.
그는 감기가 오는 것을 느꼈다.

live from hand to mouth 그날그날 벌어서 살아가다, 간신히 지내다

[SYN] live without saving for the future; have just enough

When my father was out of work, my family had to **live from hand to mouth**.
아버지가 실직했을 때 우리는 그 날 벌어 그 날 먹고살아야 했다.
Most people **lived from hand to mouth** during the war.
전시에는 대부분 사람들이 모두 어렵게 살았다.

go down (값·질이) 떨어지다, (바람이) 자다

[SYN] fall; drop; calm down

The price of apartments will never **go down**.
아파트 값은 결코 떨어지지 않을 것이다.
During the night the wind **went down**, and people could sleep peacefully.
밤 동안 바람이 약해져서 사람들은 편하게 잠들 수 있었다.

for one's part …로서는

[SYN] so far as one is concerned

For my part, I don't want to take part in the writing contest.
나로서는 작문 대회에 참여하고 싶지 않다.
For his part, I don't think there is reason to have other opinions than that.
그로서는 그것 외 다른 의견을 가질 이유가 없다고 나는 생각한다.

correspond to (구조·기능·양 등이) 상당하다, 부합하다, 상응하다

[SYN] answer to; agree; match

The article in the newspaper does not **correspond**

to what the politician actually said.
신문에 실린 기사는 그 정치인이 실제로 말했던 것과 일치하지 않는다.
His answer **corresponds to** my expectation.
그의 대답은 내가 기대했던 그대로다.

on (the) air 방송 중인, 계속 방송되고 있는

The radio station has been **on the air** since 1990.
그 라디오 방송국은 1990년부터 방송하고 있다.
Is the cooking program still **on the air**? I haven't watched it for a long time.
그 요리 프로 아직도 하니? 오랫동안 보지 못했어.

[SYN] being broadcast

without question / beyond the question / out of the question 1. 의심할 바 없이, 틀림없이, 물론 2. 전혀 불가능한

John is **without question** a great genius in our generation.
존은 의심할 바 없이 우리 세대의 위대한 천재다.
Without question you are as pretty as a picture.
말할 필요도 없이 너는 그림처럼 예쁘다.

[SYN] 1. without doubt; certainly; surely; without fail 2. cannot possibly happen

within [at] a stone's throw of [from] …에서 매우 가까운 곳에

I found that the girl was living **within a stone's throw of** my house.
나는 그 소녀가 우리 집에서 아주 가까운 곳에 산다는 것을 알았다.
The movie theater is **within a stone's throw of** the church.
영화관은 교회에서 아주 가깝다.

[SYN] near; close by; not far from

pretend to+동사 …인 체하다, …같이 꾸미다, 가장하다, 속이다

She **pretended** not **to** know me at the party.
그녀는 파티에서 나를 모른 척했다.
He **pretends to** admire me, though he privately hates me.
그는 마음속으로는 나를 미워하면서 겉으로는 나를 칭찬하는 척한다.

[SYN] make believe to; feign; deceive
cf. pretend to+명사 …을 주장하다 (=insist on; assert), 자인하다 (=admit), …인 체하다 (=pretend; feign)

wear away 닳아 없애다[없어지다], 마멸하다

The dog scratched at the door and **wore away** the paint.
개가 문을 긁어서 칠이 벗겨졌다.

[SYN] cause to lose shine, smoothness, paint, etc.; erode

The names on the tombstones have **worn away** over the years.
묘비에 쓰여진 이름들은 세월이 흐르면서 닳아 읽을 수 없게 되었다.

remember A to B A의 일을 B에게 잘 전달하다(전언하다)

Please **remember** me **to** your family.
당신 가족에게 안부를 전해 주시오.
He begs to be **remembered to** you.
그가 당신에게 안부를 전해 달라더군요.

[SYN] give one's best regards to someone

zealous for …을 열망하는, 갈망하는

There are none but are **zealous for** liberty, wealth and fame.
자유와 부귀 그리고 명성을 갈망하지 않는 사람은 없다.

[SYN] eager for; yearning for

not to mention …은 말할 것도 없고, …은 물론

He can speak German, **not to mention** English.
그는 영어는 말할 것도 없고 독일어도 잘 한다.
He's rich and **not to mention**, he's handsome, too!
그는 부자이며 게다가 물론 잘 생겼다!

[SYN] to say nothing of; not to speak of

wait up for 자지 않고 기다리다

I may be very late, so don't **wait up for** me.
많이 늦을지도 모르니 기다리지 말고 자.
You'll probably be very late, so I won't **wait up for** you.
당신은 아마 상당히 늦을 것 같으니까 먼저 자겠어요.

[SYN] put up going to bed until

찾아보기

INDEX

A

a bit	30
a bit of	40
a brace of	36
a couple of	33, 36
a dash of	40
a few	36
a good deal of	80
a good many	80
a great many	70
A is to B as C is to D	189
a large amount of	49
a large number of	49
a little	30
a lot of	49
a pair of	33, 36
a piece of	40
a rainy day	144
a scrap of	40
a short cut	117
abandon oneself to	212
abide by	149
abide by one's promise	78
able to+동사	37
abound in (with)	154
about as many times as not	10
above all	20, 72
above all (things)	8
abstain from	187
according as	150
according to	9, 91
account for	35
accountable for	42
accuse A of B	185
act on (upon)	185
add to	40
add up to	159
address oneself to	244
adhere to	129, 168
admit of	172
afraid of	113
after all	12, 40, 45
again and again	212
against a rainy day	18
against one's will	172, 173
agree on	10
agree with	178, 243, 246
agreeably to	91
ahead of time	66
aim at	152
aim for	162
alight from	62, 128
all aspects	231
all at once	15
all being counted	50
all but	107, 166, 223
all day (long)	23
all ears	196
all except	166
all in all	181
all of a sudden	15
all the more	58, 178
all the same / just the same	136
all the same	213
all the time	9, 123
all the way	140
all the year round	31, 170
all together	13
allow for	151, 228

allude to	91	as a rule	141
almost alike	48	as a whole	13, 151
along with	147, 156, 195	as an honor to	147
among all things	8	as best one can (may)	221
amount to	159	as C is to D, so A is to B	189
amuse oneself with (by)	159	(as) compared with	235
and so on / and so forth	30	as evidence of	244
and that	154	as far as	21, 42
and the like	30	as far as ... goes / as far as	
and what not	30	... is concerned	212
and yet	35	as follows	246
another way	11	as for	155
answer for	145, 175	as good as	127, 223
answer to	250	as if	15, 122
anxious to	164	as if it really were	31
apart from	179, 241	as is often the case (with)	84
appeal to	182	as it happened	158
apply for	152	as it is	138
apply oneself to	118, 205	as it is called	34
apply to	179	as it were	31, 65
approve of	86, 178	as likely as not	84
arise from	106	as long as	47
arrive at	21, 43, 49	as many	16
arrive at a conclusion	177	as many as	89, 126
arrive in	30	as much	12
as ... as	26	as much as	89, 157
as ... as any + 단수명사	221	as much as to say	201
as ... as ever	202	as often as not	10
as ... as possible	126	as payment	63
as ..., so ~	217	as regards	21, 114, 205
as a general rule	57	as soon as	6, 200
as a matter of course	19	as such	145
as a matter of fact	8, 44	as such degree	12
as a representative of	167	as the case may be	217
as a result (of)	36, 135, 231	as the respective of	26

찾아보기 255

as the result	124	at any time	37, 123
as they say	34	at best / at the best	6
as though	15, 122	at bottom	194
as usual	25	at close hand	134
as well	13, 217	at every place	28
as well as	4, 21, 97, 156, 217	at first	27
as yet	142	at first hand	111
ascribe A to B	196, 217	at first sight	4
ashamed of	127	at full length	151
aside from	179, 241	at hand	142
ask a favor of	201	at heart	194
ask after	92	at home	147
ask for	152, 157	at large	141, 151, 179
ask to	182	at last	26, 40
ask to be excused	47	at least	28
aspire to	58	at leisure	111, 159
assent to	187	at length	45, 151, 179
associate with	239	at liberty	111
assume control of	175	at once	14, 24, 78, 95, 134, 181
as (so) often happens	84	at once A and B	146
at (the) best	102	at one and the same time	14
at (the) most	19	at one time	95
at (the) worst	104	at one's astonishment	16
at a distance	139	at one's best	146
at a glance	194	at one's disposal	193
at a loss	91	at one's highest point	146
at a moment's notice	37	at one's peak	146
at a time	95	at one's will	216
at all	28	at one's wit's (wits') end	193
at all costs	128, 168	at peace	149
at all events	143, 168	at present	4, 39
at all times	9, 123	at random	148
at any moment	37	at sea	29
at any price	128	at a short distance	134
at any rate	55, 139	at short notice	191

at some distance	139
at some time	56
at some time or other	21
at stake	191
at that time	63
at the back of	9
at the beginning of	155
at the bottom of	166
at the cost of	144
at the down side of	148
at the end of	158
at the expense of	144
at the first blush	194
at the foot of	148
at the last point	158
at the mercy of	116
at the present	4
at the price of	144
at the proper time	91
at the risk of	137
at the same time	14, 95
at the sight of	61
at the start	27
at this time	4
at times	20
at times / at intervals	150
at will	193, 216
at work	149
attach A to B	187
attach oneself to	129
attempt to	131
attend on (upon)	160
attend to	6, 16, 44, 73, 152
attribute A to B	217
avail oneself of	156
avoid someone's company	231

B

back and forth	41
back up	31, 184, 243
backwards and forwards	120
badly off	79
ballot against	160
ballot for	87
be able to	5
be abound in	8
be about to	172, 182
be above average	36
be absent from	8, 231
be absorbed in	87, 118, 141, 177, 205, 221, 233
be accountable for	5, 135
be accustomed to	4, 44
be acquainted with	123
be affluent in	154
be agreeable	23
be akin to	184
be alive to	153
(be) all eyes	230
be all gone	179
(be) all smiles	222
be angry with (at) +사람	60
be anxious about	16
be anxious for	53
be anxious to	53
be apt at	23
be apt to	4, 17
(be) assured of	201

be astonished at	125	(be) conscious of	94
be at a loss	176, 193	be constrained to	145
be at home in	123	be contented with	151
be at one's own wit	123	be contrary to	163
be at the point of	172	be convinced of	168, 184, 201, 218
be attracted to	141	be crowded with	13, 84
be aware of	39, 94, 137	be crowned with	13
be away from	231	be dependent on (upon)	60, 64
be based on	214	be desirous of	53
(be) bent on	187	be devoid of / be destitute of	187
be better off	134	be devoted to	87
be better than	36	be disgusted with	49
be better to do	54	(be) dressed in	38
be born of	29	be due to + 명사	46
be born with	181	(be) due to + 동사	27
be bound for	33	be eager for	53, 64
be bound to	145	be endowed with	181
be brought about by	106	be engaged in	87, 221
be brought to a standstill	109	be entitled to	168
be capable of	5	(be) equal to	5, 37, 53
(be) characteristic of	191	be equipped with	140
be careful about	110	be expected to do	49
be caught in	151	be exposed to	143
be caught in a shower	25	be faithful to	149
be caused by	5, 199	be familiar to	44, 66
be certain to	145	be familiar with	7, 123
be close to	240	be famous for	31
be coated with	13	be famous to	38
be compelled to	5, 16, 113, 130, 145	be fascinated with	221
be competent for	5	be fond of	33, 96, 109
be composed of	15, 167	be forced to	5, 113, 130
be concerned about	110	be free from	147, 220
be concerned with	95	be free of	21
be conductive to	96	be friendly with	239
be confronted by	151	be full of pride	46

be gifted with	181	be not in	231
be given to	228	be obligation of	249
be going to	27	be obliged to	5, 16, 113, 130
be good at	4, 23, 55, 151	be occupied in (with)	87
be grateful	130	be of (the) opinion that	179
be guilty of	135	be on good terms (with)	71
be hard up for	179	(be) on the brink of	182
be impatient of+일	173	be on the point of	172
be impelled to	145	(be) open to	51
be imposed on	214	be opposed to	52
be in accord with	10	be originated in	124
be in agony	159	be out of harmony with	163
be in despair	133	be out of the question	242
be in existence	32	be persuaded of (that)	218
be in haste	35	be possessed of	43
be in need	205	be present at	44
be in need of	55	be proficient in	152
be in one's best days	164	be proud of	46, 74, 142, 210
be in the act of	172	be ready for	74, 95
be in want	205	be refused to	190
be in want of	55	be resolved to	95
be incapable of	50	be responsible for	5, 135, 145, 166
be inclined to	17, 45	be resulted from	106, 124
be indulged to	187	be rich in	8, 154
be intended to do	49	(be) satisfied with	42, 151
be jammed	84	be saved from	147
(be) known by	76	be scheduled to	27
(be) known to (as)	38, 76, 153	be sensible of	137
be liable for	135	be sensible to	94
be liable to	4	be sensitive to	84
be like to (that)	4, 17	be short of	179
be linked to	179	be sick of	49
be lost in	126, 233	be similar to	66, 184
be lost to	190	be skilled in	151
be made up of	15, 27, 167	be skillful in	4

be subjected to	151
be superior to	36
be supposed to	49
be sure of	43, 168, 201, 218
be sure to (do)	14, 18, 99
be surprised at	48, 125
be surprised to+동사	81
be taken aback	48
be thronged	84
be tired from (with)	38
be tired of	49
be too much for	209
be true to	149
be true to one's promise	78
be unable to	50
be unwilling to	33
be up and doing (coming)	181
be used to+(동)명사	4, 44
be wasteful of	136
be weary of	133
be weary with	38
be welcome to do something	141
be well acquainted with	7
be well off	42
be well versed in	7
be wet through	172
be willing to	23, 33
be without	6
be worried about	16
(be) worth -ing / It is worthwhile to+동사원형	50
bear fruit	154
bear in mind	79, 92, 101
bear out	139
bear up	159
because of	14, 20, 36, 100
become accustomed to	8
become acquainted	162
become acquainted with	96
become extinct	95
become fond of	141, 186
become friends again	167
become of	76
become responsible	63
become worse	43
before long	18, 46, 155
beg to	182
behind one's back	9
behind the times	57
believe in	22
belong to	27
beneath one's dignity	198
beside oneself	17
beside the point	198
bestow praise on	10
between ourselves	218
beware of	110
beyond (a) doubt	14, 20
beyond description	101
beyond one's means	202
beyond question	87
bits and pieces	139
blame for	115
blow up	111
boast of	74
both ... and	4
both (at once) ... and	21
brag of	74
break a promise	244
break free from	132

break in	173	by and by	46, 155
break into	96, 173, 229	by and large	62
break into pieces	136	by any chance	107
break off	209	by any means	59, 128
break out	117	by birth	118
break the ice	237	by chance	24, 29, 107, 157
break up	136	by daily wages	143
break with	209	by day	34
breathe one's last	150	by degrees	41
bring about	105, 199	by design	59
bring around	178	by dint of	36, 142, 146
bring back	93	by far	101, 107
bring down	124	by halves	30
bring for	162	by leaps and bounds	191
bring forth	249	by little and little	60
bring home to	200	by means of	36
bring in	196	by mistake	39
bring on	119	by name	30
bring oneself to do	224	by nature	99
bring out	135, 175	by no means	56
bring to an end	19	by oneself	32
bring to light	191	by reason	240
bring to notice	134	by the day	143
bring together	240	by the dozen	67
bring up	121	by the hour	27
brood over	247	by the hour-fair system	27
bud out	190	by the light of	197
build up	138	by the power of	142
bump into	85, 90	by the side of	107
burst into	96	by the skin of one's teeth	200
but for	11, 22, 34, 48	by the strength of	142
but that	202	by the way	35
by a hair's breadth	200	by trade	110
by accident	24, 29	by turns	9, 247
by all means	59, 168	by twos and threes	226

by virtue of	146
by way of	67

C

call down	247
call for	79, 219
call it a day	192
call off	119
call on	36
call out	59
call to attention	134
call together	240
call up	75
calm down	250
can't make head(s) or tail(s) of	233
cannot ... too	65
cannot but+동사원형	16, 54
cannot help but+동사원형 / cannot help+동명사	5, 54
cannot(never) fail to	14
can(can't) afford to	218
care about	16, 110, 193
care for	16, 33, 58, 109, 141, 193, 244
care nothing for	143
carry on	23
carry out	22
carry through	111
catch hold of	102
catch up	215, 233
catch up with	249
cause to stop	15
cease to exist	117
centralize upon	103

chance to	44, 62
change into	100
change one's course	248
change one's mind	248
cheer up	122
chip into	229
choke down	129
clad in	38
clear away	128, 131
clear of	121
clear off	131
clear out	241
clear up	237
cling to	126, 129
close at hand	75, 134
close by	29, 116, 251
collide with	85, 90
come about	209
come across	9, 68, 90, 246
come across one's mind	174
come after	120
come along	66
come by	166
come close to	204
come down	124
come from	29, 190, 219
come home to	203
come in effect to	43
come in touch with	84
come into	34
come into being	166
come into existence	166
come into use	128
come in(into) contact with	84
come near -ing	217

262 Index

come near to	204	conform to	10, 163
come of age	161	confuse A with B	221
come off	209	congenial to	195
come on	250	consent to	187
come out	11	considering that	47
come over	194	consist in	32
come to	169	consist of	15, 27
come to a conclusion	177	contend with	14
come to a standstill	109	contrary to	185
come to an agreement	180	contrast with	185
come to an end	81	contribute to	45, 96
come to life	135	controlled by	171
come to light	177	convert into	187
come to mind	86, 174	cope with	5, 184, 217, 247
come to one's expectation	201	correspond to	159, 250
come to one's senses	169	correspond with	162
come to pass	195	count for much	189
come to terms (with)	180	count off	243
come true	84	count on	61, 116
come up to	210	cover up	192
come up with	215	cross out	170, 203
come what may	180	curious to say	55
command a fine view	125	cut a (fine) figure	221
comment on	156	cut in	229
commit a crime	135	cut it fine (close)	190
compare to	100	cut out	189
compare with	19, 185		
compensate for	89, 174, 184		
compete with	184		
competent for+명사	37		
competent to+동사	37	**D**	
comply with	187		
concentrate on (upon)	103, 118, 205	dare to	109
concentrate one's strength on	155	date from (back to)	210
conflict with	85	day after day	74, 160
		day in and day out	74, 160
		deal in	81

deal out	233
deal out equally	39
deal with	70, 71, 247
decide on	123
defend against	46
depend on A for B	201
depend on (upon)	61, 64, 125, 110, 206, 214
deprive A of B	61, 173
derive from	124
describe as	239
destined to	232
devote oneself (to)	103, 118, 205, 233
devote to	119
die from	41
die of	32
die out	95
directly to someone	22
disagree with	133
disappointed at	118
disapprove of	207, 220
dispatch forward	190
dispense with	6, 238
dispose of	173
distinguish A from B	108, 134
distinguish between	192
divide by	53
divide equally	39
divide into	39, 53
divide up	137
do a favor	85
do all one can	85
do away with	32, 229, 238
do away with oneself	160
do damage	93
do for	244
do good to + 사람	53
do harm	93
do injury	93
do justice to / do ... justice	94
do nothing but	6
do one's best	85, 109
do one's utmost	85, 109
do well	99
do well to	100
do with	247
do without	6, 238
do without fail	99
do + 사람 + good	53
drag up	242
draw a conclusion	177
draw on	206
draw out	135
draw up	57, 242
drink a toast	130
drink to	130
drop across	68
drop by	79
drop in	38
due to	14, 20
during the day	34
dwell in	70
dwell on (upon)	247
dying to	235

E

each other	7
eager for	252
eager to (do)	164, 187

earn one's living	107
encircled by	24
encouraged by	178
engaged in	37
enjoy oneself	7
enjoy oneself with	159
enter into	65
envious of	234
escape from	132, 147
escort into	178
essential to	161
establish oneself as	211
even if (though)	48, 157
ever since	54
ever so	120
every inch	208
(every) now and then / now and again	4, 20
every other (second) day	47
every two days	47
exactly the same as	81
except for	48, 241
exchange A for B	215
exchange for	67
exclusive of	174
excuse oneself	47
excuse+사람+from	93
exert oneself	46, 232
exert oneself to the utmost	85
exist in	32
explain in detail	176
exposed to	106
express in words	218
express oneself	92
express praise of	10
extend the hand	98, 131

F

face bravely	56
face to face	37
face without shame	56
facing each other	37
fall (a) victim to	231
fall back on	60, 64, 110, 116
fall in love	175
fall in with	246
fall on (upon)	249
fall short	205
fall to	163
famed for	31
famous for	26
fancy oneself	213
far and wide	104
far away	37
far from -ing	248
farm out	242
fasten oneself on	129
feed off	109
feed on	51, 109
feel anxious	16
feel around for	129
feel for	129
feel inclined to do	224
feel like -ing	64, 79, 224
feel sure	20
fight it out	205
figure out	57, 101
fill up	72

find by chance	9
find fault with	112, 247
find out	25, 190
find pleasure in	96
finish with	223
first of all	8, 20, 22, 30, 72
fix on (upon)	123, 162
fix up	99, 155
flatter oneself	213
focus upon	103
follow after	244
follow up on	216
following one another	5
fool around with	244
for a change	220
for a moment	13, 59
for a rainy day	18
for a short time	13
for a spell	59
for a while	22, 59, 65
for a whole day	23
for all	33, 40
for all I know	235
for all that	98
for all the world	231
for an instant	13
for any price	231
for anything	231
for fear of	113, 213
for fear that	60
for fear that ... may (might) / lest ... should	213
for good	76
for hour after hour	27
for lack of	248
for nothing	226
for now	65
for one's age	100
for one's good sake of	66
for one's interest	116
for one's own efforts	59
for one's own sake	59
for one's part	250
for oneself	59
for sale	125
for some time	22, 59, 61
for sure	29, 78
for the benefit of / for one's benefit	116
for the first time	81
for the good of	167
for the life of one	216
for the most part	7
for the present	61, 65
for the purpose	48
for the purpose of -ing	112
for the sake of / for one's sake	26, 61, 66, 116, 240
for the time being	61, 65
for what reason	54
force an entrance into	173
force down	130
form the habit of -ing	131
for (from) want of	248
for (with) the purpose of	61
free of charge	226
from hand to mouth	8
from now on	25
from one's point of view	226
from that time on	54

from the distance	140	get the better (best) of	88
from time to time	4, 20	get through	177
from year to year	34	get through with	169
frown on (upon)	220	get to	30, 43
furnish A with B	240	get to know better	51
furnish with	143	get used to	8
		get well	66, 99
		getting to know	39
G		get (be) wet to the skin	172
		give ... one's best regard	42
gain control	175	give a full explanation	176
gain the support of	239	give a hint	73
gaze at	56, 162	give attention to	74, 229
generally speaking	13, 72	give away	236
get along (with)	62	give back	227
get along well	71	give birth to	249
get at	73	give control of	115
get away	164	give credit	22
get back	115	give heed to	152
get better	19	give importance	81
get down	128	give in	96, 105
get in	75	give off	208
get into a temper	88	give one's compliments to	42
get lost	9	give one's mind to	110
get off	62, 128	give oneself up to	177
get on	52, 62	give out	190
get on in life	211, 220	give rise to	93
get on in the world	227	give up	73, 187, 232
get on with	71	give vent to	197
get out of	232	give warning to	148
get out of temper	88	give way to	242
get over	19, 195	glance at	103
get ready	87, 99	go a long way	238
get rid of		go after	114
32, 88, 122, 136, 146, 189, 233, 239		go against	163

go away	236	had rather	80
go back on	244	hand back	234
go back to	210	hand down	45
go beyond	101	hand in	105, 133
go by	52, 117	hand out	233
go down	250	hand over	115, 127, 236
go for	162	hang around	196
go forward	176	hang on	126
go from bad to worse	43	hang up	74
go in for	152, 198	happen to	44, 62
go insane	176	happen to meet	77
go mad	80	hardly ... before	6
go off	164	hardly ... when	6
go on	114	have a contempt for	13
go on a visit to	36	have a disliking for	109
go on with	110	have a fine view	125
go out of one's way	232	have a good mind to	230
go over	249	have a good reason that	23
go so far as to	169	have a good time	7
go through	130, 223	have a hard time -ing	37
go through with	211	have a liking for	33, 96, 109, 186
go to sea	77	have a ride in	52
go without	6	have a right	168
good at	195	have a seeing eyes	223
good for nothing	98	have a share in	87
grow familiar (with)	8	have an effect on	99
grow into	114	have an eye for	223
grow on	247	have an inclination to	45
grow out of	235	have bad effects on	133
grow up	152	have by heart	204
		have charge of	44
		have difficulty (in) -ing	37
H		have done with	109, 208
		have fun	7
had better	54, 80, 100	have influence on	99

have just enough	250	hold up	159
have no alternative	168	hope for	58
have no choice but to+동사원형	5, 54	how about	58
have no connection with	71	hundreds of	38
have no other choice	168	hunt out	190
have nothing to do with	71	hurry up	35
have one's day	164	hurt one's honor	198
have only to	60	hurt oneself	45
have qualification	168		
have respect for	12		
have room for	172		
have seen(known) better days	176		

I

have something to do with	71	idle away	108
have something to oneself	211	if (the) weather permits	97
have trouble to+동사	38	if any	139
have trouble with	176	if anything	90
have trust in	22	if follows that	126
have(be) to do with	71	if it should happen	55
have(take) a look at	11	if it were not for	11, 34
head for	86	if not	22
hear about	96	if only	52
hear from	62	if or not	54
hear of	86	impose on	179
help oneself to	10	impute A to B	217
here and now	160	in (the) face of	28
here and there	35, 41	in a bad mood	185
hesitate to	220	in a good mood	228
hit on(upon)	52, 77, 153	in a sense	46
hold back	121	in a way	46
hold good	106	in a word	12, 17, 197
hold on to	129	in accordance with	9, 91
hold one's breath	128	in addition (to)	
hold one's tongue	236		13, 97, 147, 154, 156, 179, 248
hold out	131, 196	in advance	66
hold the time	140	in all	50

in all directions	104	in honor of	147
in all likelihood	225, 235	in itself	24
in anticipation	66	in knots	226
in any case	55, 139, 143	in lieu of	80
in any manner	28	in line	28
in arrangement	40	in most cases	113, 144
in brief	97, 137	in nine cases out of ten	152
in case (that)	55	in no time	112
in case of	36, 119	in no way	166, 225, 234
in charge of	172	in one's company	195
in company	140	in one's line	195
in company with	156	in one's opinion	179
in comparison with	112, 235	in one's place	25, 43
in confidence	155	in one's presence	159
in confirmity to	91	in one's way	106
in conformity with	9	in order	5, 28, 40
in consequence (of)	14, 135, 231	in order to (that)	34, 48, 70
in contrast to	235	in other respect	26
in danger of	137	in other words	11, 65, 144
in defiance of	231	in part	19
in detail	45, 151, 179	in particular	42
in disobedience to	231	in person / in the flesh	18, 111
in due course / in due time / in good time / in the course of time / in time	91	in place of	25, 43, 80, 167
		in plain words	28
		in poor condition	63
in earnest	205	in practice	44
in effect	90	in private	155
in every direction	28, 120	in process of	112
in every part	145	in progress	119
in fact	8, 44, 90, 92	in proof of	244
in fairness to	207	in proportion as	142, 150
in favor of	150	in proportion to	125, 142
in general	57, 141, 151, 181	in public	57
in good relationship with	114	in pursuit of	56, 244
in good (high, great) spirits	228	in reality	44, 92, 194

in regard of	114	in the first place (instance)	20, 72
in regard to	114, 155	in the future	25
in respect of (to)	174	in the interest of someone	
in return	63	(something)	240
in rotation	9	in the least	33
in search (quest) of	56	in the light of	167
in secret	155	in the long run	66
in short	12, 17, 97, 197	in the main	62, 141, 145
in sight	143	in the matter of	110
in sight of	99	in the method of	36
in single file	5	in the name of the God	32
in some measure	148	in the near future	18
in some respects	33	in the open	57
in some way but not in all	46	in the power of	116
in some ways	33	in the presence of	159
in someone's presence	22	in the recent past	63
in spite of	28, 40, 51	in the sequel	124
in spite of oneself	172	in the short time	18
in store (for)	234	in the teeth of	51
in succession	5, 46	in the usual way	25
in summary	137, 181	in the way	106
in support of	150	in the world	32, 117
in terms of	110	in the wrong order	63
in testimony of	244	in those days	63
in that	47	in time	56
in the air	157	in token of	244
in the beginning	27	in total	181
in the cause of	47	in turn	53
in the company of	147	in view of	99, 167
in the course of	112	in view of the fact	199
in the distance	37	Indeed ..., but	135
in the early part of	155	indulge (oneself) in	37, 212
in the end	26, 40, 45	inferior to	230
in the event of	36, 119	inflict punishment on	188
in the face of	224	influence on	185

찾아보기 *271*

inquire after	92
inquire into	56, 158
inside out	145
insist on (upon)	27, 168
instead of	25, 43, 80
interfere with	103
into the bargain	248
in (on) behalf of	167
irrespective of	91, 127
it (so) happens that	44
it goes without saying that	17
it is doubtful whether	212
it is natural that	23
it is needless to say that	17
It is no exaggeration to say that ...	237
it is no use -ing	121
it is no use (good) -ing	18
(it is) no wonder (that)	153
it is not too much to say that ...	65, 237
it is not until ... that ~	115
it is of no use	121
it is past time	239
It may fairly be said that ...	237
it will not be long before	155
it's high time	239

J

jeer at	89
join in	23
joking apart (aside)	222
judge by	208
judging from	88

just about	78
just as	81
just as much	26
just as soon	224
just when	81
just (right) on time	158

K

keep ... from -ing	68
keep ... in mind	92
keep abreast of	227, 235, 242
keep aloof from	223
keep an agreement	78
keep at a distance / keep at arm's length	231
keep away	108
keep away from	219, 223
keep body and soul together	183
keep company	162
keep early (good) hours	222
keep good time	214
keep in mind	79, 110, 193
keep in touch with	69
keep off	108
keep on	110
keep on -ing	69
keep one's promise (word)	78
keep one's temper	204
keep one's (an) eye on (upon)	213
keep pace with	227, 242
keep secret	183
keep silence	236
keep to	163

keep to oneself	183
keep touch with	69
keep up	87, 114
keep up with	23, 227
keep watch	213
kill oneself	160
kill time	92
know A from B	134
know better than to	216
know by heart	204
know of	135

L

lack nothing	181
later on	76
laugh at	69
lay aside (by)	169, 186
lay blame on	185
lay by	131, 186, 238
lay off	242
lay out	233
lay up	186
lead astray	214
lead back to	210
lead to	49, 93
lean on	116
learn by heart	64
learn from	79
leave no stone unturned	237
leave nothing to be desired	225
leave off	218, 242
leave out	203, 219
leave something to be desired	249
lest ... should	60, 113
let alone	71, 138, 247
let go of	203
let out	21
let's	58
let (leave) alone	88
levy on	179
liable to	51
lie in	32
lift up	159
like so many	111
likely to (that)	7
little by little	60
live beyond one's means	108
live from hand to mouth	250
live in	70
live on	51
live up to	201
live within one's means	108
lock up	60
long ago	28
long for	49, 88
longing for	164
look after	16, 33, 44, 66, 244
look at	11
look back on (upon) / look back to	243
look down on (upon)	13
look for	48, 193, 229
look forward to	64
look in the eye (face)	56
look into	56, 158
look on	12
look on (upon) A as B	245
look out	115, 213

look out for	229
look over	229
look through	132, 229
look to	125
look to A for B	201
look up	80
look up to	12
lose heart	133
lose no time (in) -ing	186
lose one's heart	175
lose one's life	161
lose one's mind	176
lose one's temper	88
lose one's way	9
lose oneself / get lost	9, 77
lose oneself in	126
lose sight of	248
lots (plenty) of	49, 70

M

mail out	190
maintain life	183
major in	162
make a boast of	74, 142
make a clean breast of	176
make a comparison	19
make a decision	57
make a display of	144
make a distinction between	192
make a fool of	202
make a fortune	186
make a go of	195
make a good of it	32
make a habit of -ing	131
make a living	107
make a long story short	172
make a note of	130
make a point of -ing	214
make a request	201
make a resolution	57
make a search for	48
make a special study of	222
make a speciality of	222
make a spring at	101
make a start	65
make a voyage	108
make advance	250
make allowance(s) for	228
make amends for	174, 184
make an attempt to	131
make an effort	178
make an exchange	67
make an excuse	47
make application (for)	152
make believe	77
make both ends meet	128
make calm	130
make efforts (an effort)	46, 124, 232
make ends meet	128
make for	45, 101
make free	21
make friends	162
make friends with	51
make fun of	69
make good	32, 174, 195
make happen	105
make haste	35, 41
make it a rule to	51

make light (little) of	13, 69, 143	mind one's own business	162
make little account of	69	misappropriate to oneself	10
make much of	81	miss out on	246
make no difference	200	mix up	195, 221
make nothing of	203	more and more	58
make one's living	107	more often than not	45
make one's way	176	more or less	51, 137
make oneself at home	89	more than half the time	45
make oneself understood	15	more than once	171, 212
make out	57, 101, 210	more than others	42
make peace with	43	most importantly	22
make preparations	87, 99	most of all	22
make progress	66	move up	221
make reference	91	much more	11
make room for	94	mull over	246
make sense	166		
make someone realize	146		
make sure	20	**N**	
make the best of	41		
make the most of	93	nail down	245
make up	167	name ... after	71
make up for	89, 174, 184	narrow down	222
make up one's mind	57	near at hand	29
make use of	19, 150, 156	near by	75
make (pull) faces (a face)	238	near (close) at hand	97
making progress	119	needless to say (that)	17, 19, 71
manage to	50	never ... but	75
manage without	6	never without	75
many a	52	never (cannot) fail to	99
may as well	100	never (not) ... but ~	102
may as well (...as not)	50	never (not) ... without ~	102
may well	23	next door	132
meet by chance	9, 85, 90, 246	next to	107
meet with	174	next to nothing	243
mess around with	244	next (second) to none	188

no better than	213
no fewer than	102
no less than	89, 102
no longer	24
no matter if	48
no matter + 의문사 ... may	73
no more ... than	69
no more than	58
no sooner ... than	68, 200
no sooner than	6
none other than	240
none the less	98
none too	212
(not) at all	33, 58, 113, 212, 248
not ... at all	79, 225
not ... because ~	213
not ... but	69
not ... until (till)	59
not a bit	58
not a few	73
not a little	68
not because ... but because ~	76, 204
not better than	230
not by any means	56
not fail to	18
not far off	29
not forget to	18
not in season	202
(not) in the least	33, 58, 113, 248
not in the slightest degree	79
not knowing what to do	29
not less ... than	90
not long ago	63
not more than	19
not much of a	90
not only ... but (also) ~	4, 21, 97
not separating	13
not so much A as B	114
not so much as	107
not that ..., but that ~	76, 204
not to mention	71, 88, 138, 247, 252
not to speak of	88, 138, 247, 252
not ... any longer	24
not ... any more than	69
noted for	26
nothing but	75, 213
nothing except	75
not (without) even	107
not (little) ... still less	236
now and again	20
now and then	149
now that	89

O

object to	52, 161
occupied with	37
occur to	52, 153, 174
odds and ends	139
of course	29
of importance	25, 130
of its own accord	36
of late	63
of moment	130
of necessity	119
of no use	80
of one's own	110
of one's own accord (free will)	224
of oneself	36

of the same number	16	on the brink of	224
of value	54, 103	on the condition that	103
off and on / on and off	171	on the contrary	26, 171
off duty	164	on the earth	28
off guard	120, 164	on the ground that (of)	240
offer for	175	on the move	182
on (the) air	251	on the occasion of	119
on a daily basis	143	on the one hand ... on the other	
on a ship	121	(hand)	95, 215
on a sudden	15	on the other hand	26
on account of	14, 20, 36, 240	on the part of	131
on alternate days	47	on the pretext of	240
on an errand	105	on the side of	150
on an (the) average	113	on the spot	24, 134
on bad terms with	114	on the strength of	178
on behalf of	26, 43	on the subject of	110
on board	121	on the verge of	182, 224
on business	105	on the way to	33
on commercial business	105	on the whole	62, 151
on condition that	248	on the (one's) way	61
on duty	163, 164	on time	67
on earth	32, 117	once and for all	241
on end	98	once in a while	4, 53
on foot	78	once upon a time	28
on good terms with	114	one ..., the other ~	161
on guard	163	one after another	5, 9, 98
on no account	166	one after the other	247
on occasion	20	one and all	178
on one's account	66	one and the same	208
on one's part	131	one at a time	5
on opposition to	185	one by one	5
on pretence of	206	one thing, another	32
on purpose	59	only too	185
on second thought(s)	238	open someone's eyes	146
on speaking terms with	245	opposed to	161

originate in	210
out of (the) reach of	85
out of breath	202
out of date	57
out of earshot	116
out of one's mind	80, 208
out of order	63, 79
out of season	202
out of sight	143, 215
out of sorts	185
over and over (again)	74, 212
owe A to B	228
owing to	20, 67, 231

P

parcel out	137
part company with	148
part from+사람	148
part with	15, 236
partake of	241
participate in	65, 87, 198
partly ... partly	95
pass away	32, 117
pass by	72, 150, 223
pass for (as)	153
pass on (upon)	161
pass over	219, 249
pass through	223
pat on the back	210
pay a visit to	36
pay attention to	110, 152
pay no attention	219
pay respect to	12
pay (give) attention to	6
peculiar to	147
peel off	218
perform one's duty	64
persist in	27, 168
persuade ... of	219
persuade oneself of (that)	184
phase out	188
pick out	65, 136
pick up	77
picture to oneself	184
place one's hope on	125
place (lay) the responsibility on	115
play a joke on	202
play a part (role)	64
play along with	205
play the part for	133
play up to	186
play with	244
plenty of	80
point out	134
point to	134, 243
poke fun at	69, 202
ponder on	199, 247
ponder over	246
prefer A to B	102
preferable to	224
prepare oneself for	95
presence of mind	227
press down	130
presume to	109
pretend to+동사	251
prevail on (upon)	129, 183
prevent ... from -ing	68, 106
previous to	109

pride oneself on	142, 210	put to use	49, 128
prior to	100, 109	put up	74, 159
proficient in	23, 195	put up with	6
protect ... from	46		
prove unsuitable for	133		
provide ... with	72		
provide against	183	**Q**	
provide for	87	queue up	230
provided (providing) that	10, 52, 103, 248	quiet down	204
		quite a few	17
pull one's leg	192		
pull oneself together	215		
pull out	223	**R**	
pull together	169	rain cats and dogs	194
pull up	186, 242	raise up	77
push around (about)	192	range oneself	195
put ... together	156	reach (out) for	98
put an end to	229	reach a conclusion	21
put aside	129, 169	reach in	30
put away	128, 131	reach out	196
put down	130, 206, 210	read between the lines	180
put down in writing	40	read into	181
put forth	175	read over	232
put forward	196	read up on	234
put in mind of	94	refer to	91
put in order	237	reflect on (upon)	199
put in writing	206	refrain from	187, 243
put it bluntly	28	regard A as B	245
put off	175	regardless of	91, 127
put on	157, 206	release one's hold on	203
put on sale	136	relieve A of B	233
put out	49	reluctant to	216
put something on record	40	rely on (upon)	60, 61, 64, 110, 116
put to death	188	relying upon	178
put to good use of	150		

remain in effect	106
remain in force	106
remember -ing	101
remember A to B	252
remember to	106
remind ... of ~	94
remind of	93, 239
replace A by (with) B	215
resort to	203
respond to	124
responsible for	42
rest on (upon)	214
result from	199
result in	43, 78, 120
return for	50
rid A of B	122
rid oneself of	220
right after	191
right away / right now	75, 78, 134
right now	24, 160
ring up	75
rise in life	220
rise in the world	220
rob A of B	61, 173
roll in	192
round up	240
rouse from sleep	146
rub it in	194
rule out	245
run across	9, 68
run against	85, 90
run away	122, 164, 241
run away with	203
run down	132
run into	77, 85
run out of	85
run over	79, 229
run short of	105, 132
rush upon	101

S

safe and sound (sure)	31
say good-bye to	144
say hello to	42
say to oneself	199
scarcely ... before	6
scarcely ... when	6
scores of	70
scrape together	206
search for	48, 193, 229
second to none	167
see A off	12
see much of	177
see through	124
see to	193
see to it that	167
seeing (that)	199
seek after	193, 244
seek favor with	186
seek for	152, 162
seek out	190
sell on	178
send for	104
send forth	190
send out	190, 208
send up	159
separate from	122
serve oneself	10

set ... free	21	side by side	28
set a goal of	152	side with	195, 243
set about	65, 90	similar to	48
set against	19	since then	54
set apart	108	single out	183
set aside	129, 131, 186	sit down	154
set down	206	sit in on	183
set forth	218	sit up	145
set in	44	slip by	117
set off	91	slow down	141
set one's sights on	152	so (that) ... may	70
set out	108, 218, 223	so ... as to	155
set sail	158	so ... that	55
set to work	105	so and so	93
set up	99	so as to	34, 48, 70
settle down	96	so far	20, 142
settle on	123	so far as	10, 15
several hundred	38	so far so	47
shake hands (with)	43	so long as	10
shake someone by the hand	43	so that	48
shake up	136	so that ... may	48
share A with B	140	so that ... not	60, 213
share out	137	so to speak	65
shoot down	124	so-called	57
short of	160	some or other(s)	149
shortly after	18	something before now	28
shout out	127	something like	223
shove off	91, 218	something of	137
show into (in)	178	soon enough	56
show off	144	sooner or later	21, 56
show to the world	191	so (as) far as ... (be) concerned	211
show up	11, 137, 219	speak for itself	222
shrink from	211	speak ill (evil) of	42
shut off	15	speak of	157
shut up	60	speak out (up)	98

speak well (highly, much) of	10
speaking of	123, 155
specialize in	162, 222
spell out	176
spend A on B	113
split on	220
split up	53
spring from	29, 219
spring up	190
stand by	12
stand for	14
stand in for	133
stand in need of / be in need of	219
stand on ceremony	235
stand out	159, 218
stand up for	31
stare at	56, 57
start up	153
starve to death	142
stay at	70
stay away from	231
stay level with	235
steal B from A	173
step by step	41
step out of	62
stick to	99, 129, 168
still more	11, 58
stir up	136
stop in for a short visit	38
stop short	227
store up	130, 131
strange to say (tell)	55
stretch out	98, 131
strictly speaking	103
strike one's mind	52
strip oneself	156
strive for (after)	174
subject to	51, 171
submit to	239
subsist on	51, 109
substitute A for B	224
substitute for	244
succeed in	32
succeed to	34
such ... as	120
such ... that	55
such and such	93
such as it is	225
such being the case	245
suffer from	159
sufficient for	124
suggest itself to	174
suitable for	148
suitable to	118
suited for (to)	118
sum up	139, 172
supply A with B	143
support oneself	183
surrounded by (with)	24
suspect A of B	171
switch off	15

T

take (it) for granted	170
take a fancy (liking) to (for)	109, 186
take account of	104, 175
take advantage of	19, 49, 153, 156
take after	66

take as a matter of course	153
take away	131, 146
take away B from A	173
take back	93, 189
take by force	61
take by surprise	194
take care	44
take care of	12, 16, 33, 44, 147, 160, 189, 193, 244
take charge of	63, 175
take down	129, 210
take for granted	153
take heart	133
take heed to	110
take hold of	111
take in	210
take in hand	172
take interest in	16, 95
take into account	104, 151
take into consideration	104, 151, 175, 228
take it easy	192
take leave of	144, 223, 236
take off	156, 189, 218
take offense (at)	236
take on	157
take one's place	151, 154
take one's seat	44, 154
take one's time	198
take out	135, 223, 239
take over	34, 175
take pains	124, 232
take part (in)	23, 87, 198
take part[sides] with / take part of	195
take place	117, 209
take pleasure in	96
take pride in	142, 210
take side with	12
take somebody by surprise	116
take someone into service	157
take the place of	151
take the trouble	124
take the trouble to	180
take to	65, 141
take turns	154
take up	77, 91, 158
take up for	195
taking advantage of	206
take place	195
talk about	156
talk out of	246
talk over	129
talk+사람+into -ing	220
talking of	123
tattle on	220
tear down	225
tell A from B	134
tell all about	176
tell from	192
tell off	243
tell on	220
ten to one	153
ten to ten	225, 235
tend to	45
thanks to	80, 142, 146, 178
that ... this	39
that is (to say)	11, 144
the day before yesterday	67
the former ... the latter /	

that ... this ~	39, 138
the minute (that)	200
the one ... the other	39
the same number of	16
the whole day	23
the 비교급, the 비교급	58
then and there	134
there is no -ing	118
there is no room for	68
there is no use (in) -ing	18
there is no use (whatever) -ing	121
there is nothing for it but to	168
these days	39
think a great deal of / think a lot of / think much of	197
think better of	248
think light of	69
think nothing of	143
think of	86
think on	199
think over	129, 247
this time	58
this way and that	41
through and through	208
through thick and thin	207
throughout the day	23
throughout the year	31
throw away	136, 173
tide over	195
tidy up	237
tie up	152
tire out	108, 156
to a (high) degree	189
to a great extent〔degree〕	168, 189
to a man	200
to advantage	118
to and fro	112, 120
to be exact	103
to be frank with you	28
to be sure	29
to begin with	30
to cut a long story short	12, 17
to do+사람〔사물〕+justice	207
to make a long story short	97, 197
to make matters worse	158
to one's advantage	66
to one's cost	199
to one's credit	199
to one's disappointment	154
to one's face	22
to one's heart's content	198
to one's honor	199
to one's regret	154
to one's satisfaction	198
to one's surprise	16
to one's taste	170
to put it shortly	97
to put it another way	11
to say about	155
to say nothing of	71, 88, 138, 247, 252
to say the least (of it)	193
to some degree	148
to some extent / to a certain extent	19, 51, 148
to speak honestly	28
to start with	30
to sum up	97
to tell the truth	92
to tell you the truth	8
to the best of one's ability	170, 188

to the degree that	150
to the effect that	188
to the full	186, 198
to the letter	146
to the life	193
to the minute	158
to the point	140
to the purpose	138, 140
together with	147, 195
too ... not to	141
too ... to	14, 55
toy with	244
track down	241
trade in	81
trifle with	225
true to life	180
trust on	64
try on	86
try one's best	109
turn back	243
turn down	63
turn in	133
turn off	15, 92
turn on	92
turn one's gaze through	132
turn out (to be)	120
turn over	127
turn over a new leaf	229
turn to account	150
turn to advantage	150
turn up	11, 137
twice as ... as	149

U

under (the) cover of	206
under construction	73
under no circumstances	234
under the best condition	6
under the circumstances	214
under the influence (of)	229
under the sun	32
under way	119
until now	20, 142
up and down	120
up to	42
up to date	81
up to now	20
upside down	127
use for	244
use up	90, 108
used to+동사	72

V

veer off	230
venture to	109
verge on	240
very thing	86
vote against	160
vote down	206
vote for	87
vote in	236
vouch for	212
vulnerable to	171

W

wait for	69
wait on (upon)	12, 160
wait up for	252
wake up	146, 169
walk out on	228
want for nothing	181
warn+사람+of (against)	148
waste away	226
watch one's step	233
watch out (for)	44, 115, 189
watch over	147
wear away	251
wear off	226
wear out	108, 220
weather permitting	97
weed out	189
weight on (upon)	122
well known for	26
were it not for	11, 34
What ... is to, ~ is to	189
what by ... what by ~	102
what do you say to	58
what for	54
What has become of ...?	70
what if	134
what is ... like	86
what is called	57
what is more	248
what is worse	158
what one has	41
what one is	35
what we (you, they) call / what is called	34, 57
what with ... what with ~	104
when confronted with	28
whether or not	54
while since	47
why don't you	58
win over	88, 239
wind up	150
wish for	53, 58
with a view to (-ing)	61, 112
with all	33, 40
with all one's effort	170
with all one's heart	170
with all one's might	170, 188
with care	107
with caution	107
with complete sincerity	170
with delight	64
with difficulty	77
with each other	7
with ease	104
with interest	126
with joy	64
with one's reach	85
with pleasure	64, 170
with reason	207
with regard to	115
with the exception of	174
with the result that	124
with the skin of one's teeth	77
within (the) reach of	85
within call	116
within hearing	116
within one's means	182
within one's reach (grasp)	132
within (at) a stone's throw of	

(from)	251
without (a) doubt	20
without (any) delay	91, 181
without (any) difficulty	104
without a break	98, 226
without defense against	116
without delay	24, 186
without doubt	87
without exaggeration	211
without exception	131
without fail	14, 71
without leave	29, 209
without notice	29
without question / beyond the question / out of the question	20, 251
without regard to	127
without reserve	227
without so much as	182
without the knowledge of	207
without warning	29
wonder if	117
work out	101, 209
worry about	16
worthy of	103
would like to / should like to ...	64
would rather	100
would (had) ... sooner than ~	97
wrinkle up	238
write down	40, 130, 210
write for	245
write in detail	237
write off	246
write up	237
wrong with	79

X out	170
year after year	34
year in, year out / year in and year out	170
yearn for	58, 88
yearning for	252
yell out	127
yield to	96, 242
zealous for	252

저자 손봉돈(孫奉敦)

tel. 02-722-3871(연구실) 오전 10시 40분~오후 6시 30분
fax. 02-722-3871

고려대학교 졸업
경희대 · 동국대 · 홍익대 · 건국대 · 세종대 · 한양대 · 경상대 · 강원대 · 충북대 · 인하대 · 원광대 · 영남대 등 특별 초빙 교수

현 코리아타임즈 편집위원

□ 코리아타임즈 해설판 18년 게재
□ 일간스포츠「영어시험 급소를 찾는다」· TOEFL 등 5년 게재
□ 스포츠서울「시험에 꼭 나오는 영어」11년 게재
□ 국방일보 생활영어 · 유머영어 3년 게재

저서

시험에 꼭 나오는 영어(10권) (스포츠 서울)
KOREA TIMES TOEFL(4권)
K · T 관광생활영어
손봉돈 TOEIC (삼지사)
손봉돈 TOEIC CD-ROM (오름기획)
손봉돈 영작문비법 I · II
손봉돈 Vocabulary I · II
손봉돈의 독해강의
떠오르는 영단어
수험영어 마라톤 (비전)
손봉돈의 배꼽빠지는 유머영어 I · II
Essence English Idioms Dictionary(영어숙어사전) 외 총 87권